THE LADIES' BOOK
OF USEFUL INFORMATION

LECTOR HOUSE PUBLIC DOMAIN WORKS

THE LADIES' BOOK OF USEFUL INFORMATION

ANONYMOUS

ISBN: 978-93-89614-44-2

Published: 1896

LECTOR HOUSE LLP
E-MAIL: lectorpublishing@gmail.com

THE LADIES' BOOK OF USEFUL INFORMATION.

COMPILED FROM MANY SOURCES.

1896.

PREFACE.

To the ladies of America is this little work, "The Ladies' Book of Useful Information," dedicated. It is a book written expressly for women. This book is full from cover to cover of useful and necessary information for women. Never before has so much knowledge with which women should be acquainted been printed in one book. It is a perfect storehouse of useful facts. Almost every lady spends many dollars every year for cosmetics, medicines, household articles, etc., which this book would save her.

This is a book which every lady should have, and which every mother should place in the hands of her daughters as they come to years of understanding. Every girl of twelve and upwards should read this valuable work.

Many books costing from three to five dollars do not contain half the information contained in this work. Everything described in this preface is taught in this book.

It teaches ladies the secret of Youth, Beauty, Health.

The first chapter teaches all about Personal Beauty.

Every lady desires to be beautiful, and it is the duty of every woman to be as attractive as possible. All may enhance their charms and be lovely by following the directions of this book. Few persons know how to improve their natural looks so as to captivate, charm, and win the admiration of those whom they meet. This book tells the wonderful secret—all the ancients ever knew, and all that has been discovered since. It teaches how to wonderfully improve the person in loveliness. The real secret of changing an ordinary looking person into one of great beauty makes this book of great value. Nature does something for us, but art must make the perfect man or woman.

If you desire bright, melting eyes, a clear, soft, rose-tinted complexion, beautiful hands and graceful figure, well-developed and perfect, use the knowledge which you will find in this book.

It teaches how to acquire a beautiful, delicate loveliness which cannot be surpassed, and which can be retained to a very late age. By means of this teaching a woman of thirty-five or forty can easily pass for a girl of twenty-five.

It teaches how to conceal the evidence of age, and how to make the most stubbornly red and rough hands beautifully soft and white. Remember that "The Ladies' Book of Useful Information" does not teach the use of paint and powder, which is injurious to the skin, but how to make the *cheek glow* with health, and the *neck*, *arms* and *hands* to rival the lily in whiteness. It teaches how to cure Greasy

Skin, Freckles, Pimples, Wrinkles, Blackheads, Crow's-feet, Blotches, Face Grubs, Tan, Sunburn, Chapped Hands, Sore Lips, etc.

It teaches how to cure and prevent redness and roughness, and to make the skin soft, smooth, white and delicate, producing a perfectly natural appearance. It teaches how to cure and refine a coarse skin, so that it will be clear and white.

It tells what has never before been published: How to restore a fair, rosy complexion to its original freshness, after it has become sallow and faded. This is a wonderful secret, and is sure in its results. It will also cause those who have always been pale to have beautiful, bright, rosy cheeks, and the eyes to be brilliant and sparkling.

It teaches how to have soft, white and attractive hands, even though compelled to do housework. Every lady desires to have nice hands, and all may do so by following the directions of this book. The most coarse, rough, red hands will, by following this teaching, become beautifully delicate and white, and it causes very little trouble to care for them.

It teaches how to care for the hair so as to improve the growth and to have a beautiful and luxuriant head of hair; how to keep the skin of the scalp healthy, to cure Dandruff, to prevent the hair falling, and to have it of a nice glossy hue.

It teaches how to have clear and brilliant eyes, with beautiful, long, drooping lashes; also, how to cure sore and weak eyes.

It teaches how to care for the teeth so as to have them white and sound, telling how to treat those that are decayed, and how to prevent the decay of sound ones.

It teaches how to have beautiful ripe red lips, and how to cure sore and chapped lips.

It teaches how to cure Warts, Corns, Bruises, Sprains, Cold Feet, Bad Breath, etc.

It teaches how to bleach, purify and whiten the most stubbornly red, rough skin, so that it will be beautifully clear and white; and a complexion that is naturally passable will be admired by all who see it after being treated as here described.

The second chapter teaches: The different human temperaments; how to tell to which temperament you belong yourself, and also the temperaments of those whom you meet;

The fortunate and unfortunate days of the month, and their importance at the hour of birth;

Important advice to females regarding their thirty-first year;

How to know whom you will marry;

The signs of a good genius;

All about Electrical Psychology, or Psychological Fascination—Mesmerism;

How to make persons at a distance think of you (this is a purely natural phenomenon);

How to win the affection of the person of the opposite sex whom you sincerely love. There is no black art about this, but merely psychological attraction, and by its use you can win the love of the person whose affection you desire.

When you desire the "love" of any one whom you meet, you can very readily reach him if you observe the directions here given.

Chapter three is a special chapter for young women, on a special subject, and contains advice which every young lady should study.

It teaches them: What marriage is, and explains how highly injurious it is to entertain low ideas regarding it;

How a young lady should act in the presence of young men;

What a girl should do when a prospect of marriage occurs.

It tells some of the most prolific sources of matrimonial difficulties, and how to remedy them;

What ladies should do who desire that their husbands should be amiable and kind;

What attentions are due to you *as a lady*.

Cautions against the failing of young ladies making themselves too cheap.

Tells what "woman" is formed to be.

Warns against indiscretions before marriage, and teaches that under all circumstance a lady will be looked to to resist any advances, and maintain her purity and virtue.

Tells what is the nature, naturally, of young women;

How a young woman should act when receiving the attentions of a young man;

How you will know when the young man whom you *should marry* presents himself to you;

What a man needs a wife for, and how to qualify yourself for the position;

About misunderstandings in early married life;

How a young mother feels towards her first-born.

Tells the good influence of virtuous love;

What young people should know before they become engaged.

Chapter four teaches about Love and Marriage; the attraction of the sexes for each other; what love is; what causes it; individual loves; fondness for cousins; different kinds of love; flirtation; the object of marriage; should marriage be for life.

Chapter five: When to Marry—How to Select a Partner on Right Principles.

Treats of the proper age to marry; which marriages are the most happy; which are the most productive of handsome children; how nature assists art in the choice of partners; the attributes of a handsome couple, etc.

Chapter six: Sexual Intercourse—Its Laws and Conditions—Its Use and Abuse.

There is an alarming and increasing prevalence of nervous ailments and complicated disorders that could be traced to have their sole origin in the ignorance, which is so universal, of the laws of these organs.

This chapter teaches all about sexual morality; how men and women should live; the law from the age of puberty to marriage; the law of marriage; what a man who truly loves a woman will do; a true union; how women are protected; the false and the true sense of duty; what is the most powerful restraint from evil.

The above is discussed in a chaste, simple, manner, and should be read by every lady. There is nothing impure in this book from beginning to end, but subjects in which women are woefully ignorant are discussed in a plain, moral manner to which no objection can be raised.

Chapter seven: Marriage.

What marriage is; how far back the marriage tie has existed; polygamy, what it is; monogamy, what it is; polyandry, and what it is; marriage customs; the basis of a happy marriage, etc.

Chapter eight: Pregnancy—Labor—Parturition.

Perhaps there is no more eventful period in the history of woman than that in which she first becomes conscious that the existence of another being is dependent upon her own, and that she carries about with her the first tiny rudiments of an immortal soul.

This chapter explains all the signs of pregnancy; the changes that take place in the face and neck; the suppression of the monthly flow; changes in the breast, etc.

Then it gives a sure test for the detection of pregnancy. It tells how a pregnant woman should live during the period of gestation.

Childbirth is not necessarily either painful or dangerous. It can be accomplished easily and safely and with comparatively no pain by following the directions given in "THE LADIES' BOOK OF USEFUL INFORMATION."

Numerous instances are known where ladies who had previously suffered with severe labor in childbirth have, by attending to the directions here given, been delivered of fine, healthy children with comparative ease.

No mother who has attended to the teaching here given but has blessed the knowledge of it, and it has saved many a young mother much needless terror.

It tells all about the ailments that almost always torment women during the trying time of pregnancy, making life itself seem a burden.

These troubles are: Morning Sickness, Toothache, Palpitation of the Heart, etc. It shows that there is no necessity for women suffering as they almost invariably do during this time; but that these troubles may be overcome by simple, safe remedies which are described in this book, and which may be safely taken by the patient.

It tells all about the medicine which is taken by the Indian women of North

America during the period of gestation. It is well known that the women of these tribes suffer very little during childbirth, and it is almost all due to the effects of this wonderful medicine.

The recipe for this medicine, "Parturient Balm," was obtained from an Indian doctor, and is given in this book, together with instructions as to how it is to be taken.

This chapter alone is worth the price of the book to any lady. Every mother, and everyone who ever expects to become a mother, should carefully study the above chapter, as it may be the means of saving her much pain and suffering.

The same chapter explains all about a case of labor; the signs that show when labor has commenced; what to give to help the patient; the different kinds of pains; the length of time between the pains; the length of time the pains should last, etc.; the taking of the child from the mother; how to care for the child; the taking away of the afterbirth; what to do in case of flooding; how to relieve afterpains, etc.

It also explains what "Abortion" is; what causes abortion; what causes premature labor; the difference between the two; symptoms of threatened abortion, and how to prevent the same if possible; what to do for miscarriage, and to try and prevent it, etc.

The ninth chapter teaches all about: Menstruation—Change of Life—Falling of the Womb, etc. Tells the time of life at which the menses should appear.

Every mother should watch her young daughter as she nears this critical time. The health for many years to come depends to a great extent on how a girl passes this period. This chapter tells all the symptoms of the near approach of the monthly flow. It shows a mother how to care for her daughter, and to see that she has proper attention during this time.

It tells the age at which the periodical flow should commence; the symptoms of its approach; how a girl should be treated at this time; how to cure Chlorosis, or Green Sickness; how to relieve and cure painful and suppressed menstruation, etc.

If the instructions of this book are followed in cases like the above, it will save many young girls much needless suffering.

This chapter also treats on: Whites, or Flour Albus, and Falling of the Womb.

Many delicate women suffer great agony through these two distressing complaints. This chapter describes all the symptoms of these complaints, and gives simple, safe remedies for them. A lady can easily attend to herself and avoid exposure.

It also treats on Change of Life.

By the phrase "Change of Life," or "The Critical Period," we understand the final cessation or stoppage of the menses. This chapter explains all about this trying time, the symptoms of its appearance, and the ages at which it usually occurs.

With proper care this period may be safely passed, and a happy and comfortable old age be spent. All the dangers incident to this period are described, and how to successfully combat them.

Chapter ten: Collection of valuable Medical Compounds.

Any of the formulas in this chapter will be readily filled by your druggist. Each recipe will give an article which is the *very best* thing that can be used for the disease which it is recommended to cure.

The first is "Magic Kidney and Liver Restorer."

Most people are afflicted to some extent with Kidney and Liver trouble. This medicine is a sure cure.

Do you have: A frequent headache over the eyes;
A susceptibility to chills and fever;
A bitter or oily taste in the mouth;
A sour stomach;
A complexion inclined to be yellow;
A great depression of spirits;
Specks before the eyes, and flushed face;
A done-out, tired feeling;

besides many other symptoms too numerous to mention? If you have, you are afflicted with Kidney and Liver complaint, and should use "Magic Kidney and Liver Restorer." This great remedy will do away with all these disagreeable symptoms, and will make you feel like a new person. It is a splendid spring medicine, cleansing the blood and purifying and toning up the system.

Another formula given is "Dyspeptic Ley."

This is a *sure, certain* cure for dyspepsia. It never fails.

- The symptoms of dyspepsia are:
- Feeling of weight in the stomach;
- Bloated condition after eating;
- Belching of wind;
- Nausea;
- Vomiting of food;
- Water brash;
- Pain in the stomach;
- Heartburn;
- Bad taste in the mouth in the morning;
- Palpitation of the heart;
- Cankered mouth; loss of flesh;
- Fickle appetite; depression of spirits;
- Lack of energy; headache and constipation.

If you have *any or all* of the above symptoms, then you are afflicted with Dyspepsia, and should endeavor to obtain relief. "Dyspeptic Ley" is a certain cure. It is easily prepared, and should be taken by everyone who is afflicted with any of the above distressing symptoms.

The same chapter tells how to cure Ague, Intermittent Fever, Neuralgia, Sick

Headache, Neuralgic Headache, Rheumatism, Dysentery, Epileptic Fits, Hysteria, Bleeding of the Lungs, Coughs, Bowel Complaint, Scrofula, Worms, Sore Eyes, Cholera, Piles, Warts, Corns, Deafness, Inverted Toe-nail, etc.

All these diseases are described, together with the best method of treating them.

Chapter eleven teaches how to Prepare Nourishment for the Sick Room. Very few people know how to prepare nourishment for the sick. This chapter teaches how to prepare a great number of nourishing dishes. Every lady should know how to prepare food for the sick, as at some time or other there is almost certain to be sickness in every family. There are over forty recipes given in this chapter for food for the sick and convalescent.

Chapter twelve describes things Curious and Useful.

It tells: How to get clear of mosquitoes; how to get rid of bedbugs; to obtain fresh-blown flowers in winter. By this process the buds of flowers can be gathered in summer and autumn and kept until the winter, when they can be used as required. The flowers open and are as beautiful as though fresh plucked from the garden. Any one can understand the process, as it is very simple.

Also: How to transfer all kinds of pictures on to glass—a very pretty art; how to prevent horses being teased by flies; how to prevent flies lighting on to windows, pictures, mirrors, etc.; to render paper fireproof; to render boots waterproof; how to extract the essential oil from any flower; how to take leaf photographs; to cure drunkenness; to make different kinds of perfumes; to write secret letters, etc.;

To prepare flowers so that their beauty will remain unimpaired for years. Roses and other flowers can be had to last for years by this beautiful art. The process is very easy, and the directions are so simple that a child may follow them.

Chapter thirteen treats of Home Decoration.

It teaches how to arrange a house so as to furnish it cheaply and harmoniously. It gives complete instructions for every room—Hall, Parlor, Library, Dining-room, Bedrooms, etc., and attends to every detail. This is a splendid guide to all who wish to make their home attractive.

Chapter fourteen teaches all about caring for House Plants. It tells the right temperature to keep them in; the proper soil for potting; how to make plants grow luxuriantly; how to have plenty of blossoms; to keep plants without a fire at night; to destroy bugs and rose-slugs; to raise plants with the least trouble; the best varieties of plants to raise, etc.

It tells how to preserve autumn leaves so that they can be bent in any form desired, and so that they will retain their color.

It tells how to prepare skeleton leaves—a very pretty amusement.

Chapter fifteen is devoted to The Laundry.

It tells: How to make washing fluid; to take out scorch; to make plain, fine, and coffee starch; to make enamel for shirt bosoms, so that any housekeeper can do them up as nicely as they do at the laundry; to clean velvets and ribbons; to take grease out of silks, woolens, paper, floors, etc.; to take out fruit stains; to take out iron rust and mildew; to wash woolen goods and blankets so that they will not shrink, etc.

The sixteenth chapter teaches how to do all kinds of Stamping.

In this chapter are given full instructions for wet and dry stamping; for making stamping powder; how to mix white paint for dark goods, and dark paint for light goods; it tells how to prepare all the necessary articles for stamping; how to prepare transfer paper; how to transfer any pattern you may see; how to make a distributor; how to enlarge designs; how to prepare all kinds of stamping powder; how to do French indelible stamping; what kind of a brush to use; and how to care for patterns. If the directions here given are followed the stamping will always be satisfactory.

Chapter seventeen teaches how to do Bronze Work.

Bronzing is the latest improvement in wax work, and if properly made cannot be detected from the most expensive, artistic bronze. It is used for table, mantel and bracket ornaments, and may be exposed to dust and air without sustaining the slightest injury. It can be dusted like any piece of furniture, and makes a very desirable, inexpensive ornament. The colors it is made in are Gold, Silver, Copper, Fire, and Green Bronze. Among the articles described are a vase in bronze, a motto in bronze, a floral basket in bronze, animals and birds in bronze, statuary in bronze, flowers and leaves in bronze.

The art of making each of the above articles is carefully described so that any one can follow the directions.

The art of Decalcomania is also taught in this chapter. This is used upon almost everything for which ornamentation is required, such as Crockery, China, Porcelain, Vases, Glass, Bookcases, Folios, Boxes, Lap desks, Ribbons, etc. It is a very pretty art, and is much admired.

Chapter eighteen gives twelve recipes for articles needed in every household. It will tell you how to save a large percentage of household expenses, and also how to have a great many of the articles you use in your daily housework of a superior quality, vastly better than the ones you are using at the present time.

It is a fact not generally known, that a great many of the articles used in daily household work cost little more than one-tenth of the price the consumer pays. We purpose to show the readers of this book how to have, in most instances, better articles than those they buy, for a small percentage of the cost. To do this, we have, by our own personal investigation, gathered a number of valuable recipes together, and have paid for the privilege of using them.

We give in "The Ladies' Book of Useful Information" twelve recipes which have never before been published, and which, if you once possess, you will never wish to be without, as they are truly valuable secrets.

The list is as follows: Healing salve; Magnetic croup cure; Worm elixir; Brilliant self-shining stove polish; Wonderful starch enamel; Royal washing powder;

Magic annihilator; I X L baking powder; Electric powder; French polish or dressing for leather; Artificial honey.

It also contains a list of all the poisons and their antidotes. It describes the symptoms of poisoning and how to proceed in each case.

CONTENTS

CHAPTER I.
PERSONAL BEAUTY.

Teaches all about Personal Beauty. Every woman desires to be beautiful, and every woman may enhance her charms and be lovely by following the directions of this book. Few persons know how to improve their natural looks so as to captivate, charm, and win the admiration of those whom they meet. This book tells this wonderful secret—all the ancients ever knew, and all that has been discovered since. It teaches how to wonderfully improve the person in loveliness. The real *secret* of changing an ordinary looking person into one of great beauty makes this book of great value. Nature does something for us, but art must make the perfect man or woman. If you desire bright, melting eyes; a clear, soft, rosy-tinted complexion; beautiful hands; and graceful figure, well-developed and perfect, use the knowledge which you will find in this book.

It teaches how to conceal the evidence of age; how to make the most stubbornly red and rough hands beautifully soft and white. Remember that "The Ladies' Book of Useful Information" does not teach the use of paint and powder, which is injurious to the skin, but how to make the cheek glow with health, and the neck, arms, and hands to rival the lily in whiteness. It teaches how to cure Greasy Skin, Freckles, Wrinkles, Pimples, Blackheads, Crow's-feet, Blotches, Face Grubs, Tan, Sunburn, Chapped Hands, Sore Lips, etc. It teaches how to cure and prevent redness and roughness, and to make the skin soft, smooth, white and delicate, producing a perfectly healthy and natural appearance. It teaches how to cure and refine a coarse skin, so that it will be clear and white.

It teaches how to have soft, white and attractive hands, even though compelled to do housework. Every lady desires to have nice hands, and all may do so by following the directions of this chapter.

It teaches how to care for the hair so as to improve the growth and to have a beautiful and luxuriant head of hair; how to keep the skin of the scalp healthy; to cure dandruff; to prevent the hair falling, and to have it of a nice color.

It teaches how to have clear and brilliant eyes, with beautiful, long, drooping lashes. Also, how to cure sore and weak eyes.

It teaches how to care for the teeth so as to have them white and sound, telling how to treat those that are decayed, and how to prevent the decay of sound ones.

It teaches how to have beautiful ripe red lips, and how to cure sore and chapped lips.

It teaches how to cure Warts, Corns, Bruises, Sprains, Cold Feet, Bad Breath, etc.

The following formulas for Toilet Preparations are all given in this book. They are vastly superior to the much-advertised cosmetics which flood the market. Your druggist will fill any of these recipes for a very small sum, and you will always have a superior article. Each of these preparations will do exactly what is claimed for it.

The following is a list of what is given in the first chapter: Lotion to remove freckles and tan; To expel freckles; Cleopatra's Freckle Balm; Lemon Cream, for sunburn and freckles; Wash to prevent sunburn; Grape lotion, for sunburn; Pate Axerasive of Bozin, to soften and whiten the skin; To remove red pimples; To remove black specks or flesh-grubs; Preparation for whitening the face and neck (bleaches and whitens the skin); To cure profuse perspiration; Cleopatra's Enamel for whitening the hands and arms; To cure freckles, and parched, rough skin; To purify the breath; To bleach and purify the skin of the face and neck; To permanently remove black specks or flesh-worms; French face-wash (purifies and brightens the complexion); To remove pimples; Kalydor for the complexion—for pimples, freckle-tanned skin, or scurf on the skin; To improve the skin; Wash a la Marie Antoinette (gives a beautiful brilliancy to the complexion); Liquid Rouge (harmless), a perfect imitation of nature; Milk of Roses, a cosmetic; Circassian Cream; Toilet Vinegar; Bloom Rose; Certain cure for eruptions, pimples, etc.; To clear the complexion and reduce the size of the face; To cure and refine a stippled or blotched skin; To cure and prevent wrinkles; Wash for wrinkles; To remove wrinkles; How to have brilliant, beautiful eyes; To cure weak eyes; To improve the eyelashes; To cure weakness of eyes; How to have beautiful eyelashes; To cure watery and inflamed eyes; To strengthen the sight; What to do for nearsightedness; How to have a beautiful mouth and lips; To make lip salve; French lip salve; German lip salve;

CHAPTER II.

TREATING OF MISCELLANEOUS MATTERS.

CHAPTER III.

A SPECIAL CHAPTER FOR YOUNG WOMEN.

CHAPTER IV.

LOVE AND MARRIAGE.

CHAPTER V.

WHEN TO MARRY—HOW TO SELECT A PARTNER ON RIGHT PRINCIPLES.

CHAPTER VI.

SEXUAL INTERCOURSE—ITS LAWS AND CONDITIONS— ITS USE AND ABUSE.

CHAPTER VII.

MARRIAGE.

CHAPTER VIII.

PREGNANCY—LABOR—PARTURITION.

CHAPTER IX.

MENSTRUATION.

CHAPTER X.

COLLECTION OF VALUABLE MEDICAL COMPOUNDS.

CHAPTER XI.

THINGS FOR THE SICK ROOM.

CHAPTER XII.

THINGS CURIOUS AND USEFUL.

CHAPTER XIII.

HOME DECORATION.

CHAPTER XIV.

FLORAL.

CHAPTER XV.

THE LAUNDRY.

CHAPTER XVI.

HOW TO DO YOUR OWN STAMPING AND MAKE YOUR OWN PATTERNS.

CHAPTER XVII.

BRONZE WORK.

CHAPTER XVIII.

CHAPTER I.

PERSONAL BEAUTY.

Teaches all about Personal Beauty. Every woman desires to be beautiful, and every woman may enhance her charms and be lovely by following the directions of this book. Few persons know how to improve their natural looks so as to captivate, charm, and win the admiration of those whom they meet. This book tells this wonderful secret—all the ancients ever knew, and all that has been discovered since. It teaches how to wonderfully improve the person in loveliness. The real *secret* of changing an ordinary looking person into one of great beauty makes this book of great value. Nature does something for us, but art must make the perfect man or woman. If you desire bright, melting eyes; a clear, soft, rosy-tinted complexion; beautiful hands; and graceful figure, well-developed and perfect, use the knowledge which you will find in this book.

It teaches how to conceal the evidence of age; how to make the most stubbornly red and rough hands beautifully soft and white. Remember that "The Ladies' Book of Useful Information" does not teach the use of paint and powder, which is injurious to the skin, but how to make the cheek glow with health, and the neck, arms, and hands to rival the lily in whiteness. It teaches how to cure Greasy Skin, Freckles, Wrinkles, Pimples, Blackheads, Crow's-feet, Blotches, Face Grubs, Tan, Sunburn, Chapped Hands, Sore Lips, etc. It teaches how to cure and prevent redness and roughness, and to make the skin soft, smooth, white and delicate, producing a perfectly healthy and natural appearance. It teaches how to cure and refine a coarse skin, so that it will be clear and white.

It teaches how to have soft, white and attractive hands, even though compelled to do housework. Every lady desires to have nice hands, and all may do so by following the directions of this chapter.

It teaches how to care for the hair so as to improve the growth and to have a beautiful and luxuriant head of hair; how to keep the skin of the scalp healthy; to cure dandruff; to prevent the hair falling, and to have it of a nice color.

It teaches how to have clear and brilliant eyes, with beautiful, long, drooping lashes. Also, how to cure sore and weak eyes.

It teaches how to care for the teeth so as to have them white and sound, telling how to treat those that are decayed, and how to prevent the decay of sound ones.

It teaches how to have beautiful ripe red lips, and how to cure sore and chapped lips.

It teaches how to cure Warts, Corns, Bruises, Sprains, Cold Feet, Bad Breath, etc.

The following formulas for Toilet Preparations are all given in this book. They are vastly superior to the much-advertised cosmetics which flood the market. Your druggist will fill any of these recipes for a very small sum, and you will always have a superior article. Each of these preparations will do exactly what is claimed for it.

The following is a list of what is given in the first chapter: Lotion to remove freckles and tan; To expel freckles; Cleopatra's Freckle Balm; Lemon Cream, for sunburn and freckles; Wash to prevent sunburn; Grape lotion, for sunburn; Pate Axerasive of Bozin, to soften and whiten the skin; To remove red pimples; To remove black specks or flesh-grubs; Preparation for whitening the face and neck (bleaches and whitens the skin); To cure profuse perspiration; Cleopatra's Enamel for whitening the hands and arms; To cure freckles, and parched, rough skin; To purify the breath; To bleach and purify the skin of the face and neck; To permanently remove black specks or flesh-worms; French face-wash (purifies and brightens the complexion); To remove pimples; Kalydor for the complexion—for pimples, freckle-tanned skin, or scurf on the skin; To improve the skin; Wash a la Marie Antoinette (gives a beautiful brilliancy to the complexion); Liquid Rouge (harmless), a perfect imitation of nature; Milk of Roses, a cosmetic; Circassian Cream; Toilet Vinegar; Bloom Rose; Certain cure for eruptions, pimples, etc.; To clear the complexion and reduce the size of the face; To cure and refine a stippled or blotched skin; To cure and prevent wrinkles; Wash for wrinkles; To remove wrinkles; How to have brilliant, beautiful eyes; To cure weak eyes; To improve the eyelashes; To cure weakness of eyes; How to have beautiful eyelashes; To cure watery and inflamed eyes; To strengthen the sight; What to do for nearsightedness; How to have a beautiful mouth and lips; To make lip salve; French lip salve; German lip salve; To care for the teeth; To cure toothache; Premium tooth powder; Feuchtwanger's tooth paste; Fine tooth powder; Rye tooth powder; To cure foul breath; To have white and beautiful teeth; For decayed teeth; To remove yellow color from teeth; Camphor paste; Powerfully cleansing dentifrice; Infallible cure for toothache; Mixture for decayed teeth; To whiten and beautify the teeth.

How to have soft, white and beautiful hands; How to care for the hands; Bleaching lotion for the hands (renders them beautifully white); To remove stains from hands; To make the hands white and delicate; Remedy for chapped hands; To whiten coarse and dark-skinned hands; To cure red hands; Almond paste for the hands; To care for the nails.

To cause the skin to become satin-smooth and to smell like violets.

To cause those who have lost the bloom and fairness of early youth to regain them.

How to care for the hair; How often to wash the hair; To improve the growth and luxuriance of the hair; To make the hair glossy; To impart curliness or waviness to the hair when it is naturally straight; On changing the color of the hair; To have elegant hair; Wild Rose curling fluid; To cause the hair to grow very thick; Lola Montez hair coloring; Hair Restorative; For bald heads; Excellent hair wash; To cure baldness; Stimulants for the hair; The golden hair secret; For keeping the hair crimped or curled in summer; To bleach the hair; For improving the hair; Pomade for preserving the hair; To make the hair grow and to prevent it from falling; To make the hair grow quick; Wash for scald heads, etc.

Powders and their use: Boston Burnet powder for the face; Queen Bess complexion wash.

Treating of the Care of the Skin, Hair, Teeth, and Eyes, so as to have each arrive at the highest degree of beauty of which each is capable.

A great object of importance, of care to every lady, is the care of her complexion. There is nothing more pleasing to the eye than a delicate, smooth skin; and besides being pleasing to the eye, is an evidence of health, and gives additional grace to the most regular features. The choice of soaps has considerable influence in promoting and maintaining this desideratum. These should invariably be selected of the finest kinds, and used sparingly, and never with cold water, for the alkali which, more or less, mingles in the composition of all soaps has an undoubted tendency to irritate a delicate skin; warm water excites a gentle perspiration, thereby assisting the skin to throw off those natural secretions which, if allowed to remain, are likely to accumulate below the skin and produce roughness, pimples, and even eruptions of an obstinate and unpleasant character. Those soaps which ensure a moderate fairness and flexibility of the skin are the most desirable for regular use.

Pomades, when properly prepared, contribute in an especial manner to preserve the softness and elasticity of the skin, their effect being of an emollient and congenial nature; and, moreover, they can be applied on retiring to rest, when their effects are not liable to be disturbed by the action of the atmosphere, muscular exertions or nervous influences.

The use of paints has been very correctly characterized as "a species of corporeal hypocrisy as subversive of delicacy of mind as it is of the natural complexion," and has been, of late years, discarded at the toilette of every lady.

The use of cosmetics has been common in all ages and in every land. Scripture itself records the painting of Jezebel; and Ezekiel, the prophet, speaks of the eye-painting common among the women; and Jeremiah, of rending the face with painting—a most expressive term for the destruction of beauty by such means. For the surest destroyers of real beauty are its simulators. The usurper destroys the rightful sovereign.

That paint can ever deceive people, or really add beauty for more than the duration of an acted charade or play, when "distance lends enchantment to the view," is a delusion; but it is one into which women of all times and nations have fallen—from the painted Indian squaw to the rouged and powdered denizen of London or Paris.

Milk was the favorite cosmetic of the ladies of ancient Rome. They applied plasters of bread and ass's milk to their faces at night, and washed them off with milk in the morning.

As a cosmetic, milk would be harmless, but we doubt its power of improving the skin. As a beverage, no doubt, it whitens the complexion more than any other food.

But before we speak of improving the complexion, it will be well to explain to our readers the nature and properties of the skin.

This is what an American physician has recently told us about it:—

THE SKIN—ITS BEAUTY, USES, CONSTRUCTION, MANAGEMENT, ETC.

Every person knows what the skin is, its external appearance, and its general properties; but there are many of my readers who may not be aware of its peculiar and wonderful construction, its compound character, and its manifold uses. It not merely acts as an organ of sense, and a protection to the surface of the body, but it clothes it, as it were, in a garment of the most delicate texture and of the most surpassing loveliness. In perfect health it is gifted with exquisite sensibility, and while it possesses the softness of velvet, and exhibits the delicate hues of the lily, the carnation, and the rose, it is nevertheless gifted with extraordinary strength and power of resisting external injury, and is not only capable of repairing, but of actually renewing itself. Though unprotected with hair, wool or fur, or with feathers or scales, as with the brute creation, the human skin is furnished with innumerable nerves, which endow it with extreme susceptibility to all the various changes of climate and of weather, and prompt the mind to provide suitable materials, in the shape of clothing, to shield it under all the circumstances in which it can be placed.

The importance of the due exposure of the body to daylight or sunlight cannot be too strongly insisted on. Light and warmth are powerful agents in the economy of our being. The former especially is an operative agent on which health, vigor, and even beauty itself, depend. Withdraw the light of the sun from the organic world, and all its various beings and objects would languish and gradually lose those charms which are now their characteristics. In its absence, the carnation tint leaves the cheek of beauty, the cherry hue of the lips changes to a leaden-purple, the eyes become glassy and expressionless, and the complexion assumes an unnatural, cadaverous appearance that speaks of sickness, night and death. So powerful is daylight, so necessary to our well-being, that even its partial exclusion, or its insufficient admission to our apartments, soon tells its tale in the feeble health, the liability to the attacks of disease, and the pallid features (vacant and sunken, or flabby, pendent and uninviting) of their inmates. Even the aspect of the rooms in which we pass most of our time, and the number and extent of their windows, is perceptible, by the trained eye, in the complexion and features of those that occupy them. So in the vegetable world—the bright and endlessly varied hues of flowers, and their sweet perfumes—even their very production—depend on sunlight. In obscure light plants grow lanky and become pale and feeble. They seldom produce flowers, and uniformly fail to ripen their seeds. In even partial darkness the green hue of their foliage gradually pales and disappears, and new growths, when they appear, are blanched or colorless.

The best method of keeping the skin clean and healthy, by ablution and baths, may here be alluded to. The use of these, and the washing of the skin that forms part of the daily duties of the toilet, appear to be very simple matters, but writers on the subject differ in opinion as to the methods to be followed to render them perfect cleansers of the skin. Some of them regard the use of soap and water applied in the form of lather with the hands, and afterwards thoroughly removed from the skin by copious affusions, rinsing or sluicing with water, or immersion in it, as the best method. This is probably the case when the skin is not materially dirty, or its pores or surface obstructed or loaded with the residual solid matter of the perspiration or its own unctuous exudation and exuviæ. To remove these completely and readily, something more than simple friction with the smooth hand is generally required. In such cases the use of a piece of flannel or serge, doubled and spread across the hand, or of a mitten of the same material, will be most ready and effective. Friction with this—first with soap, and afterwards with water to wash the soap off—will be found to cleanse the skin more thoroughly and quickly than any other method, and, by removing the worn-out portion of its surface, to impart to it a healthy glow and hue that is most refreshing and agreeable. This effect will be increased by wiping and rubbing the surface thoroughly dry with a coarse and moderately rough, but not a stiff, towel, instead of with the fine, smooth diapers which are now so commonly employed. At the bath, the fleshbrush usually provided there will supersede the necessity of using the flannel.

The small black spots and marks frequently observed on the skin in hot weather, particularly on the face, generally arise from the accumulation of the indurated solid matter of the perspiration in its pores. When they assume the form of small pimples (*acne punctata*), and often when otherwise, they may be removed by strong pressure between the fingers, or between the nails of the opposite fingers, followed by the use of hot, soapy water.

The subsequent daily application of a weak solution of bichloride of mercury—as in the form commonly known as Gowland's lotion—or of sulphate of zinc, will completely remove the swelling, and generally prevent their re-formation.

Eruptions are too well known to need any lengthy description here. They are usually classified, by writers on the subject, into: animalcular eruptions, or those due to the presence of animalcula (minute acari) in the scarfskin, which occasion much irritation, and of which the itch furnishes a well-marked example; papular eruptions, or dry pimples; pustular eruptions, or mattery pimples, of which some forms are popularly known as crusted tetters; scaly eruptions, or dry tetters; and vesicular eruptions, or watery pimples.

The treatment of all of the above, except the first, in simple cases, where there is not much constitutional disarrangement, consists mainly in attention to the general principles of health, cleanliness, exercise, food, ventilation, and clothing. Occasional doses of mild saline aperients (Epsom salts, cream of tartar, or phosphate of soda, or of sulphur combined with cream of tartar) should be taken, and warm or tepid bathing, preferably in sea-water, or, if not convenient, rain water, frequently had recourse to. Stimulants of all kinds should be avoided, and the red meats, ripe fruits, and the antiscorbutic vegetables should form a considerable portion of the diet. Lemonade, made by squeezing the juice of a lemon into a half-pint tumbler full of water, and sweetening with a little sugar, should be frequently and liberally taken as one of the best beverages in such cases. To relieve the itching and irritation (except in the pustular, crusted, and vesicular varieties), brisk friction with a fleshbrush or a fleshglove may be employed. The parts should also be wetted with an appropriate lotion after each friction or bath, or the use of soap and water.

In all the scaly eruptions, iodide of potassium internally, and ioduretted or sulphuretted lotions or baths are invaluable. In many of them of a malignant or obstinate character, as *Lepra Psoriasis*, *Lupus*, etc., small doses of solution of arsenite of potassa (liquor arsenicalis; the dose, from 3 to 5 drops, gradually and cautiously increased to 7 to 9 drops, twice a day, after a meal) prove highly serviceable. In the forms of psoriasis popularly called baker's itch, grocer's itch, and washer-woman's itch, the application of ointment of nitrate of mercury, diluted with ten or twelve times its weight of lard, has been highly recommended. A course of sarsaparilla is also in most cases advantageous.

The small, hard, distinct pimples—"acne, or acne simplex" of medical writers—that occur on the forehead, and occasionally on the temples and chin, generally yield to stimulating lotions, consisting of equal parts of strong vinegar, or spirit, and water, or to weak lotions of sulphate of zinc, assisted by occasional doses of cooling laxatives, as the salines, or a mixture of sulphur or cream of tartar.

Freckles, or the round or oval-shaped yellowish or brownish-yellow spots, resembling stains, common on the face and the backs of the hands of persons with a fair and delicate skin who are much exposed to the direct rays of the sun in hot weather, are of little importance in themselves, and have nothing to do with the general health. Ladies who desire to remove them may have recourse to the frequent application of dilute spirit, or lemon juice, or a lotion formed by adding acetic, hydrochloric, nitric, or sulphuric acid, or liquor of potassa, to water, until it is just strong enough to slightly prick the tongue. One part of good Jamaica rum to two parts of lemon juice or weak vinegar is a good form of lotion for the purpose. The effect of all these lotions is increased by the addition of a little glycerine.

The preceding are also occasionally called "common freckles," "summer freckles," and "sun freckles." In some cases they are very persistent, and resist all attempts to remove them while the exposure that produces them is continued. Their appearance may be prevented by the greater use of the veil, parasol or sun-shade, or avoidance of exposure to the sun during the heat of the day.

Another variety, popularly known as cold freckles, occur at all seasons of the year, and usually depend on disordered health or some disturbance of the natural functions of the skin. Here the only external application that proves useful is the solution of bichloride of mercury and glycerine, or Gowland's lotion.

The Itch—"psora" and "scabies," of medical authors; the "gale" of the French,—already referred to, in its common forms is an eruption of minute vesicles, generally containing animalcula (acari), and of which the principal seats are between the fingers, bend of the wrist, etc. It is, accompanied by intense itching of the parts affected, which is only aggravated by scratching. The usual treatment is with sulphur ointment (simple or compound) well rubbed in once or twice a day; a spoonful (more or less) of flowers of sulphur, mixed with treacle or milk, being taken at the same time, night and morning. Where the external use of sulphur is objectionable, on account of its smell, a sulphuretten bath or lotion, or one of chloride of lime, may be used instead. In all cases extreme cleanliness, with the free use of soap and water, must be strictly adhered to.

The small, soft discolorations and excrescences of the skin, popularly called moles, may be removed by touching them every second or third day with strong acetic or nitric acid, or with lunar caustic. If covered with hair they should be shaved first.

Extreme paleness of the skin, when not symptomatic of any primary disease, generally arises from debility, or from the languid circulation of the blood at the surface of the body; often, also, from insufficient or improper food, want of out-door exercise, and the like. The main treatment is evident. Warm baths, friction, and stimulating lotions and cosmetics may be here employed, together with a course of some mild chalbeate (as the lactate, protophosphate, or ammonia-citrate of iron) and hypophosphate of soda.

Roughness and Coarseness of the skin, when not depending on any particular disease, may be removed or greatly lessened by daily friction with mild unguents or oil, or by moistening the parts, night and morning, with a weak solution of bichloride of mercury containing a little glycerine.

Rashes and redness of the skin, of a common character, often arise from very trifling causes, among which indigestion, suppressed perspiration, irritation, and the like, are the most frequent. Nettle rash or urticaria, so called from the appearance and tingling sensations resembling those caused by the sting of nettles, in some people, is very apt to follow the use of indigestible and unwholesome food. It is usually of short duration and recurrent. The treatment consists in the administration of mild saline aperients, and, in severe cases, of an emetic, particularly when the stomach is still loaded with indigestible matter. These should be followed by copious use of lemonade made from the fresh expressed juice. The patient should be lightly but warmly clothed during the attack, and exposure to the cold, or to draughts of cold air, should be carefully avoided. The further treatment may be similar to that noticed under "eruptions." To prevent the recurrence of the attack, the objectionable articles of food, and any other known exciting causes, must be avoided. Red rash, red blotch, or fiery spot, a common consequence of disordered health, a sudden fit of dyspepsia, and, in females, of tight lacing, and rose rash, false measles, or roseola, having commonly a similar origin to the preceding, for the most part require the same treatment.

Scurf—"furfur or furfura"—is a formation depending on the natural and healthy exfoliation of the skin on every part of the body on which hair or down grows, but most extensive and observable on the scalp, on account of the abundance and darker color of the hair there. Scurfiness, or excessive scurfiness, is the result of morbid action, and may be treated by the frequent use of the fleshbrush or hairbrush, ablution with soap and water, and the use of mild stimulating, astringent, or detergent lotions.

Scurvy—"scorbutus" of medical writers—is a disease which, even in its incipient and early stages, when its presence is often unsuspected, is most injurious to the skin and complexion. It usually commences with unnatural sallowness, debility, and low spirits. As it proceeds, the gums become sore, spongy, and apt to bleed on the slightest pressure or friction; the teeth loosen, and the breath acquires a fœtid odor; the legs swell, eruptions appear on different parts of the body, and at length the patient sinks under general emaciation, diarrhœa, and hemorrhages. Its chief cause is improper food, or, rather, the absence or insufficient supply of fresh meat and vegetables in the diet; to which cold, humidity, want of exercise and fresh air may be added as secondary ones. Hence its frequent, fatal visitations formerly on shipboard, and its still occasional occurrence in ill-victualled ships during long voyages. The treatment mainly consists in adopting a liberal diet of fresh animal food and green vegetables, with ripe food and an ample allowance of mild ale or beer, or lemonade made from the fresh expressed juice, as beverages. In serious cases, tonics, as quinine and steel, should also be administered.

Wrinkles and looseness of the skin depend chiefly on the attenuation of the cutis or true skin and the reduction in the bulk of the underlying surfacial portions of the body. They cannot be regarded as a disease of the skin; but are the result of long continued bad health, anxiety and study, and of general emaciation and old age. Cleanliness, nutritious food, vigorous outdoor exercise, agreeable occupation of the mind, and an equable and happy temper, retard their formation. Whatever tends to promote the general health and to increase the bulk of the body, and particularly the disposition of fat in the cellular tissues, also tends to remove them and to increase the smoothness and beauty of the skin. The free and frequent use of warm water and soap, followed by the daily use of mild, stimulating, cosmetic lotions or fomentations, or friction with warm oil of a like character, and cod-liver oil internally, is all that art can do for the purpose.

Excoriations, in popular language, are those cases of soreness produced by chafing under the arms, behind the ears, and in the wrinkles and folds of the skin generally. They occur chiefly in infancy, and in stout persons with a delicate skin, who perspire excessively. Extreme cleanliness, and carefully wiping the parts dry after washing, with the subsequent use of a little violet powder, or finely powdered starch, or French chalk scraped or grated very fine, dusted over the parts once or twice a day, will generally remove them and prevent their recurrence.

WASHES FOR THE FACE.

We do not approve of face washes, but as some ladies will use them, we recommend the following as harmless: Dampen with glycerine tempered with rose-water, then powder with the finest magnesia. It imparts a charming whiteness.

Less harmless, but more frequently used, is to procure five cents' worth of bismuth, of flake white, and of powdered chalk; mix with five cents' worth of rose-water. Great care must be taken to wash off this preparation before retiring to rest, as the bismuth is of a hurtful nature.

To Remove Freckles.—Freckles are of two kinds: Those occasioned by exposure to the sunshine, and consequently evanescent, are denominated "summer freckles"; those which are constitutional and permanent are called "cold freckles." With regard to the latter, it is impossible to give any advice which will be of value. They result from causes not to be affected by mere external applications. Summer freckles are not difficult to deal with, and with a little care the skin may be kept free from this cause of disfigurement by using either of the following lotions:—

First: Scrape horse-radish into a cup of sour milk, let it stand twelve hours, strain, and apply two or three times a day.

Second: Into half a pint of milk squeeze the juice of a lemon, with a spoonful of brandy, and boil, skimming well; add a dram of rock alum. Apply freely.

Magic Lotion for Removing Freckles.—Dissolve three grains of borax in five drams each of rose-water and orange-flower water. A splendid and harmless remedy is equal parts of pure glycerine and rose-water, applied every night and allowed to dry on the skin.

To Remove Freckles and Tan.—Tincture of benzoin, one pint; tincture of tolu, one-half pint; oil rosemary, one-half ounce. Put one teaspoonful of the above mixture in one-quarter pint of water, and then with a towel thoroughly bathe the face. Do this every night and morning.

To Expel Freckles.—Finely powdered nitre is excellent. Apply it to the face with the finger moistened with water and dipped in the powder.

Cleopatra's Freckle Balm.—A splendid article. Venice soap, one ounce; lemon juice, half ounce; oil of bitter almonds, quarter ounce; deliquidated oil of tartar, quarter ounce; oil of rhodium, three drops. Dissolve the soap in the lemon juice, then add the two oils, and put the whole in the sun till it acquires the consistency of ointment, and then add the oil rhodium. Anoint the freckly face at night with this balm, and wash in the morning with pure water.

Lemon Cream for Sunburn and Freckles.—Put two spoonfuls of sweet cream into half a pint of new milk, squeeze into it the juice of a lemon, add half a glass of genuine French brandy, a little alum and loaf sugar; boil the whole, skim it well, and when cool it is fit for use.

Wash to Prevent Sunburn.—Take two drams of borax, one dram of Roman alum, one dram of camphor, half an ounce of sugar candy, one pound of ox-gall. Mix and stir well together, and repeat the stirring three or four times a day until it becomes transparent; then strain it through filtering or blotting paper, and it will be fit for use. Wash the face with the mixture before you go into the sun.

Grape Lotion for Sunburn.—Dip a bunch of green grapes in a basin of water; sprinkle it with powdered alum and salt mixed; wrap the grapes in paper, and bake them under hot ashes; then express the juice, and wash the face with the liquid, which will remove either freckles, tan or sunburn.

To Soften and Whiten the Skin—Pate Axerasive of Bozin.—This celebrated perfume has the distinction of being highly commended by the French Royal Academy of Medicine. It is better for toilet use than soaps, which contain alkali.

Take powder of bitter almonds, eight ounces; oil of the same, twelve ounces; savon vert of the perfumes, eight ounces; spermaceti, four ounces; soap powder, four ounces; cinnabar, two drams; essence of rose, one dram. Melt the soap and spermaceti with the oil in a bath water; add the powder, and mix the whole in a marble mortar. It forms a paste which softens and whitens the skin better than any soap.

To Remove Red Pimples.—Sulphur water, one ounce; acetated liquor of ammonia, quarter ounce; liquor of potassa, one grain; white wine vinegar, two ounces; distilled water, two ounces.

To Remove Black Specks or Flesh-worms.—Squeeze them by pressing the skin, and then wash with warm water and rub well with a towel. Then apply the following lotion: Liquor of potassa, one ounce; cologne, two ounces.

Preparation for Whitening the Face and Neck.—For bleaching and purifying the skin of the face and neck, making them beautifully smooth and white: Terebinth of Mecca, three grains; oil of sweet almonds, four ounces; spermaceti, two drams; flour of zinc, one dram; white wax, two drams; rose-water, six drams. Mix in a bath water, and melt together. After washing, before retiring (use water as hot as can be borne), anoint the face and neck freely with this preparation.

To Cure Profuse Perspiration.—Bathe the hands, feet, and parts of the body where the perspiration is greatest, with a cold infusion of rosemary and sage, and afterwards dust the stockings and under-garments with a mixture of two drams of camphor, four ounces of orris root, and sixteen ounces of starch, the whole reduced to a fine powder. Put the mixture in a coarse muslin bag, and shake it over the clothes.

Cleopatra's Enamel for Whitening the Hands and Arms.—One ounce of myrrh, four ounces of honey, two ounces of yellow wax, six ounces of rose-water. Mix well together the wax, honey and rose-water in a dish held over boiling water, and add the myrrh while hot. Rub this thickly over the skin before going to bed.

To Cure Freckles and Parched or Rough Skin.—Take one ounce of sweet almonds, or of pistachia nuts, half a pint of elder or rose-water, and one ounce of pure glycerine; grate the nuts and put the powder in a little linen or cotton bag, and squeeze it for several minutes in the rose-water; then add the glycerine and a little perfume. Use it by wetting the face two or three times a day. This is a grateful application for a parched, rough skin, and is good for the removal of freckles. It should be allowed to dry thoroughly. When it feels pasty or sticky it may be washed off with a little warm water without soap.

TO PURIFY THE BREATH.

There is nothing more disagreeable to people with whom we associate than for them to be able to detect a bad odor from our breath when in their company. Yet a great many are afflicted in this way. The following will purify and sweeten the breath: Chlorate of lime, seven drams; vanilla sugar, three drams; gumeratic, five drams. Mix well with warm water to a stiff paste, and cut into lozenges. Take a lozenge occasionally.

TO BLEACH AND PURIFY THE SKIN OF THE FACE AND NECK.

A celebrated physician gives the following as a good skin bleacher and purifier: Half a pint of skim milk; slice into it as much cucumber as it will cover, and let it stand an hour; then bathe the face, neck, and hands. Wash them off with clean soft water when the cucumber extract is dry. If the skin is rough from exposure to the wind, an application of buttermilk at night, washed off with fine carbolic soap in the morning, will make the skin smooth and natural.

To Permanently Remove Black Specks or "Flesh-worms."—Sometimes little black specks appear about the base of the nose, or on the forehead, or in the hollow of the chin, which are called flesh-worms, and are occasioned by coagulated lymph that obstructs the pores of the skin. They may be squeezed out by pressing the skin, and ignorant people suppose them to be little worms. They are permanently removed by washing with very warm water, and severe friction with a towel and then applying a little of the following preparation: Liquor of potassa, one ounce; cologne, two ounces; white brandy, four ounces.

French Face Wash Purifies and Brightens the Complexion.—Take equal parts of the seeds of the melon, pumpkin, gourd, and cucumber, pounded till they are reduced to powder; add to it sufficient fresh cream to dilute the flour, and then add milk enough to reduce the whole to a thick paste. Add a grain of musk and a few drops of the oil of lemon. Anoint the face with this, leave it on twenty or thirty minutes, or over night if convenient, and wash off with warm water. It gives a remarkable purity and brightness to the complexion.

Or, try this; splendid.—Infuse a handful of well-sifted wheat bran for four hours in white wine vinegar; add to it five yolks of eggs and two grains of musk, and distill the whole. Bottle it, keep carefully corked for fifteen days, when it will be fit for use. Apply over night, and wash in the morning with tepid water.

To Remove Pimples.—There are many kinds of pimples, some of which partake almost of the nature of ulcers, which require medical treatment; but the small red pimple, which is most common, may be removed by applying the following twice a day: Sulphur water, one ounce; acetated liquid of ammonia, one-quarter ounce; liquor of potassa, one grain; white wine vinegar, two ounces; distilled water, two ounces. These pimples are sometimes cured by frequent washing in warm water and prolonged friction with a coarse towel. The cause of these pimples is obstruction of the skin and imperfect circulation.

To Remove Tan.—*Creme de'l Enclos.*—New milk, half a pint; lemon juice, one-quarter ounce; white brandy, half ounce. Boil the whole and skim it clear from all scum. Use night and morning.

A Cosmetic Bath.—Take two pounds of barley or bean flour, eight pounds of bran, and a few handfuls of Borage leaves. Boil these ingredients in a sufficient quantity of spring water. This both cleanses and softens the skin in a superior manner.

Kalydor for the Complexion.—For pimples, freckle-tanned skin, or scurf on the skin. Take emulsion of bitter almonds, one pint; oxymuriate of quicksilver, two and one-half pints; sal ammoniac, one dram. To be used moderately by means of a sponge, after washing the face and hands with pure soap and warm water.

To Improve the Skin.—Take two ounces of Venice soap and dissolve it in two ounces of lemon juice. Add one ounce of the oil of bitter almonds and a like quantity of the oil of tartar. Mix the whole and stir it well till it has acquired the consistence of soap, and use it as such for the hands. The paste of sweet almonds, which contains an oil fit for keeping the skin soft and elastic and removing indurations, may be beneficially applied to the hands and arms.

Wash a la Marie Antoinette.—Gives a beautiful brilliancy to the complexion. Take half a dozen lemons and cut them in small pieces, a small handful of the leaves of white lilies and southernwood, and infuse them in two quarts of cows milk, with an ounce and a half of white sugar and an ounce of rock alum. These are to be distilled in palneum mariæ. The face at bedtime is to be rubbed with this liquid, and it will give a beautiful luster to the complexion. It is a safe application, and its effects are certain.

Liquid Rouge.—Harmless—a perfect imitation of nature. For ladies who wish to use a little artificial bloom the following is recommended. A liquid rouge to produce a perfect imitation of the colors of nature is prepared as follows: Add to a pint of French brandy, half an ounce of benzoin, an ounce of red sandalwood, half an ounce of Brazil wood and the same quantity of rock alum. Cork the bottle carefully, shake it well once a day, and at the end of twelve days it will be fit for use. The cheeks are to be lightly touched with it.

Milk of Roses.—This is a cosmetic. Pound an ounce of almonds in a mortar very finely; then put in shavings of honey soap in a small quantity. Add enough rose-water to enable you to work the composition with the pestle into a fine cream; and in order that it may keep, add to the whole an ounce of spirits of wine, by slow degrees. Scent with otto of roses. Strain through muslin. Apply to the face with a sponge or a piece of lint.

Circassian Cream.—This celebrated preparation is made, according to a published recipe, in this way: Castor oil, one pint; almond oil, four ounces; liquid potassa, three drams; essence of bergamot, oil of cloves, and oil of lemon, in equal quantities; and about a dozen drops of otto of roses.

Toilet Vinegar.—Add to the best malt vinegar, half a pint of cognac and a pint of rose-water. Scent may be added, and if so, it should be first mixed with the spirit before the other ingredients are put in.

Bloom Rose.—This is a preparation of carmine for the face and lips. Take a quarter of a dram of carmine and place it in a phial with half a dram of liquid ammonia; keep for a few days, occasionally shaking the mixture; then dilute with two ounces of rose-water, to which half a dram of essence of roses has been added. Draw off and keep a week or ten days, then apply with the corner of a soft hand-kerchief, taking care that if the color is too bright it is reduced by means of pure water.

Certain Cure for Eruptions, Pimples, Etc.—Having in numerous instances seen the good effects of the following prescription, I can certify to its perfect rem-edy: Dilute corrosive sublimate with the oil of almonds, apply it to the face occa-sionally, and in few days a cure will be effected.

To Clear the Complexion, and Reduce the Size.—It is essential that the blood should be cleansed. Take a teaspoonful of powdered charcoal, mixed with water or honey, for three successive nights, then use a seidlitz powder to remove it from the system. It acts splendidly upon the system and purifies the blood; but under no circumstances must the physic be neglected to carry the chemicals from the system; if not, ill effects are certain to follow.

To Cure and Refine a Stippled or Blotched Skin.—A small dose of teraxacum every other night will most materially aid in refining the skin. It is a month's or six weeks' job to accomplish the desired result. You must also wear a mask of quilted cotton, wet in cold water, over night. Do not get discouraged, for it is worth the trouble.

TO CURE AND PREVENT WRINKLES.

Pomade d'Hebe.—This pomade is used for the removal of wrinkles. To make: Melt white wax, one ounce, to gentle heat; add juice of lily bulbs, two ounces; add honey, two ounces; rose-water, two drams; and otto of roses, a drop or two. Use twice a day.

Lotion for Wrinkles.—Beautifies the face, preserves the freshness of youth, and gives a beautiful brilliancy to the skin. Take the second water of barley, one pint, and strain through a piece of fine linen; add a dozen drops of the balm of Mecca; shake it well together until the balm is thoroughly incorporated with the water, which will be effected when the water assumes a whitish or turgid appear-ance. Before applying, wash the face with soft water. If used once a day, this lotion will beautify the face, remove wrinkles, preserve the freshness of youth, and give a surprising brilliancy to the skin.

Wash for Wrinkles.—Take two ounces of the juice of onions, two ounces of the white lily, two ounces of Norboune honey, and one ounce of white wax; put the whole into a new earthen pipkin until the wax is melted, then take the pipkin (crock) off the fire, and continue stirring briskly until the mixture grows cold. This should be applied on going to bed and allowed to remain on till the morning.

To Remove Wrinkles.—To one fluid ounce of tincture of gum benzoin add seven fluid ounces of distilled rose-water and one-half ounce of glycerine. Bathe face, neck, and hands with it at night, letting it dry on. Wash off in the morning with a very little pure white castile soap and soft water. This is a famous cosmetic, and has been sold under various names. It is an excellent remedy for tan, freckles, and sunburn also.

HOW TO HAVE BRILLIANT, BEAUTIFUL EYES.

Beautiful eyes are the gift of nature; but even those of the greatest beauty may owe something to the toilet, while those of an indifferent kind are very susceptible of improvement. We entirely discountenance any tampering with the eye itself, with a view to giving it luster or brightness. The sight has often been injured by the use of belladonna, preparations of the calabar bean, eyebright, and other substances having a strong effect on the eyes. But without touching the eye itself, it is possible to give the effect of brightness, softness, etc., by means of the eyelids and eyelashes. Made-up eyes are by no means desirable, and to many are singularly displeasing; but the same may be said of made-up faces generally. Some ladies are, however, persuaded that it adds to their charms to give the eyes a long, almond shape—after the Egyptian type—while very many are persuaded that the eye is not seen to advantage unless its apparent size is increased by the darkening of the lids. Both these effects are produced by kohl, a black powder, which may be procured at the chemist's, and is mixed with rose-water and applied with a camel's-hair brush.

To Cure Weak Eyes.—It is well to have on the toilet table a remedy for inflamed eyes. Spermaceti ointment is simple and well adapted for the purpose. Apply at night, and wash off with rose-water in the morning. Golden ointment will serve a like purpose. Or, there is a simple lotion made by dissolving a very small piece of alum and a piece of lump sugar of the same size in a quart of water. Put the ingredients into water cold and let them simmer. Bathe the eyes frequently with it. Sties in the eyes are irritating and disfiguring. Foment with warm water; at night apply a bread and milk poultice. When a white head forms, prick it with a fine needle. Should the inflammation be obstinate, a little citerine ointment may be applied, care being taken that it does not get into the eye, and an aperient should be tried.

To Improve the Eyelashes.—Many people speak highly of this secret. Trim the tiny points slightly, and anoint with this salve: Two drams of ointment of nitric oxida of mercury, and one dram of lard. Mix the lard and ointment well, and anoint the edges of the eyelids night and morning, after each time, with milk and water. This will restore the lashes when all other remedies fail. It is not known in this country, and is a valuable secret.

To Cure Weakness of Eyes.—Sulphate of copper, fifteen grains; camphor, four grains; boiling water, four ounces. Mix, strain, and when cold make up to four pints with water. Bathe the eyes night and morning with a portion of the mixture.

How to Have Beautiful Eyelashes.—The effect of the eyes is greatly aided by beautiful eyelashes. These may be secured to a certain extent by a little care, especially if it is taken early in life. The extreme ends should be cut with a pair of small, sharp scissors, care being taken to preserve the natural outline, not to leave jagged edges. Attention to this matter results in the lengthening of the lashes. Dyeing them is another expedient often resorted to for increasing their effect. A good permanent black is all that is needed, and for this use Indian ink. As an impromptu expedient to serve for one night, a hairpin held for a few seconds in the flame of a candle, and drawn through the lashes, will serve to color them well, and with sufficient durability. It need scarcely be added that the hairpin must be suffered to grow cold before it is used, or the consequence may be that no eyelash will be left to color. Good eyebrows are not to be produced artificially. It is possible, however, to prevent those that are really good from degenerating through neglect. When wiping the face dry after washing, pass a corner of the towel over the forefinger and set the eyebrows in the form you wish them to assume. And when oiling the hair, do not forget to oil the eyebrows also.

To Cure Watery and Inflamed Eyes.—Foment frequently with decoction of poppy heads. When the irritation and inflammation occur, a teaspoonful of cognac brandy in four ounces of spring water may be used three or four times in the course of the day as a strengthening lotion.

General Care of the Eyes.—The eyes, of all the features, stand pre-eminent for their beauty and ever-varying powers of expression, and for being the organs of the most exalted, delicate and useful of the senses. It is they alone that "reveal the external forms of beauty to the mind, and enable it to perceive them, even at a distance, with the speed of light. It is they alone that clothe the whole creation with the magic charms of color, and fix on every object the identity of figure. It is the eyes alone, or chiefly, that reveal the emotions of the mind to others, and that clothe the features with the language of the soul. Melting with pity, or glowing with hope, or redolent with love, benevolence, desire, or emulation, they impart to the countenance those vital fascinations which are the peculiar attributes of man." "And when the mind is subdued by fear, anxiety or shame, or overwhelmed by sorrow or despair, the eyes, like faithful chroniclers, still tell the truthful story of the mental disquietude. And hatred, anger, envy, pride, and jealousy, ambition, avarice, discontent, and all the varied passions and emotions that torment, excite or depress the human soul, and find a resting place in the human breast, obtain expression in the eyes. At one moment the instruments of receiving and imparting pleasure, at another the willing or passive instruments of pain, their influences and changes are as varied and boundless as the empire of thought itself." Through their silent expressions the mind reveals its workings to the external world in signs more rapid and as palpable as those uttered by the tongue. It is "the eyes alone that stamp the face with the outward symbol of animation and vitality," and which endue it with the visible "sanctity of reason." The eye is, indeed, the chief and most speaking feature of the face, and the one on whose excellence, more than any other, its beauty depends.

Theories have been based on even the peculiar color of the eyes. Thus, it is said that dark blue eyes are found chiefly in persons of delicate, refined or effeminate mental character; light blue eyes, and more particularly gray eyes, in the hardy and active; hazel eyes, in the masculine, vigorous, and profound; black eyes, in those whose energy is of a desultory or remittent character, and who exhibit fickleness in pursuits and affection. Greenish eyes, it is asserted, have the same general meaning as gray eyes, with the addition of selfishness or a sinistrous disposition. These statements, however, though based on some general truths, and supported by popular opinion, are liable to so many exceptions as to be unreliable and valueless in their individual applications.

Shakespeare is said to have had hazel eyes; Swift, blue eyes; Milton, Scott, and Byron, gray eyes. Wellington and Napoleon are also said to have had gray eyes.

A beautiful eye is one that is full, clear, and brilliant; appropriate in color to the complexion, and in form to the features, and of which the connected parts — the eyelids, eyelashes, and eyebrows, which, with it, in a general view of the subject, collectively form the external eye — are also beautiful, and in keeping with it.

To increase the beauty and expression of the eyes, various means are occasionally had recourse to, nearly all of which, except those herein mentioned in connection with the eyelashes and eyebrows, are not merely highly objectionable, but even dangerous. Thus, some fashionable ladies and actresses, to enhance the clearness and brilliancy of their eyes before appearing in public, are in the habit of exposing them to air slightly impregnated with the vapor of prussic acid. This is done by placing a single drop of the dilute acid at the bottom of an eyecup or eyeglass, and then holding the cup or glass against the eye for a few seconds, with the head in an inclined position. It has also been asserted, and I believe correctly, that certain ladies of the demimonde rub a very small quantity of belladonna ointment on the brow over each eye, or moisten the same part with a few drops of tincture of belladonna. This produces dilation of the pupil, and gives that peculiar fullness and an expression of languor to the eyes which, by some, is regarded as exceedingly fascinating. The use of these active medicinals in this way must be manifestly injurious; and when frequent, or long continued or carried to excess, must necessarily result in impaired vision, if not in actual blindness.

The following means of repairing and restoring the sight, which has for some time been going the round of the press, being based on scientific principles, may be appropriately inserted here:

For nearsightedness, close the eyes and pass the fingers, very gently, several times across them outward, from the canthus, or corner next the nose, towards the temple. This tends slightly to flatten the corner and lens of the eye, and thus to lengthen or extend the angle of vision. The operation should be repeated several times a day, or at least always after making one's toilet, until shortsightedness is nearly or completely removed. For long sight, loss of sight by age, weak sight, and generally for all those defects which require the use of magnifying glasses, gently pass the finger, or napkin, from the outer angle or corner of the eyes inward, above and below the eyeball, towards the nose. This tends slightly to "round up" the eyes, and thus to preserve or to restore the sight. It should be done every time the eyes are washed, or oftener.

TO HAVE A BEAUTIFUL MOUTH AND LIPS.

The beauty of the human mouth and lips, the delicacy of their formation and tints, their power of expression, which is only inferior to that of the eyes, and their elevated position as the media with the palate, tongue, and teeth, by which we communicate our thoughts to others in an audible form, need scarcely be dilated on here. The poet tells us that:

"The lips of woman out of roses take
The tints with which they ever stain themselves.
They are the beautiful, lofty shelves
Where rests the sweetness which the young hours make,
And which the earnest boy, whom we call Love,
Will often sip in sorrow or in play.
Health, when it comes, doth ruddiness approve,
But his strong foe soon flatters it away!
Disease and health for a warm pair of lips,
Like York and Lancaster, wage active strife:
One on his banner front the White rose keeps,
And one the Red; and thus with woman's life,
Her lips are made a battle-field for those
Who struggle for the color of a rose."

A beautiful mouth is one that is moderately small, and has a well-defined and graceful outline; and beautiful lips are gracefully molded, neither thick nor thin, nor compressed nor lax, and that are endowed with expression and are tinted with the hues of health.

The ladies of Eastern nations commonly heighten the hue and freshness of their lips by means of cosmetics, a practice which in Western Europe is only adopted on the stage, and occasionally by courtesans and ladies of the demimonde.

Chapped lips most frequently occur in persons with pale, bluish, moist lips and a languid circulation, who are much exposed to the wind or who are continually moving from heated apartments to the external air. East and north-east winds are those that generally produce them. The occasional application of a little cold cream, lip salve, spermaceti ointment, or any other mild unguent, will generally prevent them, and remove them when they have already formed. A still more elegant and effective preventive and remedy is glycerine diluted with about twice its weight of eau-de-rose, or glycerinated lip salve or balsam.

The moist vesicular eruption of the lips, referred to above, may also generally be prevented by the use of glycerine, or any of the preparations just mentioned. After its accession, the best treatment is to freely dust the affected portion of the lips with violet powder, finely powdered starch, prepared chalk, or French chalk or talc reduced to an impalpable powder by scraping or grating it.

The following formulas of preparations are all valuable for beautifying and preserving the beauty of the lips:—

White Lip Salve—No. 1.—Take half a pound spermaceti ointment, liquify it by the heat of warm water, and stir in one-half dram neroli or essence de petit-grain. In a few minutes pour off the clear portion from the dregs (if any) and add twenty drops of oil of rose. Lastly, before it cools, pour it into jars.

Lip Salve—No. 2.—This indispensable adjunct to the toilet is made by melting in a jar, placed in a basin of boiling water, a quarter of an ounce each of white wax and spermaceti; flour of benzoin, fifteen grains; and half an ounce of oil of almonds. Stir till the mixture is cool. Color red with two-penny worth of alkanet root. Splendid for keeping the lips healthy and of a beautiful crimson color.

French Lip Salve.—Lard, twenty-six ounces; white wax, two ounces; nitre and alum in fine powder, of each one-half ounce; alkanet to color.

German Lip Salve.—Butter of cacao, one-half ounce; oil of almonds, one-quarter ounce; melt together with a gentle heat, and add six drops of essence of lemon.

THE CARE OF THE TEETH.

The influence which the teeth are capable of exercising on the personal appearance is usually known and admitted.

The teeth have formed especial objects of attention, in connection with the toilet and cosmetic arts, from almost the earliest ages of the world to the present time. History and tradition, and the researches of archæologists among the remains of the prehistoric nations of the East, show us that even dentistry may trace back its origin to a date not very long subsequent to the "confusion of tongues."

We are told that the ancient Welsh took particular care of their teeth, by frequently rubbing them with a stick of green hazel and a woollen cloth. To prevent their premature decay, they scrupulously avoided acid liquids, and invariably abstained from all hot food and drink.

Europeans pride themselves on teeth of pearly whiteness; but many Asiatic nations regard them as beautiful only when of a black color. The Chinese, in order to blacken them, chew what is called "betel" or "betel nut," a common masticatory in the East. The Siamese and the Tonquinese do the same, but to a still greater extent, which renders their teeth as black as ebony, or more so. As the use of the masticatory is generally not commenced until a certain age, the common practice is to stain the teeth of the boys and girls with a strong preparation of it, on the former attaining the age of ten or twelve.

Keeping the lips apart and breathing through the mouth instead of the nose, and, particularly, sleeping with the mouth open, are habits which are very prejudicial to the teeth and gums. In this way the mouth forms a trap to catch the dust and gritty particles floating in the atmosphere, which soon mechanically injure the enamel of the teeth by attrition.

On the subject of cleanliness in connection with the teeth and mouth, it may be said that the mouth cannot be too frequently rinsed during the day, and that it should be more particularly so treated after each meal. Pure cold water is the best for the purpose. It not only cleans the teeth and mouth, but exerts a tonic action on the gums, which warm water, or even tepid water, is deficient in. When cold water cannot be tolerated, tepid water may be employed, the temperature being slightly lowered once every week or ten days until cold water can be borne. Every one who abhors a fœtid breath, rotten teeth, and the toothache, would do well to thoroughly clean his teeth at bedtime, observing to well rinse the mouth with cold water on rising in the morning, and again in the day once, or oftener, as the opportunities occur. With smokers, the use of the toothbrush the last thing at night is almost obligatory if they value their teeth and wish to avoid the unpleasant flavor and sensation which teeth fouled with tobacco smoke occasion in the mouth on awakening in the morning.

As to tooth powders or pastes to be used with the brush, the simplest are the best. Plain camphorated chalk, with or without a little finely powdered pumice stone or burnt hartshorn, is a popular and excellent tooth powder. It is capable of exerting sufficient friction under the brush to ensure pearly whiteness of the teeth without injuring the enamel, whilst the camphor in it tends to destroy the animalcula in the secretions of the mouth, whose skeletons or remains constitute, as we shall presently see, the incrassation popularly called "tartar." Recently-burnt charcoal, in very fine powder, is another excellent tooth powder, which, without injuring the enamel, is sufficiently gritty to clean the teeth and remove the tartar from them, and possesses the advantage of also removing the offensive odor arising from rotten teeth and from decomposing organic matter. The charcoal of the heavy hardwoods, as lignum-vitæ, boxwood, oak, are the best; and these, as to quality, range in the order given. Still more valuable as a dentifrice is areca nut charcoal, which, besides possessing the properties of the other vegetable charcoals in an eminent degree, has valuable ones peculiar to itself.

Some dentists, and some persons in imitation of them, in order to whiten the teeth, rub their surfaces with hydrochloric acid, somewhat dilute; but the practice is a most dangerous one, which, by a few repetitions, will sometimes utterly destroy the enamel and lead to the rapid decay of all the teeth so treated. Should the teeth be much discolored, and ordinary tooth powder prove ineffective, a little lemon juice used with the brush will generally render them perfectly white. It should only be employed occasionally, and the mouth should be well rinsed with water afterwards. A little of the pulp of an orange, used in the same way, is also very effective and safe, as are also ripe strawberries, which may be either rubbed on the teeth with the fingers or applied with the brush. The last form, perhaps, the very best natural dentifrice known. Besides possessing singular power in whitening and cleaning the teeth and rapidly removing tartar, they destroy the offensive odor of rotten teeth and impart an agreeable fragrance to the breath.

The importance of a judicious attention to the teeth, in connection with health, cleanliness, and personal comfort and appearance, cannot be too often alluded to and enforced.

It is no exaggeration to say that, taking the whole community, there are few, very few, who clean their teeth, or even wash their mouths, once a day. With the masses the operation, if performed at all, is confined to the Sabbath day, or to holidays; whilst refined, educated, and cleanly persons regard the operation of cleaning the teeth as a daily duty, as necessary as washing the face and hands. The dirty and vulgar—the two words are here synonymous—wholly neglect it, and too often even consider it as unnecessary, effeminate, and absurd. The consequences of the careless performance, or the neglect, of this really necessary personal duty are not long in being developed. Passing over the degradation of the other features, the offensiveness of the breath, often to a degree which renders the individual uncompanionable, and the unfavorable impression which, like other marks of uncleanliness, they convey of the taste and habits of their possessor, as the immediate effects of habitually neglected and dirty teeth, let us look at the more distant, but not less certain, ones:—

In cases of ordinary toothache, even severe ones, chewing a small piece of really good pellitory will often give relief in a few minutes. Chewing a piece of strong, unbleached Jamaica ginger will often do the same in light cases. The celebrated John Wesley recommended a "few whiffs" at a pipe containing a little caraway seed mixed with tobacco as a simple and ready means of curing the toothache. I can bear testimony to the fact that in some cases it succeeds admirably.

Scarcely anything is more disagreeable, and in marked cases, more disgusting, than fœtid breath. It is unpleasant to the person that has it, and it renders him unfit for the society of others. The cause of stinking breath may generally be traced to rotten teeth, diseased stomach, or worms. When the first are the cause, the teeth should be thoroughly cleansed and then "stopped" in the manner already indicated; or, when this is impracticable, the offending tooth, or teeth, may be removed and replaced by artificial ones. When this cannot be done, or is inconvenient, the evil may be greatly lessened by the frequent use of an antiseptic tooth powder, areca nut charcoal or camphorated chalk. Dirty teeth, even when quite sound, always more or less taint the breath. When a foul or a diseased stomach is the cause, mild aperients should be administered; and if these do not succeed, an emetic may be given, scrupulous cleanliness of the teeth being observed, as in the former case. When worms are the cause, worm medicine, under medical direction, will be necessary.

To Cure Foul Breath.—When bad breath is occasioned by teeth, or any local cause, use a gargle consisting of a spoonful of solution of chloride of lime in half a tumbler of water.

To Have White and Beautiful Teeth.—An article known as "The Queen's Tooth Preserver" is made as follows: One ounce of coarsely powdered Peruvian bark, mixed in half a pint of brandy for twelve days. Gargle the mouth (teeth and gums) with a teaspoonful of this liquid, diluted with an equal quantity of rose-water. Always wash off the teeth after each meal with water. Also, twice a day, wash the teeth with the ashes of burned bread—bread burned to ashes.

For Decayed Teeth.—There is nothing better than two scruples of myrrh in fine powder, one scruple of juniper gum, and ten grains of alum, mixed in honey. Apply often to the teeth.

To Cure Toothache.—Take equal parts of camphor, sulphuric ether, ammonia, laudanum, tincture of cayenne, and one-eighth part oil of cloves. Mix well together. Saturate with the liquid a small piece of cotton, and apply to the cavity of the diseased tooth, and the pain will cease immediately.

Premium Tooth Powder.—Six ounces prepared chalk, one-half ounce cassia powder, one ounce orris; mix well.

Mouth Pastilles for Perfuming the Breath.—First: Extract of liquorice, three ounces; oil of cloves, one and a half drams; oil of cinnamon, fifteen drops. Mix, and divide into one-grain pills.

Second: Catechu, seven drams; orris powder, forty grains; sugar, three ounces; oil of rosemary (or of cloves, peppermint, or cinnamon), four drops. Mix, and roll flat on oiled marble slab, and cut into very small tablets.

Feuchtwanger's Tooth Paste.—Powdered myrrh, two ounces; burned alum, one ounce; cream tartar, one ounce; cuttlefish bone, four ounces; drop lake, two ounces; honey, half a gallon. Mix. Reduce the proportion for a small quantity.

Fine Tooth Powder.—Powdered orris root, one ounce; Peruvian bark, one ounce; prepared chalk, one ounce; myrrh, one-half ounce. Mix.

To Remove Offensive Breath.—For this purpose, almost the only substance that should be admitted to the toilet is the concentrated solution of chloride of soda. From six to ten drops of it in a wineglassful of spring water, taken immediately after the operations of the toilet are completed.

In some cases, the odor arising from caries is combined with that of the stomach. If the mouth be well rinsed with a teaspoonful of the solution of the chloride in a tumbler of water, the bad odor of the teeth will be removed.

Rye Tooth Powder.—Rye contains carbonate of lime, carbonate of magnesia, oxide of iron, manganese, and silica, all suitable for application to the teeth. Therefore, a fine tooth powder is made by burning rye, or rye bread, to ashes, and grinding it to powder by passing the rolling-pin over it. Pass the powder through a sieve, and use.

Camphorated Chalk.—This favorite tooth powder is easily made. Take a pound of prepared chalk, and with this mix two drams of camphor very finely powdered, and moisten with spirits of wine. Thoroughly mix.

To Remove the Yellow Color from Teeth.—Take of dry hypochlorite of lime, one-half dram; red coral, two drams. Tincturate and mix thoroughly. This powder is employed in the following manner: A new brush is slightly moistened, then dipped in the powder and applied to the teeth. A few days after the use of this powder the teeth will acquire a beautiful white color.

Camphor Paste.—Take one ounce of oil ammoniac, four drams of camphor. Let the above be very finely powdered, then mix it with sufficient honey to make it into a smooth paste; triturate it until entirely smooth. This is a most excellent paste for preserving and beautifying the teeth.

Preservative Tincture for the Teeth and Gums.—Take four drams of camphor, one ounce of tincture of myrrh, one ounce of tincture of bark, and one ounce of rectified spirits of wine; mix them, and put 30 or 40 drops in a wineglassful of water. Pour a little of this upon your brush before you apply it to the powder, and when the teeth are clean, wash the mouth, teeth, and gums with the remainder. It will in ordinary cases prevent toothache.

Powerfully Cleansing Dentifrice.—Take fine powder of pumice stone, four drams; fine powder of cuttlefish bone, four drams; add one scruple of subcarbonate of soda. Mix them well together, color and scent according to taste, and then pass it through a fine sieve.

Infallible Cure for Toothache.—Take alum, reduced to an impalpable powder, two drams; nitreous spirits of ether, seven drams. Mix, and apply them to the tooth. This is said to be an infallible cure for all kinds of toothache, unless the disease is connected with rheumatism.

Mixture for Decayed Teeth.—Make a balsam with a sufficient quantity of honey, two scruples of myrrh in fine powder, a scruple of gum juniper, and ten grains of rock alum. A portion to be applied frequently to the decayed tooth.

To Whiten and Beautify the Teeth.—Take gum tragacanth, one ounce; pumice stone, two drams; gum arabic, one ounce; cream of tartar, one ounce. Dissolve the gums in rose-water, and adding to it the powder, form the whole into little sticks, which are to be dried slowly in the shade, and afterwards kept for use. Use on the brush like soap.

HOW TO HAVE SOFT, WHITE AND BEAUTIFUL HANDS.

There are very few beautiful hands, but to make the hands beautiful rests, with scarcely an exception, with the possessor. Now that chiromancy has become so fashionable as to be a part of a great many entertainments, it is very desirable that the hands should present an attractive appearance. A soft, white, delicate hand, with neatly-kept nails, forms an important factor in a pleasing personal appearance, and is something any man or woman may possess themselves of with a little care. Of course it goes without saying, that requisite is perfect cleanliness of both the hands and nails. The best and purest soap should be used, and when soft water cannot be obtained, a few drops of ammonia, or a little borax, should be added to the water in which the hands are washed, and they should always be thoroughly dried. A lotion of one ounce glycerine, one ounce rose-water, ten drops of carbolic acid, and forty drops of hamamelis, is excellent to use on the hands before they are dried each time they are washed.

Persons who do housework should wear the India rubber gloves which are made for the purpose and can be purchased in any size for from $1.00 to $1.25 as they are with or without wrists.

Rubbing the hands once or twice a day in oatmeal tends to whiten them and make them soft and flexible.

The following bleaches the hands and arms and makes them beautifully soft and white:—

Bleaching Lotion.—Bitter almonds, ten ounces; iris powder, one ounce; pulverized horse-chestnut, two ounces; essence of bergamot, one dram; carbonate of potash, two drams; mix. Use on the hands after washing, and on retiring for the night.

Five grains of chloridated lime in a pint of warm water will whiten the hands and remove all stains, but as this is not always quite harmless to a delicate skin, it is perhaps better to remove stains with a cut of lemon, and use the preparation given above for whitening them.

Tight lacing and tight sleeves, and even tight shoes, will cause the hands to be an unsightly red, for which no lotion or care is a remedy. If, however, all the clothing is worn so as to allow a free circulation, and the directions which have been given are regularly and constantly followed, any hand will become white, supple and delicate—a pleasure to both possessor and beholder; and it is really worth the care, which after a little time becomes a fixed habit and so is scarcely noticeable, to have such hands.

To Make the Hands White and Delicate.—Should you wish to make your hands white and delicate, wash them in hot milk and water for a day or two. On retiring to rest, rub them well over with palm oil, and put on a pair of woollen gloves. The hands should be thoroughly washed with hot water and soap the next morning, and a pair of soft leather gloves worn during the day; they should be frequently rubbed together to promote circulation. Sunburnt hands should be washed in lime water or lemon juice. Should they be severely freckled, the following will be good to use: Take of distilled water, half a pint; sal ammoniac, half a dram; oxymuriate of quicksilver, four grains; divide the two last in spirit, and gradually add the water to them; add another half pint of water, mix well together, and it is ready for use. It should be applied as often as desirable, with a piece of soft sponge. If rose-water is substituted for distilled water, the effect is pleasanter.

Remedy for Chapped Hands.—The simplest remedy is the camphor ball, to be obtained of all chemists. Powdered hemlock bark put into a piece of muslin and sprinkled on the chaps is highly recommended. Or, wash with oatmeal, and afterwards rub the hands over with dry oatmeal, so as to remove all dampness. It is a good thing to rub the hands and lips with glycerine before going to bed at night. A good oil is made by simmering: Sweet oil, one pint; Venice turpentine, three ounces; lard, half a pound; beeswax, three ounces. Simmer till the wax is melted. Rub on, or apply with a rag.

To Cure Red Hands.—Wash them frequently in warm, not hot, water, using honey soap and soft towel. Dry with violet powder, and again with a soft, dry handkerchief. Take exercise enough to promote circulation, and do not wear gloves too tight.

Almond Paste for the Hands.—Take one pound of sweet almonds, one-quarter of a pound of bread crumbs, one half a pint of spring water, one-half a pint of brandy, and the yolks of two eggs. Pound the almonds with a few drops of vinegar or water, to prevent them oiling; add the crumbs of bread, which moisten with the brandy as you mix it with the almonds and the yolks of eggs. Set this mixture over a slow fire, and stir it continually or it will adhere to the edges.

Almond Paste for Chapped Hands (which will preserve them smooth and white).—The daily use of the following paste will keep the hands smooth and white: Mix a quarter of a pound of unsalted hog's lard, which has been washed in common, and then in rose, water, with the yolks of two fresh eggs and a large spoonful of honey. Add as much paste from almonds (well pounded in a mortar) as will work it into a paste.

General Remarks.—The human hand, regarded either with reference to its ingenious construction and usefulness, or to its beauty, stands alone, in its superlative excellence, in the whole animal world. In no species of animal is the hand so wonderfully formed and so perfectly developed as in man.

To preserve the delicacy and beauty of the hands, some little care, and more than that which is ordinarily bestowed on them, is required. Foremost in consideration must be the subject of cleanliness. Dirty and coarse hands are no less marks of slothfulness and lowbreeding than clean and delicate hands are of refinement and gentility. To promote softness and whiteness of the skin, mild emollient soaps, or those abounding in oil or fat, should alone be adopted for common use; by which means the tendency to contract chaps and chilblains, and roughness from drying winds, will also be lessened. The coarse, strong kinds of soap, those abounding in alkali, should be rejected, as they tend to render the skin rough, dry and brittle. Rain, or soft, water is the best natural water for washing the hands, as it cleanses them more rapidly and completely than ordinary hard water, and with the use of less soap. It may be advantageously used tepid, or even warm; but hot water should be avoided. Distilled water, when obtainable, is preferable to even rain water. In the absence of these, water that has been boiled and allowed to settle and cool may be employed. With hard water the hands are cleansed with difficulty, and though it may be readily softened by the addition of a little soda, such an addition tends to make the skin of a delicate hand somewhat hard and rough. If hard water must be used to wash with, the only harmless substance that can be conveniently added to it is a little good powdered borax. This will also cause it to exert a genial action on the skin. Oatmeal and warm water used every night and morning as a wash will whiten and soften the roughest and darkest hands.

Coarse, Red, Dark-Skinned Hands may be whitened by the occasional use of a few grains of chloride of lime, with warm water, in the manner mentioned above.

Roughness of the Hands, induced by exposure to cold and drying winds, may, in general, be removed by the use of a little powdered pumice stone with the soap in washing them. The subsequent application, particularly at night, of the above lotions, or of two or three drops of almond or olive oil, well rubbed in, will usually effect the object completely.

The hands may be preserved dry for delicate work by rubbing a little club moss (lycopodium), in fine powder, over them. So repellent is this substance of moisture, that if a small quantity of it be sprinkled on the surface of a basin of water, the hand, by a little adroitness, may be plunged to the bottom of the basin without becoming wet.

Excessive moisture or perspiration of the hands without obvious cause is generally indicative of debility, or disordered stomach, and requires corresponding treatment. Frequently washing the hands in moderately cold water often proves a local remedy for the inconvenience. The addition of a few grains of alum, sal ammoniac, or sulphate of zinc, or of a teaspoonful of vinegar, to the water greatly increases its efficacy. Extremely delicate and susceptible persons cannot always bear the excessive perspiration of their hands to be thus suddenly lessened, and therefore some discretion should be exercised by them in their attempts to check it.

The Finger Nails require special attention if we desire to preserve them in their highest condition of beauty and usefulness. To keep them clean, the nail-brush and soap and water should be used once or oftener daily, as circumstances demand. Once a day at least, on wiping the hands after washing them, and whilst they are still soft from the action of the water, the free edge of the scarfskin, which, if not attended to, is apt to grow upward over the nails, should be gently loosened and pressed back in a neatly rounded form, by which the occurrence of cracks and sores about their roots (agnails, nail springs, etc.) will be prevented, and a graceful, oval form, ending in a crescentlike space of white, will be ensured. The skin, as a rule, should never be cut, pared, picked or torn off, as is commonly done, and the less it is meddled with, otherwise than in the way just mentioned, the better. The ends or points of the nails should be pared once every week or ten days, according to the rapidity of their growth, which somewhat varies with the season of the year and the habit of the individual. This is best done with a sharp penknife or nail-knife. Scissors are less convenient for the purpose, and have the disadvantage of straining and distorting the nails during the process.

The length and shape of the nails, both for beauty and use, should exactly correspond with the tips of the fingers. Nails extending beyond the ends of the fingers are vulgar, clawlike, and inconvenient; whilst if shorter, particularly much shorter than the fingers, they are unsightly and of little use, and cause the tips of the fingers to become thick and clumsy. Biting the nails should be avoided as a dirty and disagreeable habit, and one utterly destructive to their beauty, strength, and usefulness.

To remove stains and discolorations of the nails, a little lemon juice or vinegar and water is the best application. Should this fail, a few grains of salt of sorrel, oxalic acid, or chloride of lime, each diluted with warm water, may be applied, care being taken to thoroughly rinse the hands in clean water, without soap, afterwards. Occasionally a little pumice stone, in impalpable powder, or powdered cuttlefish bone, putty powder (polisher's peroxide of tin), may be used along with water and a piece of wash-leather, flannel, or the nailbrush, for the same purpose. The frequent use of any of these substances is, however, injurious to the healthy growth, strength, and permanent beauty of the nails. The common practice of scraping the surface of the nails cannot be too strongly censured, as it causes them to become weak and distorted. Blows on the nails, and, indeed, violence to them in any form, also distorts and marks them.

The ladies of Oriental nations commonly dye the nails; and amongst many savage tribes the same practice is adopted, and is not confined to the gentler sex. Amongst Western Europeans, and Americans, white and regularly-formed nails are alone esteemed.

Chapped Hands are common among persons with a languid circulation, who are continually "dabbling" in water during cold weather, and particularly among those with a scrofulous taint, who, without the last, expose their ungloved hands to bleak, cold winds. The best preventives, as well as remedies, are the use of warm gloves out of doors, and the application, night and morning, of a little glycerine, diluted with twice its weight of water, or a little cold cream, spermaceti cerate, salad oil, or any other simple unguent or oil, which should be well rubbed in, the superfluous portion being removed with a towel. This treatment will not only preserve the hands from the effects of cold and damp, but also tend to render them soft and white. Deep chaps which have degenerated into sores should be kept constantly covered with a piece of lint wetted with glycerine or spread with spermaceti ointment, the part being at the same time carefully preserved from dirt, cold, and wind. It is said that a once favorite actress, celebrated for the beauty of her hands, even when in the "sere and yellow leaf," covered them nightly with the flare of a calf or lamb, with the fat attached, over which was drawn a glove or mitten of soft leather. The application of a little glycerine or fatty matter, in the way just indicated, would have been equally effective.

Warts, like chilblains, are too well known to require description. They chiefly attack the hands, and particularly the fingers, but sometimes occur on other portions of the body. They may be removed by rubbing or moistening their extremities every day, or every other day, with lunar caustic, nitric acid, concentrated acetic acid, or aromatic vinegar, care being taken not to wash the hands for some hours after. The first is an extremely convenient and manageable substance, from not being liable to drop or spread; but it produces a black stain, which remains till the cauterized surface peels off. The second produces a yellow stain, in depth proportioned to the strength of the acid employed. This also wears off after the lapse of a few days. The others scarcely discolor the skin.

To Cause the Skin to become Satin-smooth, and to Smell like a bunch of Violets.—Any one using the following preparation will be noted for the fair softness of her complexion and the delicate perfume which emanates from her person. For ladies who like perfume, and care for a satin-smooth skin, the following is an invaluable toilet preparation:—

Have your druggist mix for you one ounce tincture of orris, one ounce tincture of benzoin, ten drops oil of neroli, and ten drops oil of lemon. To use this perfume, add a tablespoonful of it to about a pint of warm water. It will turn as white as milk, and the real perfume will be given off, whereas while in the bottle it has anything but a pleasing odor. Now, after your bath, just take a soft cloth and go over yourself with this milk, dry thoroughly, and you will smell like a bunch of violets. The perfume may be altered to suit you, or you may add any handkerchief extract, but don't omit the benzoin, for that is what gives permanence to the perfume and softness and smoothness to the skin.

To Cause Those Who have Lost the Bloom and Fairness of Early Youth to Regain Them.—Many ladies who as young girls were fair with a lovely rosy bloom, lose these beauties very early in life; very many do this at twenty, or very little later, and become sallow and heavy-eyed, thus losing their principal charm. Now, this is very easily remedied. Go to your druggist and ask him for some iron pills and for some simple purgative to take with them. Get from him directions for taking both, and take strictly according to his directions. In a very short time you will again be fair and rosy and your eyes bright and sparkling; in fact, you will seem to have renewed your youth, and, indeed, you will feel like another person, so light-hearted will you become, in addition to your return of beauty.

THE HAIR.

Its Estimation, Structure, Growth, Management, Etc.—The hair is not only invaluable as a protective covering of the head, but it gives a finish and imparts unequalled grace to the features which it surrounds. Sculptors and painters have bestowed on its representation their highest skill and care, and its description and praises have been sung in the sweetest lays by the poets of all ages. Whether in flowing ringlets, chaste and simple bands, or graceful braids artistically disposed, it is equally charming, and clothes with fascination even the simplest forms of beauty.

> O wondrous, wondrous, is her hair!
> A braided wealth of golden brown,
> That drops on neck and temples bare.

If there is one point more than another on which the tastes of mankind appear to agree, it is that rich, luxuriant, flowing hair is not merely beautiful in itself, but an important, nay, an essential, auxiliary to the highest development of the personal charms. Among all the refined nations of antiquity, as in all time since, the care, arrangement and decoration of the hair formed a prominent and generally leading portion of their toilet. The ancient Egyptians and Assyrians, and other Eastern nations, bestowed on it the most elaborate attention. The ancient Jews, like their modern descendants, were noted for the luxuriance and richness of their hair and the care which they devoted to it. Glossy flowing black hair is represented to have been the glory of the ancient Jewess, and in her person to have exhibited charms of the most imposing character; whilst the chasteness of its arrangement was only equalled by its almost magic beauty. Nor was this luxuriance, and this attention to the hair, confined to the gentler sex, for among the pagan Orientals the hair and beards of the males were not less sedulously attended to. Among the males of Judah and Israel, long flowing ringlets appear to have been regarded as highly desirable and attractive. The reputed beauty and the prodigious length and weight of the hair of Absalom, the son of David, as recorded in the sacred text, would be sufficient to startle the most enthusiastic modern dandy that cultivates the crinal ornament of his person. Solomon the Wise, another son of David, conceived the beauty of hair sufficiently dignified to express figuratively the graces of the Church.

The hair, though devoid of sensibility and unsusceptible of expression under the influence of the will and the ordinary mental feelings, like the mobile portions of the face, and though it may be popularly regarded rather in the light of a parasitic growth than as an essential portion of the body, is capable of being affected by the stronger emotions and passions, and even of aiding their expression in the features. Who is there that, at some period or other of his life, if only in childhood, in a moment of sudden terror or horror, has not experienced the sensation popularly described as "the hair standing on end?" Or who is there that, at some time or other, has not witnessed the partial erection of the hair in children or females under like violent emotions, or seen the representation of it in sculptures or paintings? Those passions, so aptly styled by Gray the "vultures of the mind," frequently affect with wonderful rapidity the health of both the body and the mind, which wreck the hair soon sympathizes with and shares. Instances are recorded in which violent grief in a few weeks has blanched the hair and anticipated the effects of age; and others in which intense terror or horror has affected the same with even greater celerity, the change having occurred in a few days or even in a few hours.

Besides daily attention to the hair, something else is necessary to insure its cleanliness and beauty and the perfect health of the skin of the head from which it springs. For this purpose the head should be occasionally well washed with soap and water, an abundance of water being used and great care being subsequently taken to thoroughly rinse out the whole of the soap with the water in which the head has been washed. The water may be either tepid or cold, according to the feelings or habit of the person; and if the head or hair be very scurfy or dirty, or hard water be used, a few grains of soda (not potash or pearlash) may be advantageously added to the water. This will increase its detersive qualities. After the hair has been washed, which should be done quickly, though thoroughly, it should be freed as much as possible by pressure with the hands and then wiped with a soft, thick towel, which should be done with care, to avoid entangling it. After laying it straight, first with the coarse end of the dressing comb and then with the finer portion, it may be finally dressed.

In ordinary cases once every two or three weeks is often enough to wash the hair and head. The extreme length of ladies' hair will sometimes render the process of washing it very troublesome and inconvenient. In such cases the patient and assiduous use of a clean, good hairbrush, followed by washing the partings and the crown of the head with soap and water, may be substituted.

The occasional washing of the head is absolutely necessary to preserve the health of the scalp and the luxuriance and beauty of the hair when much oil, pomatum or other greasy substance is used in dressing it.

Medical writers have frequently pointed out the ill effects of the free or excessive use of oily or greasy articles for the hair; but their warnings appear to be unheeded by the mass of mankind. Some object to their use altogether. There are, however, exceptions to every rule, and some of these exceptions are noticed elsewhere in this volume. The ill effects referred to chiefly occur from their being used when not required, and in excess, and are aggravated by the neglect of thorough cleanliness.

To improve the growth and luxuriance of the hair, when languid or defective, the only natural and perfectly safe method that can be adopted is to promote the healthy action of the scalp by increasing the vigor of the circulation of the blood through its minute channels. For this purpose nothing is so simple and effective as gentle excitation of the skin by frequent continued friction with the hairbrush, which has the convenience of ease of application and inexpensiveness. The same object may be further promoted by the application of any simple cosmetic wash or other preparation that will gently excite or stimulate the skin or exercise a tonic action on it without clogging its pores. Strong rosemary water or rosemary tea, and a weak solution of the essential oil of either rosemary or garden thyme, are popular articles of this kind. They may be rendered more stimulating by the addition of a little ammonia or a little spirit, or both of them. The skin of the head should be moistened with these on each occasion of dressing the hair, and their diffusion and action promoted by the use of a clean hairbrush. Aromatized water, to which a very little tincture or vinegar of cantharides (preferably the former) has been added, may also be used in the same way, and is in high repute for the purpose. When the skin is pale, lax, and wrinkled, astringent washes may be used. Strong black tea is a convenient and excellent application of this kind. When the skin and hair are dry, and the latter also stiff and untractable, a little glycerine is an appropriate addition to each of the preceding washes or lotions. The occasional use of a little bland oil, strongly scented with oil of rosemary or of origanum, or with both of them, or with oil of mace, or very slightly tinctured with cantharides, is also generally very serviceable when there is poorness and dryness of the hair. When the hair is unnaturally greasy and lax (a defect that seldom occurs), the use of the astringent washes just referred to, or of a little simple oil slightly scented with the essential oil of bitter almonds, will tend to remove or lessen it.

All the articles named above promote the glossiness and waviness of the hair, and are also among the simplest, safest, and best applications that can be employed when the hair is weak and begins to fall off.

To impart some degree of curliness or waviness to the hair when it is naturally straight, and to render it more retentive of the curl imparted to it by papers or by other modes of dressing it, various methods are often adopted and different cosmetics employed. The first object appears to be promoted by keeping the hair for a time in a state intermediate between perfect dryness and humidity, from which different parts of its structure, being unequally affected in this respect, will acquire different degrees of relaxation and rigidity, and thus have a tendency to assume a wavy or slightly curly form, provided the hair be left loose enough to allow it. For this purpose nothing is better than washing the hair with soap and water, to which a few grains of salt of tartar (carbonate of potash) have been added; or it may be slightly moistened with any of the hair washes mentioned in the last paragraph, in each half-pint of which a few grains of the carbonate (say ten or twelve), or a teaspoonful of glycerine, has been dissolved. The moistened hair, after the application of the brush, should be finally loosely adjusted as desired with the dressing-comb. The effect occurs as the hair dries. When oils are preferable to hair washes, those strongly scented with the oil of rosemary, to which a few drops of oil of thyme or origanum may be added, appear to be the most useful.

To cause the hair to retain the position given to it in dressing it, various methods and cosmetics are commonly employed. When the arrangement is a natural one and the hair healthy and tractable, the free use of the hairbrush will usually be sufficient for the purpose. When this is insufficient, the application of a few drops of oil, or, better still, moistening the hair with a little simple water, will effect the object satisfactorily. In very elaborate and unnatural styles of dressing the hair, and to cause it to remain in curl or to retain its position during dancing, or violent exercise, bandoline and cosmetique or hard pomatum are the articles commonly employed in fashionable life. Mild ale or porter has a similar effect, and is often substituted for the preceding expensive cosmetics. The frequent use of any of these articles is objectionable, as they clog up the pores of the skin and shield both it and the hair from the genial action of the atmosphere, which is essential to their healthy vigor. They should, hence, be subsequently removed by carefully washing the head with a little soap and tepid water. Their use may be tolerated in dressing for the ballroom, but on no other occasion. Simple water skillfully employed, as noticed elsewhere, is the best and safest mixture, and under ordinary circumstances is amply sufficient for the purpose.

The practice of artificially changing the color of the hair, and particularly of dyeing it, has descended to us from remote antiquity, and though not so common in Western Europe as formerly, is still far from infrequent at the present day. This might be inferred from the multitude of nostrums for the purpose continually advertised in the newspapers, and from the number of persons who announce themselves as practicing the art, even though the keen and experienced eye did not frequently detect instances of it, as it now does, in the hair and beards of those we see around us. The recent rage after light auburn or reddish hair in fashionable life has, unfortunately, greatly multiplied these instances. The consideration of the subject, however, in its ethical relations does not come within the province of the present work, and I shall confine myself to pointing out how the color of the hair may be changed in the safest and most satisfactory manner.

To change the color of the hair various methods and preparations are employed. The principal of these are intended to darken it, but sometimes the contrary is aimed at. Whichever object is desired, it is necessary that the article or preparation employed to carry it out be not of a caustic or irritant nature, capable of injuriously affecting the delicate skin to which it is applied, or that it may be liable to come in contact with, as is the case with many of the nostrums vended for the purpose. Some of the substances that necessarily enter into the composition of hair strains and hair dyes, or that are used in connection with them, possess these objectionable properties in a high degree, and can, therefore, only be safely employed in a state of proper dilution and combination. If any doubt exists respecting such an article, it is a wise precaution to regard it with suspicion and to test its qualities before applying it for the first time. This may be done by placing some of it on the soft skin of the inner side of the wrist or fore-arm, and allowing it to remain there as long, and under the same conditions, as it is ordered to be left in contact with the hair or skin of the head or face. In this way the injury or loss of the hair, sores, and other serious consequences that too often follow the use of advertised and ill-prepared hair dyes may be generally avoided.

To gradually darken the shade of the hair on these principles, provided its normal sulphur be still secreted by the hair-bulbs and be still present in its structure, it will, therefore, generally be sufficient to occasionally employ a weak solution of any of the milder salts of iron as a hair wash. The menstruum may be water, to which a little spirits and a few drops of oil of rosemary to increase its stimulating qualities have been added. In applying it, the head being first washed clean, care should be taken to thoroughly moisten the whole surface of the hair and the skin of the head with the wash; and its absorption and action should be promoted by the free use of a clean hairbrush. Wine is the favorite solvent for the iron; ale and beer are also sometimes so employed. Most of the fashionable ferruginous hair washes also contain a few grains of acetate of copper or distilled verdigris, the objections to which have been already pointed out.

The daily use of oil or pomatum, with which a few grains of carbonate of lead, lead plaster, or trisnitrate of bismuth, have been blended by heat and careful trituration, has generally a like effect on the hair to ferruginous solutions; so also has a leaden comb, but its action is very uncertain. None of these last are, however, safe for long-continued use. Atrophy of the scalp, baldness, and even local paralysis, have sometimes, though rarely, been caused by them.

When the normal sulphur of the hair is absent, or deficient, the preceding substances fail to darken the hair. In this case the desired effect may often be produced by also moistening the head, say twice a week, with water, to which a little sulphuret of potassium or hydrosulphuret of ammonia has been added.

When it is desired to dye or darken the hair more rapidly, as in a few hours, or even a few minutes, plumbite of lime, plumbite of potassa, or nitrate or ammonia—nitrate of silver—is usually employed. The first is commonly produced by the admixture of quicklime with oxide of lead (litharge), carbonate of lead, or acetate of lead. These ingredients should be in appropriate proportions, but very generally the reverse is the case in those of the shops.

It may be laid down as a rule that when the lime is in greater proportion than about two to one of the oxide, and to the corresponding equivalents of the other substances mentioned, or when the lime has not been prepared in a proper manner, the compound is not safe, and very likely to prove injurious to the skin and hair-bulbs, and perhaps to act as a depilatory. The effects of these lead dyes arise partly in the way previously described and partly by direct chemical action between the sulphur of the hair and the lead which they contain, sulphuret of lead being formed in the surfacial portion of the hair. It is on the last that their more immediate effect depends. If there be no sulphur in the hair, they will not darken it. After the necessary period of contact, they should be gently but thoroughly removed from the hair and skin by rubbing them off with the fingers, and by the use of the hairbrush, the head being then washed clean with tepid water. Should the tint imparted by them not be deep enough, or be too fiery, it may be darkened and turned on the brown or black by moistening the hair the next day with a very weak solution of sulphuret of potassium, or of hydrosulphuret of ammonia.

None of the compounds of lead stain the skin, an advantage which has led to a preference being given to them by many persons who are clumsy manipulators, and to the more extensive use of them than of other hair dyes.

The salts of silver above referred to are more rapid in their action as hair dyes than those containing lead. It is only necessary to wash the hair quite clean and free from grease, then to moisten it with a weak solution of one of them, and, lastly, to expose it to the light, to effect the object in view. Sunlight will fully darken it in a few minutes, but in diffused daylight it will take two or three hours, or longer, to acquire the deepest shade. To avoid this delay and inconvenience, the common practice is, a few minutes after applying the silver solution, to moisten or wet the hair with a solution of sulphuret of potassium, or of hydrosulphuret of ammonia. The effect is immediate, and the full depth of shade which a silver solution of the strength employed is capable of imparting is at once produced. A few minutes later and the hair and skin may be rinsed with tepid water, gently wiped dry, and the hair finally adjusted with the comb. The effect of its application, its rapid action, and the satisfactory nature of the effect produced, all tend to render a solution of nitrate of silver the favorite hair dye of those who have sufficient skill and steadiness of hand to use it properly.

It will be useful here to inform the inexperienced reader that all solutions and compounds which contain nitrate of silver stain the skin as well as the hair, if they be allowed to touch it. These stains may be removed, when quite recent, by rubbing them with a piece of rag or sponge wetted with a weak solution of potassium, of hydrosulphuret of ammonia, or of iodide of potassium; but as this is attended with some trouble and inconvenience, the best way is to avoid the necessity of having recourse to it. The hairdressers commonly adopt the plan of smearing hard pomatum or cosmetique over the skin immediately surrounding the hair to be operated upon, in order to protect it from the dye. By very skillful manipulation, and the observance of due precautions, the hair may be thoroughly moistened with the silver solution without touching the adjacent skin; but this can only be done when the hair of the head is under treatment by a second party.

In reference to the tone and shades of color given by the substances commonly employed to dye the hair, it may be useful to state that the shades given by preparations of *iron* and *bismuth* range from dark brown to black; those given by the salts of silver, from a fine natural chestnut to deep brown and black, all of which are rich and unexceptional. The shades given by lead vary from reddish-brown and auburn to black; and when pale or when the dye has been badly applied or compounded, are generally of a sandy, reddish hue, often far from agreeable. However, this tendency of the lead dyes has recently led to their extensive use to impart that peculiar tint to the light hair of ladies and children which is now so fashionable. Other substances, hereafter referred to, are, however, preferable, as imparting a more pleasing hue.

The reddish tint produced by lead, as already hinted, may be generally darkened into a brown, more or less rich, by subsequently moistening the hair with a weak solution of either sulphuret of potassium or hydrosulphuret of ammonia.

The favorite compounds for external use in baldness, and, perhaps, the most convenient and best, are such as owe their stimulating quality to cantharides or Spanish flies, or to their active principle, cantharidine. This application of these drugs has received the sanction of the highest medical authorities, both in Europe and America. The leading professional hair-restorers now rely almost exclusively on cantharides, and all the more celebrated advertised nostrums for restoring the hair contain it as their active ingredient.

Oils and pomades, very strongly impregnated with the essential oil of garden thyme (origanum) and rosemary, and lotions or liniments containing ammonia with a like addition of these essential oils, probably come next in the frequency of their use as popular restoratives of the hair in actual and incipient baldness.

To Have Elegant Hair.—Every girl should have thick, magnificent hair. It is essential to clip the ends of the hair once a month after a child is four years of age. Ammonia and warm water is an excellent wash for the hair and scalp, and gives life and vigor to it when all other articles fail.

Wild Rose Curling Fluid.—Take two drams (avoirdupois) dry salt of tartar; (carbonate of potassa) powdered cochineal, half dram; liquor of ammonia and spirit de rose, each one fluid dram; glycerine, one-fourth ounce; rectified spirit, one and one-half imperial fluid ounces; distilled water, eighteen ounces; digest with agitation for a week, and then decant or filter. The hair to be moistened with it, and then loosely adjusted. The effect occurs as it dries.

To Cause the Hair to Grow very Thick.—One of the most powerful stimulants for the growth of the hair is the following: Take a quarter of an ounce of the chippings of alkanet root, tie in a scrap of coarse muslin, and suspend it in a jar containing eight ounces of sweet oil for a week, covering it from the dust. Add to this sixty drops tincture of cantharides, ten drops oil of rose, sixty drops of neroli, and sixty drops oil of lemon. Let this stand twenty days, closely corked, and you will have one of the greatest hair-invigorators and hair-growers that this world has ever produced.

Lola Montez Hair Coloring.—This celebrated woman published the following, and claimed that it was as harmless as any preparation that would really color the hair: Ten grains of gallic acid, one ounce of acetic acid, one ounce of tincture of sesgurichloride of iron. Dissolve the gallic acid, sesgurichloride, and add the acetic acid. Wash the hair with soap and water; when dried, apply the dye by dipping a fine comb in it and drawing through the hair so as to color the roots thoroughly. Let it dry, then oil and brush well.

Hair Restorative.—Four drams oxide bismuth, four drams spermaceti, four ounces pure hog's lard. The lard and spermaceti should be melted together. When nearly cool, stir in the bismuth and perfume. Prevents the hair from turning gray, and restores gray hair.

For Bald Heads.—A most valuable remedy for promoting the growth of the hair is an application, once or twice a day, of wild indigo and alcohol. Take four ounces of wild indigo and steep it about a week or ten days in a pint of alcohol and a pint of hot water, when it will be ready for use. The head must be thoroughly washed with the liquid, morning and evening, application being made with a sponge or soft brush.

Another excellent preparation is composed of three ounces of castor oil, with just enough alcohol to cut the oil, to which add twenty drops tincture of cantharides, and perfume to suit. This not only softens and imparts a gloss to the hair, but also invigorates and strengthens the roots of the hair.

Excellent Hair Wash.—Take one ounce of borax, half an ounce of camphor; powder these ingredients very fine and dissolve them in one quart boiling water. When cool the solution will be ready for use. Dampen the hair frequently. This wash effectually cleanses, beautifies, and strengthens the hair, preserves the color, and prevents early baldness. The camphor will form into lumps after being dissolved, but the water will be sufficiently impregnated.

To Cure Baldness.—Cologne water, two ounces; tincture of cantharides, two drams; oil of lavender or rosemary, of each ten drops. These applications must be used twice a day for three or four weeks, but if the scalp becomes sore they may be discontinued for a time or used at longer intervals.

When the hair falls off, from diminished action of the scalp, preparations of cantharides are excellent. The following will cause the hair to grow faster than any other preparation: Beef marrow (soaked in several waters, melted and strained), half a pound; tincture cantharides (made by soaking for a week one dram of powdered cantharides in one ounce of proof spirit), one ounce; oil of bergamot, twelve drops.

Stimulants for the Hair.—Vinegar and water form a good wash for the roots of the hair. A solution of ammonia is often used with good effect for the same purpose. For removing scurf, glycerine diluted with a little rose-water will be found of service. Any preparation of rosemary forms an agreeable and highly cleansing wash. The yolk of an egg beaten up in warm water is a most nutritious application to the scalp. A very good application is made in this way: Take an ounce of powdered borax and a small piece of camphor and dissolve in a quart of boiling water. The hair must afterwards be washed in warm water. Many heads of hair require nothing more in the way of wash than soap and water. The following recipe will strengthen the hair and prevent its falling out: Vinegar of cantharides, half an ounce; eau de cologne, one ounce; rose-water, one ounce. The scalp should be brushed briskly until it becomes red, and the lotion should then be applied to the roots of the hair twice a day.

The Golden Hair Secret.—The rage for light, gold color, or even red hair, which has prevailed for some time, has led to various expedients for procuring it. Many ladies have sacrificed fine heads of hair, and in place of their own dark tresses have adopted light wigs; but the prevailing absurdity has been the use of strong alkalies for the purpose of turning dark hair light. This is the purpose of the ausicomus fluid, which may be procured of any hairdresser; but we warn our fair readers that the use of these products is apt to be disappointing. They certainly will turn black to a brick-dust hue, but the color is often disagreeable. It is apt to present itself in patches in different hues, and the effect on the hair is terrible—it often rots and crumbles away. In place of this absurd practice, we recommend the following as available for trying the effect for dress purpose: Procure a packet of gold powder of the hairdresser. Have ready a very weak solution of gum and water, and one of the small perfume vaporizers now in use. When the hair has been dressed, sprinkle it with gum and water by means of the vaporizer and then shower on the gold powder. It may be put on thick enough to hide the color of the hair, and owing to the gum it cannot be danced off. The effect by artificial light is beautiful.

For Keeping the Hair Crimped or Curled in Summer.—A quarter of an ounce of gum tragacanth, one pint rose-water, and five drops of glycerine; mix and let stand over night. If the tragacanth is not dissolved, let it remain half a day longer; if it is thick add more rose-water and let it remain for some hours. If then it is a smooth solution, nearly as thin as glycerine, it is fit for use. Dampen the hair before crimping or curling.

To Bleach the Hair.—It has been found in the bleaching of hair that gaseous chlorine is the most effectual. The hair should be cleaned for that purpose by a warm solution of soda and washed afterwards with water. While moist it is put into a jar with chlorine gas introduced until the air in the jar looks greenish. Allow it to remain on for twenty-four hours, and then, if necessary, repeat the operation.

A New French Remedy for Baldness.—Croton oil, one of the best French remedies for baldness, is employed by simply adding to it oil or pomade, and stirring or agitating the two together until admixture or solution is complete. The formula adopted by the eminent French physician who introduced this remedy, and who speaks in the most confident and enthusiastic way of the success attending its use, is: Take croton oil, twelve drops (minims); oil of almonds, four troy grains. Mix. A little is to be well rubbed on the scalp twice a day. Soft down, we are assured, appears in three weeks.

For Improving the Hair.—*Palma Christi oil for thickening the hair*: Take one ounce of Palma Christi oil, add oil of lavender or bergamot to scent it. Let it be well brushed into the hair for two or three months, particularly applying it to those parts where it may be most desirable to render the hair luxuriant. This is a simple and valuable oil, and not in the hands of any monopolist.

To Dye the Hair Flaxen.—We have heard the following is effective: Take a quart of lye prepared from the ashes of vine twigs, briony, celandine roots, and tumeric, of each half an ounce; saffron and lily roots, of each two drams; flowers of mullein, yellow stechas, broom, and St. John's wort, of each a dram. Boil these together and strain off the liquor clear. Frequently wash the hair with the fluid, and it will change it, we are told, in a short time to a beautiful flaxen color.

A Powder for Preserving the Hair.—The following powder has the name of facilitating the regeneration of the hair and strengthening its roots. Still more valuable properties have been ascribed to it, such as that of rousing the imagination to vigorous efforts and strengthening the memory—delightful properties if they could be realized by such simple means. Take an ounce and a half of red roses; a small quantity each of calamus aromaticus (sweet-scented flag), and of the long cyperus; an ounce of benzoin; six drams of aloes (the wood of); half an ounce of red coral, and the same quantity of amber; four ounces of bean flour; and eight ounces of the root of Florentine iris. Let the whole be mixed together and reduced to a very fine powder, to which add a few grains of musk. This powder is to be sprinkled on the hair in the same manner as hair powder is generally used, and, having remained for a time embedded with the hair, to be removed by means of comb and brush; and to be occasionally applied and removed. It is said to regenerate the hair and strengthen the roots, and to possess the properties which are above enumerated.

To Make the Hair Grow and to Prevent It from Falling.—The following recipes are selected from a work published some years ago in Paris, entitled "Manuel Cosmetique des Plantes":—

Take the roots of young vines, the roots of hemp, and young cabbages, of each two handfuls. Dry, and then burn them. Make afterwards a lye with the ashes. Before the head is washed with this lye it must be rubbed with honey, and continue both for three successive days. This will not only make the hair grow, but restore it upon bald places, under certain habits and constitutions of body. Pulverize some parsley seed, and use it as hair powder for three nights at the commencement of the year, and it will prevent your hair from falling.

To Make the Hair Grow Quick.—Dip, every morning, the teeth of your comb in the juice of nettles, and comb the hair against the grain.

Mixture for Shampoo.—Bay rum, one pint; tincture of cantharides, one dram; carbonate of ammonia, one half dram; salts tartar, one half dram. Mix.

To Prevent the Hair Falling Out.—Boxwood shavings, six ounces; proof spirit, twelve ounces; spirits of rosemary, two ounces; spirits of nutmeg, one half ounce. Mix.

Wash for Scald Heads.—Take one half ounce of sulphate of potassa, one pint of lime water, one ounce of soap liniment. Mix, and apply to the head two or three times a day.

POWDERS AND THEIR USES.

The powders usually sold by druggists are injurious to the complexion, owing to harmful ingredients. If a powder is perfectly pure, a moderate use of it will not harm the complexion, but if it is impure it soon causes the face to turn sallow and yellow. The following is perfectly pure, and is a splendid article, giving a lovely, refined complexion:—

Boston Burnet Powder for the Face.—Five cents' worth of bay rum, five cents' worth of magnesia snowflake, five cents' worth of bergamot, five cents' worth oil of lemon; mix in a pint bottle and fill up with rain water. Perfectly harmless, and splendid.

Queen Bess Complexion Wash.—Put in a vial one dram of benzoin gum in powder, one dram nutmeg oil, six drops of orange-blossom tea or apple blossoms; put in half a pint of rain water, and boiled down to a spoonful, and strained; one-pint of sherry wine. Bathe the face morning and night; it will remove all flesh-worms and freckles, and give a beautiful complexion. Or, put one ounce of powdered gum benzoin in a pint of whisky. To use: Put in water in washbowl till it is milky.

FLESH-WORMS—TO CURE.

Black specks on the nose disfigure the face. Remove by washing thoroughly in tepid water, rubbing with a towel, and applying with a soft flannel a lotion made of three ounces of cologne and half an ounce of liquor of potash.

TO WHITEN THE SKIN AND REMOVE FRECKLES AND TAN.

Bathe three times a day in a preparation of three quarts water, one quart alcohol, two ounces of cologne and one of borax, in proportion of two teaspoons mixture to two tablespoons soft water.

CHAPTER II.

TREATING OF MISCELLANEOUS MATTERS.

The Human Temperaments.—By these are meant certain types, forms or conformations of the human body, each known and distinguished from the other by certain characteristics, which enable those who are familiar with these peculiarities to readily distinguish one temperament from the others. The existence of the temperaments is believed to depend upon the development of certain parts or systems in the body, and each is accompanied by different degrees of activity of the brain, and corresponding difference in the talents and manifestations of the individual. They are four in number, viz.: Nervous, Sanguine, Bilious, and Lymphatic. When the brain and nerves are predominant, it is termed the *nervous* temperament; if the lungs and blood vessels constitutionally predominate, the *sanguine*; if the muscular and fibrous systems are in the ascendency, the *bilious*; and when the glands and assimilating organs are in the ascendency, it is termed the *lymphatic* or *phlegmatic*.

First: The nervous is indicated by fine, thin hair, small muscles, thin skin, pale countenance, brilliant eyes, with great quickness and sensitiveness to impressions, and is really the mental or intellectual temperament.

Second: The sanguine is known by a stout, well-defined form, a full face, florid complexion, moderate plumpness, firm flesh, chestnut or sandy hair, and blue eyes. This is the tough, hardy, working temperament, excessively fond of exercise and activity, and a great aversion to muscular quiescence and inactivity, and consequently averse to books and close literary pursuits.

Third: The bilious is indicated by a thin, spare face, dark skin, black hair, firm flesh, moderate stoutness, with rough, harsh, and strongly marked features. This temperament gives great will, elasticity, and powers of endurance, and, when combined with the nervous, is the great, efficient, moving temperament in the great events of the world.

Fourth: The lymphatic is indicated by paleness, roundness of the form, softness of muscle, fair hair, sleepy, half-closed eyes, and a dull, sluggish, inexpressive face. In this temperament the brain and all other parts of the body appear to be slow, dull, and languid, and the whole body little else than one great manufactory of fat. These temperaments, however, are rarely found pure, but mixed or blended in an almost endless variety of ways, producing the ever-varying peculiarities of human character and intellect.

THE FORTUNATE AND UNFORTUNATE DAYS OF EACH MONTH.
FORTUNATE.

In January, six days—the 1st, 2nd, 15th, 26th, 27th, and 28th.

In February, four days—the 11th, 21st, 25th, and 26th.

In March, two days—the 10th and 24th.

In April, five days—the 6th, 15th, 16th, 20th, and 28th.

In May, three days—the 3rd, 18th, and 31st.

In June, five days—the 10th, 11th, 15th, 22nd, and 25th.

In July, three days—the 9th, 15th, and 28th.

In August, six days—the 6th, 7th, 10th, 11th, 19th, and 25th.

In September, five days—the 4th, 8th, 17th, 18th, and 23rd.

In October, five days—the 3rd, 7th, 16th, 21st, and 22nd.

In November, three days—the 5th, 14th, and 20th.

In December, six days—the 15th, 19th, 20th, 22nd, 23rd, and 25th.

UNFORTUNATE.

In January, seven days—the 3rd, 4th, 6th, 13th, 14th, 20th, and 21st.

In February, seven days—the 3rd, 7th, 9th, 12th, 16th, 17th, and 23rd.

In March, eight days—the 1st, 2nd, 5th, 8th, 12th, 16th, 28th, and 29th.

In April, two days—the 24th and 25th.

In May, five days—the 17th, 20th, 27th, 29th, and 30th.

In June, eight days—the 1st, 5th, 6th, 9th, 12th, 16th, 18th, and 24th.

In July, four days—the 3rd, 10th, 17th, and 18th.

In August, two days—the 15th and 16th.

In September, two days—the 9th and 16th.

In October, six days—the 4th, 9th, 11th, 17th, 27th, and 31st

In November, four days—the 3rd, 9th, 10th, and 21st.

In December, two days—the 14th and 21st.

DAYS OF THE WEEK—THEIR IMPORTANCE AT THE NATAL HOUR.

A child born on Sunday shall be of long life and obtain riches.

A child born on Monday will be weak and effeminate.

Tuesday is more unfortunate still, though a child born on this day may, by extraordinary vigilance, conquer the inordinate desires to which he will be subject; still, in his violent attempts to gratify them, he will be in danger of a violent death.

The child born on Wednesday will be given to a studious life, and shall reap great profit therefrom.

A child born on Thursday shall attain great honor and dignity.

He who calls Friday his natal day shall be of a strong constitution, and perhaps addicted to the pleasures of love.

Saturday is another ill-omened day; most children born on this day will be of heavy, dull, and dogged disposition.

IMPORTANT ADVICE TO FEMALES.

It has often been observed, and experience has shown the observation to be a true one, that some event of importance is sure to happen to a woman in her thirty-first year, whether it prove for her good or it be some evil or temptation; therefore we advise her to be circumspect in all her actions. If she is a maiden or widow, it is probable she will marry this year. If a wife, that she will lose her children or husband. She will either receive riches or travel into a foreign land; at all events, some circumstance or other will take place during this remarkable year of her life that will have great effect on her future fortunes and existence.

THE MAGIC RING.

To know whom you will marry, and what kind of a fate you will have with them.—Borrow a wedding ring, concealing the purpose for which you borrow it; but no widow's or pretended marriage ring will do—it spoils the charm; wear it for three hours at least before you retire to rest, and then suspend it, by a hair off your head, over your pillow; write within a circle resembling a ring, the sentence from the matrimonial service beginning with, *"with this ring I thee wed,"* and round the circle write your own name at full length, and the figures that stand for your age; place it under your pillow, and your dream will fully explain whom you are to marry, and what kind of a fate you will have with them. If your dream is too confused to remember it, or you do not dream at all, it is a certain sign that you will never be married.

PHYSIOGNOMICAL SIGNS OF A GOOD GENIUS.

A straight, erect body, neither over tall nor short, between fat and thin. The flesh naturally soft. The skin neither soft nor rough, but a medium between. The complexion white, verging to a blush of redness. The hair between hard and soft, usually of a brown color. The head and face of a moderate size. The forehead rather high. The eyes manly, big, and clear, of a blue or hazel color. The aspect mild and humane. The teeth so mixed that some are broad and some narrow. A subtle tongue, and the voice between intense and remiss. The neck comely and smooth. The channel-bone of the throat appearing and moving. The back and ribs not over fleshy. The shoulders plain and slender. The hands indifferently long and smooth. The fingers long, smooth, and equally distant. The nails white, mixed with red, and shining. The carriage of the body erect in walking.

ELECTRICAL PSYCHOLOGY, OR PSYCHOLOGICAL FASCINATION.

The most easy, sure and direct mode to produce electro-psychological communication is to take the individual by the hand, in the same manner as though you were going to shake hands. Press your thumb with moderate force upon the *ulnar nerve*, which spreads its branches to the ring and little finger. The pressure should be nearly one inch above the knuckle, and in range of the ring finger. Lay the ball of the thumb flat and particularly crosswise so as to cover the minute branches of this nerve of motion and sensation. When you first take your subject by the hand, request him to place his eyes upon yours, and to keep them fixed, so that he may see every emotion of your mind expressed in the countenance. Continue this pressure for half a minute or more, then request him to close his eyes, and with your fingers gently brush downward several times over the eyelids, as though fastening them firmly together. Throughout the whole process feel within yourself a fixed determination to close them, so as to express that determination fully in your countenance and manner. Having done this, place your hand on the top of his head and press your thumb firmly on the organ of individuality, bearing partially downward, and with the other thumb still pressing the *ulnar nerve*, tell him, *You cannot open your eyes!* Remember that your manner, your expression of countenance, your motions, and your language must all be of the same positive character. If he succeed in opening his eyes, try it once or twice more, because impressions, whether physical or mental, continue to deepen by repetition. In case, however, that you cannot close his eyes, nor see any effect produced upon them, you should cease making any further efforts, because you have now fairly tested that his mind and body both stand in a positive relation as regards the doctrine of impressions. If you succeed in closing the subject's eyes by the above mode, you may then request him to put his hands on his head, or in any other position you choose, and tell him, *You cannot stir them!* In case you succeed, request him to be seated, and tell him, *You cannot rise!* If you are successful in this, request him to put his hands in motion, and tell him, *You cannot stop them!* If you succeed, request him to walk on the floor, and tell him, *You cannot cease walking!* As so you may continue to perform experiments, involving muscular motion and paralysis of any kind that may recur to your mind, till you can completely control him in arresting or moving all the voluntary parts of his system.

MESMERISM.

If you desire to mesmerize a person, who has never been put in that state, nor in the least affected, the plan is to set him in an easy posture and request him to be calm and resigned. Take him by both hands, or else by one hand and place your other gently on his forehead. But with whatever part of his body you choose to come in contact, be sure to always touch two points, answering to the *positive* and *negative* forces. Having taken him by both hands, fix your eyes upon his, and, if possible, let him contentedly and steadily look you in the face. Remain in this position until his eyes close. Then place both your hands on his head, gently pass them to his shoulders, down the arms, and off at the ends of his fingers. Throw your hands outward as you return them to his head, and continue these passes till he can hear no voice but yours. He is then entirely in the mesmeric state. When a person is in the mesmeric state, whether put there by yourself or someone else, you can awake him by the upward passes, or else do it by an impression, as follows: Tell him, "I will count *three*, and at the same instant I say *three* I will slap my hands together, and you will be wide awake and in your perfect senses. Are you ready?" If he answers in the affirmative, you will proceed to count "One, two, three!" The word three should be spoken suddenly, and in a very loud voice, and at the same instant the palms of the hands should be smitten together. This will instantly awake him.

HOW TO MAKE PERSONS AT A DISTANCE THINK OF YOU.

Let it be particularly remembered that "faith" and concentration of thought are positively needful to accomplish aught in drawing others to you, or making them think of you. If you have not the capacity or understanding to operate an electric telegraph battery, it is no proof that an expert and competent person should fail in doing so. Just so in this case; if faith, meditation, or concentration of thought fail you, then will you also fail to operate on others. First, you must have a yearning for the person you wish to make think of you; and, secondly, you must learn to guess at what time of day or night, he may be unemployed—passive—so that he may be in a proper state to receive the thought which you dispatch to him. If he should be occupied in any way, so that his nervous forces were needed to complete his task, his "human battery," or thought, would not be in a recipient or passive condition, therefore your experiment would fail at that moment. Or, if he were under heavy narcotics, liquors, tobacco, or gluttonous influences, he could not be reached at such moments. Or, if he were asleep, and you operated to effect a wakeful mind or thought, you would fail again at the moment. To make a person at a distance think of you (whether you are acquainted with him or not, matters not), I again repeat, find out or guess at what moment he is likely to be passive— by this I mean easy and careless; then, with the most fervent prayer or yearning of your entire heart, mind, soul, and strength, desire he may think of you. And if you wish him to think on any particular topic in relation to you, it is necessary for you to press your hands, when operating on him, on such mental faculties of your head as you wish him to exercise towards you. This demands a meager knowledge of Phrenology. His "feeling nature," or "propensities," you cannot reach through these operations, but when he thinks of you (if he does not know you, he imagines such a being as you are) he can easily afterwards be controlled by you, and he will feel disposed to go in the direction where you are, if circumstances permit and he is his own master, for, remember, circumstances alter cases. I said you cannot reach his "feeling," but only his "thinking," nature, truly, but after he thinks of you once his "feeling nature," or propensities, may become aroused through his own organization. In conclusion on this topic, let me say that if you wish the person simply to think of you, one operation may answer; but, on the contrary, if you wish him to meet you, or go where you are, all you have to do is to persevere, in a lawful and Christian manner, to operate, and I assure you, in the course of all natural things—that is, if no accident or very unfavorable circumstances occur— he will make his way towards you, and when he comes within sight, or reaching distance of you, it will be easy to manage him.

HOW TO CHARM THOSE WHOM YOU MEET AND LOVE.

When you desire to make any one "love" you with whom you meet, although not personally acquainted with him, you can very readily reach him and make his acquaintance, if you observe the foregoing instructions in addition to the following directions: Suppose you see him coming towards you, in an unoccupied mood, or recklessly or passively walking past you, all that remains for you at that moment is to concentrate your thought, and send it into him as before explained, and, to your astonishment, if he was passive, he will look at you, and now is your time to send a thrill to his heart, by looking him carelessly, though determinately, in the eyes, and praying him, with all your heart, mind, soul, and strength, that he may read your thought and receive your true love, which God designs we should bear one another. This accomplished, and you need not, and must not, wait for a cold-hearted, fashionable, and popular Christian introduction; neither should you hastily run into his arms, but continue operating in this psychological manner, not losing any convenient opportunity to meet him at an appropriate place, when an unembarrassed exchange of words will open the door to the one so magnetized. At this interview, unless prudence sanction it, do not shake hands, but let your manners and loving eyes speak with Christian charity and ease. Wherever or whenever you meet again, at the first opportunity grasp his hand in an earnest, sincere, and affectionate manner, observing at the same time the following important directions, viz.: As you take his bare hand in yours, press your thumb gently, though firmly, between the bones of the thumb and the forefinger of his hand, and at the very instant when you press thus on the blood vessels (which you can before ascertain to pulsate) look him earnestly and lovingly in the eyes, and send all your heart's, mind's, and soul's strength into his organization, and he will be your friend, and if you find him not to be congenial, you have him in your power, and by carefully guarding against evil influences, you can reform him to suit your own purified, Christian, and loving taste.

CHAPTER III.

A SPECIAL CHAPTER FOR YOUNG WOMEN.

A special chapter for young women: On marriage; What young women look forward to; What it is best to do when a prospect of marrying occurs; What a husband looks for; What marriage affords; On making yourself cheap; How to protect yourself; About courtship; Care of your character; How easily men are led astray, and how cautious you should be; What state of life is most honorable; Important points for your consideration; To make a husband happy; Nature of young women; On attracting the attention of young men; Young man's part; Young woman's part; Parents' wishes; How young men act in female company; Modesty; Courtship; On near relations marrying; On dress; What men need wives for; A mother's pleasure at the birth of her first child; How differently girls and boys are constituted; What young people should study before they become engaged.

MARRIAGE.

Advice upon this subject is very much needed. I am assured that it is a subject not often talked of in families—at least, as it ought to be—nor is it much alluded to in the pulpit, and the result is that young people commonly get their notions about it from those only a little older than themselves, and who therefore know but little more than they do, or from those who form their opinions from the abuse they see of it and so hold degrading and unworthy ideas respecting it. Sometimes all that is known about it amounts to this, that it is a delightful thing to be married.

It is quite true that it often is, and always ought to be, delightful; still, you know it is frequently the reverse. You cannot, then, be too cautious in the matter.

Nothing can be more orderly, right, proper, and holy than marriage. It is not, however, quite so simple an affair as you may fancy. Every good thing (and this is one of the best) requires some effort to obtain it, and unless you take the right course you must not expect to succeed.

You may often see a young woman who, from not entertaining correct views on the point, is certainly taking a wrong course, her endeavors being rather to make what she considers a good match than by acquiring kind and orderly habits to qualify herself to become worthy of a worthy husband.

That the best things are liable to the greatest abuses is notorious, and from the lamentable fact that marriage is often abused we may fairly infer its pre-eminent worth. In truth, there is nothing more valuable. It is, then, highly injurious to entertain low notions respecting it, and men who indulge in loose conversation on the subject are likely at the same time to think meanly of women. Beware of them, and if you hear them expressing such opinions in your presence, withdraw from them at once as unworthy of your company. Never fear but they will respect you the more for the rebuke.

Of course you are looking forward to settling happily, and will do your best for that purpose. On this let me remark that all happiness (that is, all that is genuine, and therefore worthy of the name) comes from connection with the one great source of all good, and He has freely and fully provided all the means necessary for our being happy, both here and hereafter. He has placed each of us where it is best for us to be, and in the circumstances that are best for us at the time, and this applies to you and to me now. Howsoever much appearances may be to the contrary, He cares as much for each of us as if we were the sole objects of His care. It is only by doing our duty in humble dependence on His assistance, which He never withholds, that we can be happy. It behooves you, then, to consider well what is your duty, in order that you may do it and may enjoy the blessings He is so ready to bestow. I hope you may have been a loving and dutiful daughter, an affectionate sister, and a faithful friend; then you may have good ground of hope for the future.

WHEN A PROSPECT OF MARRIAGE

occurs you cannot do better than consult your mother, aunt, or other discreet relative that has your welfare at heart, from whom you may reasonably expect the best and most disinterested advice; and this it will be well for you to be guided by. Women of mature years can judge far better than you whether a man is likely to make a good husband. You should likewise quietly and cautiously make your own observations among your married acquaintances, especially where you believe there is a comfortable and happy home. You will doubtless find that to a very great extent this happy home depends on the wife's management and economy. Very often it happens that when two husbands have the same income, with the same number of children, there will be comfort in the one home and discomfort in the other. Now, there must be a reason for this, and you should endeavor to find it out and profit by the lesson. It is said "Cleanliness is next to godliness," and truly the value of cleanliness cannot be overrated. In point of time, it should go before godliness, for where there is not cleanliness there can hardly be godliness; and the health of body and mind are greatly dependent on these two. Moreover, where can there be complete happiness without health?

One of the most prolific sources of matrimonial difficulties is the lack of knowledge on the part of wives of the duties of housekeeping. In these days there are a hundred young ladies who can drum on the piano to one who can make a good loaf of bread.

YET A HUNGRY HUSBAND

cares more for a good dinner than he does—as long as his appetite is unappeased—to listen to the music of the spheres. Heavy bread has made many heavy hearts, given rise to dyspepsia—horrid dyspepsia—and its herd of accompanying torments. Girls who desire that their husbands should be amiable and kind, should learn how to make good bread. When a young man is courting, he can live well at home; or, if he has to go a distance to pay his addresses, he usually obtains good meals at an hotel or an eating-house; but when he is married and gets to housekeeping, his wife assumes the functions of his mother or his landlord, and it is fortunate for her if she has been educated so as to know what a good table is. Those who are entirely dependent upon hired cooks make a very poor show at housekeeping. The stomach performs a very important part in the economy of humanity, and wives who are forgetful of this fact commit a serious mistake.

You know full well that most young men—and most young women, too—are desirous of marrying and having a family; but they do not sufficiently consider that it is God who gives them this desire, and that for the wisest of purposes; not only that this world may be peopled, but also that its inhabitants may be prepared for heaven.

Nothing is more certain than that

MARRIAGE AFFORDS

the fairest opportunities for preparing for a better world. In it we have others dearer than ourselves to think about and provide for; and in doing so, we have often to practice that very useful virtue, self-denial. Let me here impress upon you most deeply, that it is only by making others happy that we can become happy ourselves. The angels, we may be assured, are happy, because they are always actively good; and for a similar reason it is that God himself is infinitely happy. If you try to secure you own happiness by any other means than a faithful discharge of your duty to God and your neighbor, you will certainly fail.

I dare say you will find that

YOUNG MEN ARE FOND OF YOUR COMPANY,

and of paying you every polite attention, and you, as a right-minded woman, are well pleased to be so treated. It is due to you *as a woman*. Now, each of them is, or ought to be, looking out for a wife, and it is well that you should know this. It is, too, more important than you perhaps are aware, that you should be carefully making your own observations, so that when the time arrives for one of them to ask you to become his wife you may not be taken by surprise, but may know how to act on the occasion.

Let me caution you here against a failing that is common among young women. I mean that of making themselves too cheap. They feel flattered by the attentions paid to them, and are not sufficiently aware that many young men are fond of indulging in flattery; and such, if they find a young woman weak enough to be pleased with it, will perhaps play upon her feelings and gain her affections without having any honorable intentions towards her.

As a protection against such, I recommend you to have a proper respect for yourself, and to consider with what object or purpose you receive their attentions. If you respond without an object, you may be doing them wrong; if you accept them when they have no right intentions, you allow them to wrong you. For this purpose consider well what you are—a human being intended for an eternity of bliss. God has made you a woman; and, believe me, as there is no fairer, so there is no nobler creature than woman. She is formed to be her husband's helpmate and the mother of his children, and the all-important work of training these for heaven depends mainly upon her. Great, then, is her responsibility; but God has given her the requisite love and power to do her duty with satisfaction and delight. He has placed you in this beautiful world that by doing your duty as a daughter, sister, wife, mother, and friend, you may become fitted to enter His heavenly kingdom.

During your courtship let me entreat you to be very careful and circumspect. There is no period of life that can compare with this delightful season. It is, or should be, full of sunshine and sparkling with the poetry of life; but alas! to many it is the opposite. A want of judgment—a momentary indiscretion—has not only blotted out this beautiful springtime of life, but has marred, darkened, and blighted the whole of the after lifetime.

No maiden can, under any circumstances, place her character in the hands of any man before marriage. No matter how sincere the love, how ardent the protestations, how earnest or plausible the pleadings, you must not, you cannot, surrender your honor. You must preserve your prudence and virtue; it is only by possession of these that you can keep

THE LOVE AND RESPECT OF YOUR LOVER.

Be firm, be circumspect; a rash word or a false step may extinguish forever all your bright hopes and prospective joys. Even should your lover redeem his promises and take you to be his wife, this indiscretion, or crime, will surely hang over you like a curse, creating discord, trouble, and sorrow, the greatest portion of which will fall to your share.

You must know that young men, however amiable, worthy or honorable they may be, may, in a moment of intense excitement, commit a sin that in their calmer moments they would not be guilty of for worlds.

But under all circumstances you will be looked upon to resist any advances, and maintain your purity and virtue. No matter how high the tide of passion may run in unguarded moments, and set in against heaven and against society, the terrible and painful ebb will surely follow and leave you stranded forever on the bleak and barren shore of your earthly existence.

THERE IS NO STATE OF LIFE MORE HONORABLE,

useful, and happy than that of a wife and mother. There must and ever will be inequalities of station, but happiness is equally attainable in them all. To be happy, however, you must be good. Of course, I do not mean absolutely good, for "there is none good but One"; but I mean that you should be relatively good, and should aim at becoming better and more innocent as you advance in life. Now, you cannot respect yourself unless you know that you are worthy of respect; and if you do not respect yourself, you cannot expect that anybody else will; and in such case you will not be worthy of the love of any good man, and none such will be likely to pay court to you. If, however, you take the right means, in which I include prayer for divine guidance, you will have the respect and friendship of all your acquaintances, and then in God's own time, and, let me add, without your seeking it, the man whom you can make happy will present himself and propose to make you his wife, if it be God's will that you should become one.

Here are two very important points for your consideration: First, that it should be your constant endeavor to

MAKE YOUR HUSBAND HAPPY;

and, second, that before you consent to marry him, you should ascertain that he has those qualifications that will secure your happiness. It most nearly concerns yourself that you do your duty to God and your neighbor at all times, so that it becomes your habit; and you will find it much easier, and safer, too, to do it every day rather than on only particular occasions; for this would require a special effort, and for the time, perhaps, put you into a state of excitement, which, in all probability, would be followed by a depression of spirits. What you should rather aim at is a uniformly cheerful state of mind, resulting from a conscious and confident dependence on Providence. If your husband knows from experience that such is your character, he cannot fail, provided he be worthy of you, to be content and happy.

IT IS THE NATURE OF YOUNG WOMEN

to be affectionate, and it is pleasant and usual for them to have several dear friends, enjoying more or less of their confidence. Among these may be included some of their male acquaintance. Now, while they may esteem each of these as they would a dear cousin, they should know and act upon the knowledge that it is only to *one* they can give their unlimited confidence and individual affection as a wife. It is the height of cruelty and wickedness for either a man or a woman to trifle with another's affection. Such base conduct has cost many a young woman her health and peace, and even her life, and cannot, therefore, be too much depreciated and avoided.

Let me, then, advise you to be

VERY CAUTIOUS

before you allow a young man to pay you such marked attentions as may lead to marriage. It is not, you know, to terminate in seven years, like an apprenticeship or a commercial partnership, but it is an engagement for the life of one of the parties. I want you, then, to profit by the experience of others, too many of whom enter into marriage from light and low considerations, and not to settle in life till you, and also your friends, see that there is a reasonable prospect of your securing happiness, as well as comfort and a respectable position.

When a young woman has property or expects it, or is possessed of superior personal attractions, she should be especially prudent in her conduct towards the numerous admirers which such qualifications usually attract. No woman should allow herself to accept the attentions of any man who does not possess those sterling qualities which will command her respect, or whose love is directed to her fortune or beauty rather than herself. On such a one she can place no reliance, for should illness or misfortune overtake her she may find herself deprived of that love which she had valued as the great treasure of her life. Possessed of this, she feels that earthly riches are but of secondary importance, and that the want of them can never make her poor.

Moreover, a worthier man than any of her interested suitors may have a sincere respect and affection for her, but be kept in the background by the overzealous attention of his rivals. Still, if she has sufficient self-command to patiently and calmly investigate their general private character, she may find reason to decline their suit, and may discover that the more modest and retiring youth is the one that is deserving of her love.

While on this subject, let me caution you against the foolish affectation which some girls practice in order to attract the attention of young men. In their company be natural in your manners, open and friendly and ready to converse on general subjects; not appearing to expect that every one who pays you the ordinary courtesies of society is going to fall in love with you. This mode of behavior, which is more common with those who are vain of their beauty than with others, frequently leads to such young women being more neglected than their less pretending sisters; for prudent young men, who are impressed with the necessity of a right decision in the all-important step of marriage, instinctively shrink from those who seem unwilling to give them a fair opportunity of judging whether their hearts and minds are as attractive as their persons.

You may innocently admire many a young man for the noble qualities God has bestowed upon him, without at all entertaining the idea either that he would make you happy as his wife, or you him as your husband. Thank God we are constituted of such different temperaments that all may find suitable partners without clashing with each other's tastes, if they will only be content to watch and wait.

It is the part of a young man to *watch*, to be actively desirous of meeting with a suitable partner. In doing this, his first consideration should be to seek for such a one as he can make happy; not to look primarily for beauty, fortune, wit, or accomplishments—things all very good in themselves, but by no means constituting the essentials of happiness. If he is influenced by pure and simple motives, he will not find, or expect to find, more than one that can satisfy his desire, and he will not be in much danger of exciting the envy or the rivalry of his companions.

On the other hand, it is becoming in a young woman to

WAIT PATIENTLY

till, from the assiduous and respectful attentions of a young man, she can have no doubt that he is in earnest, when, and not before, she may freely give him her company, and with every expectation of a happy result. Be assured that no sensible young man is ever attracted by a young woman whom he sees on the lookout for a lover; he is more likely to think meanly of her, and to avoid her society.

It may, however, happen that a young man makes the offer before the young woman knows enough of him for it to be right for her to accept it, and before he, on his part, ought to take the step. In such case it would be well for her, even supposing she is inclined to like him, to tell him that he has taken her by surprise, and that she cannot think of entering on so important a subject without consulting her friends, to whom she accordingly refers him. It would then become her duty to intimate to him that, although his attentions are agreeable to them, he must wait a while, till, from further acquaintance, they are enabled to judge whether it will conduce to the mutual happiness of their daughter and himself for her to accept the offer he has so kindly made.

But it is not only young men who

ARE APT TO BE HASTY

in these matters. It is, as is well known, not uncommon for parents, especially mothers, very soon after a young man has begun to pay attention to their daughter, to give him to understand that they wish to know his intentions in reference to her. By such proceedings a young man may be taken aback, and either hurry into a match, which turns out unhappily, or be led to withdraw from a union which might have resulted in the happiness of all the parties concerned.

That your parents should wish you to be married is only natural, especially if their own marriage has been a happy one. It will be gratifying to them to see a worthy young man paying attention to you, and most probably they will let things take their own course. Marriage is too important a matter to admit of being hastened.

There are, I am aware, unwise parents, who, from various motives, will throw obstacles in the way of young people who are desirous of coming together. Some are so selfish as to be unwilling to part with their daughter, preferring their own happiness to hers. Others are so silly as to think no ordinary man good enough for her, and therefore, if they had their own way, would have her to become an old maid. Fortunately, such shortsighted people are not infrequently outwitted.

If your parents are, as I hope they are, reasonable in their views and expectations, one of the chief concerns of their life will be the promotion of your happiness, and it behooves you to pay the utmost deference to their opinion; and should they, from circumstances they become aware of, deem it advisable that you should either postpone or even break off an engagement, they will doubtless give you such weighty reasons as will justify you in acting on their advice. Where, however, as sometimes happens, they unwisely refuse their consent to their child's marriage at a time when she well knows from her own feelings, and also from the sanction she receives from the opinion of trustworthy and judicious friends, that she would be making a real sacrifice were she to comply with their wishes; if, I say, under such circumstances she acts disobediently and marries the man she loves, more blame attaches to the parents than to herself, and the sooner they forgive her the better.

It is very common for young men, when going into the company of young woman, together with their best dress to put on their best behavior; in fact, to assume a character which is not their natural one, but far superior to it.

Some hold the opinion that

"ALL IS FAIR IN LOVE AND WAR."

To me it appears there cannot be greater folly and wickedness than for young people who are thinking of marrying to attempt to deceive each other. What is the good of it? A very short period of married life will entirely dispel the illusion. I suppose people of the world may think it fair to overreach one another in their dealings, saying "everyone for himself." They have no intention of seeking to promote the other's happiness; present gain is all they want. But a married pair, to be happy, must

RESPECT AND ESTEEM, AS WELL AS LOVE,

each other; and this cannot be attained except by the constant endeavor to *be* as well as to *appear* true and good.

That young men should behave well in the presence of women is only natural and right; none but a fool would do otherwise. But you, long before thinking of marrying, should take all fair means to learn what is the general conduct and habits of your male acquaintance in their family circle and with their daily connections. "Are they good-humored and kind—able to bear the troubles they meet with? Are they industrious, frugal, temperate, religious, chaste? Have they had the prudence to insure against sickness and death?" Or, on the other hand, are they addicted to drinking, smoking, betting, keeping late hours, frequenting casinos, etc.? Your mother and other prudent friends will assist you to find this out. Those who do not come up to the proper standard, however agreeable they may be as acquaintance, certainly cannot make good husbands. In company of such, it behooves you to be well on your guard, and accept no attention from them. Should you marry such a one, you would be sure to be miserable.

While, however, it is quite right that you should be careful about the character of the young man who is paying court to you, it is of far more importance to you that you should be careful about your own, and this whether you marry or not. Indeed, a chief object in our being placed in this world is that we may acquire good habits, and so be fitted to associate with the just made perfect in heaven!

Be very guarded in your actions and demeanor. Cultivate purity of heart and thought.

No woman is fit to become a wife who is not perfectly modest in word, deed, and thought. No young man, who is worth having, would ever entertain the thought for a moment of taking the girl for a wife who is habitually careless in her conversation and displays a levity in her manners. Young men may like your free and hearty girls to laugh and talk with, but as to taking one for a wife, let me assure you they would not tolerate the idea for a moment.

You may at times be unavoidably compelled to hear a vulgar word spoken or an indelicate allusion made; in every instance maintain a rigid insensibility. It is not enough that you should cast down your eyes or turn your head, you must act as if you did not hear it; appear as if you did not comprehend it. You ought to receive no more impression from remarks of this character than a block of wood. Unless you maintain this standing, and preserve this high-toned purity of manner, you will be greatly depreciated in the opinion of all men whose opinion is worth having, and you deprive yourself of much influence and respect which it is your privilege to possess and exert.

COURTSHIP, AFTER ALL, IS A MOMENTOUS MATTER.

After taking all the counsel that may be offered, you must at last, in a great measure, rely on your own judgment. Within a few short months you have to decide, from what you can see of a man, whether you will have him in preference to your parents, friends, and all others that you know, to be a life companion. What can you do? How shall you judge? How arrive at a correct conclusion? My dear young girl, there is only One who can assist you. He, in His mercy to your helplessness and weakness, has given to every virtuous and pure-minded woman a wonderful, mysterious, and subtle instinct; a peculiar faculty that cannot be analyzed by reason, a faculty that men do not possess, and one in which they do not generally believe. At this all-important period, this eventful crisis in your life, this womanly instinct guides and saves you. You can feel in a moment the presence or influence of a base, sensual, and unworthy nature. An electric-like thrill animates you, and you are naturally repulsed from him. When your suitor is a man of incongruous temper, ungenial habits, and of a morose and unsympathetic disposition, this same precious, divine instinct acts, and the man feels, though he cannot tell why, that all his arts and aspirations are in vain. It will seldom be necessary for you to tell him verbally of his failure; but should such a one blindly insist upon intruding his attentions, do not hesitate to tell him kindly but firmly your decision. Should your suitor be one who is worthy, who will make you happy, this same blessed instinct will whisper in your soul the happy news. From the first interview there is frequently thrown around the maiden a peculiar, undefined spell; she will feel differently in his presence, and watch him with other eyes than she has for the rest of men, and in due time, when he shall ask her to decide upon the question which shall seal the temporal and eternal destiny of two human souls, she will gladly respond, giving in loving trustfulness that which is the most precious, the most enviable thing on earth: a maiden's heart, a woman's love.

Many persons, of both sexes, however amiable and pure their minds may be, should conscientiously abstain from marriage. This applies to all who have a tendency to consumption, scrofula, insanity, or any other of those diseases which are so frequently transmitted to offspring. This very important matter is not sufficiently known, and therefore is not attended to as it ought to be; hence the great amount of sickness and early death among children.

The tendency to inherit qualities is very evident in the case of drunkards, whose children are often inclined to practice the vice of their parents. The children of the blind, and of the deaf and dumb, are also liable to be afflicted as their parents were. These facts go far to show that it is literally true that the sins of the fathers are visited upon the children. It is, however, gratifying to know — and there are many well-attested cases to prove it — that whereas the children born to a man while he was addicted to drunkenness were similarly addicted to that vice, those born after he gave up his vicious indulgence, and by that means improved his bodily health, were free from the evil tendency.

One strong reason

WHY NEAR RELATIONS SHOULD NOT INTERMARRY

is that, as the same general tendencies prevail in families, when the parents are nearly related they are very likely to have the same evil tendency, whatever that may be; and, therefore, there is a great probability that their children will also have the same, but more strongly developed, and, consequently, the difficulty of their overcoming it will be much increased.

How plainly, then, is it the duty of those about to marry, as well as of those who are married, to strive to their utmost, with God's help, to overcome disorderly habits of every kind; for, be assured, it is only by such means they can hope to be blessed with good and healthy children, and thereby contribute to their own happiness, and at the same time to the improvement of the race as subjects both of this world and of heaven.

As it is by no means certain that you will marry, and the time may come when it will no longer be convenient to your parents to support you, it will be good for you, keeping these contingencies in mind, to qualify yourself to earn your own maintenance by some honest industry. You will then have a right feeling of independence, and not be tempted to marry, as too many young women do, not from the true principle of sincere affection, but mainly for a living. They may thus obtain a competence, and jog on comfortably, but they have no right to expect that genuine happiness which I recommend you to aim at. When, too, you see so many left widows, with small families, and, as we say, totally unprovided for, you will become sensible of the soundness of the advice I am offering you. As the Lord's tender mercies are over all His works, it is evident, from what is occurring around us, that trouble and adversity are better suited to the state of some people, to prepare them for their eternal destination, than any amount of prosperity would be. The poor are no less His children than the rich, and he cares equally — that is, infinitely — for them all. It is certainly wise, then, to be prepared to meet adversity, should He suffer it to come upon you.

Again, suppose you should not have any suitable offer of marriage, such as you would feel it your duty to accept, you are not on that account to be disheartened, and fancy yourself overlooked by Providence.

Single life is evidently the best for some persons; they escape many troubles which perhaps they would find it very hard to bear. There are many ways in which single people can lead a useful life, and be

AS HAPPY AS THE DAY IS LONG.

No one that is actively useful can be unhappy. What do you see around you? Many, I admit, who are not so happy as we should like them to be; but in most cases, if we could fully investigate the matter, it would perhaps be found to have arisen from their thinking too much about themselves and not enough for others. But, on the other hand, it not infrequently happens, when a woman is left, and sees that the support and welfare of herself and children depend on her own exertions, she is enabled to so successfully put forth her energies and to employ her talents which, till she needed them, she hardly knew she possessed, as to surprise both herself and the most sanguine of her friends.

Now, it must be confessed that we are fallen creatures, and therefore prone to evil. We are consequently always in danger of going wrong and forming bad habits, but our Heavenly Father watches over us at all times and gives us power to "refuse the evil and choose the good." We are, I know full well, too much inclined to yield to evil influences; still, as we always have divine aid if we implore it, I am not sure that, on the whole, it is not as easy to acquire good habits as bad ones. This much is certain, that whichever we acquire, they are likely to remain with us and are not easily to be got rid of.

Among the subjects deserving attention as affecting our happiness is one on which, perhaps, I am not entitled to say much. I refer to dress. Now, I hold it to be a duty for people to dress well—that is, according to their position, means, and age; and this not so much for their own sakes as for the sake of giving pleasure to others. It is, I admit, difficult to determine how much of one's income should be devoted to dress, but I think few will deny that at present dress occupies too much time, attention, and money. For my own part, I confess I am most affected by female dress, and although certainly I like to see women well dressed, and would rather see them a little too fine than slovenly, I am often pained at witnessing the extravagance and, to me, ridiculous taste exhibited. Whenever I see a handsome and expensive dress trailing in the dirt, I regard it as culpable waste and in bad taste, and when I see it accidentally trodden on I am not sorry. I am inclined to believe that many women can hardly find time or opportunity to perform any useful duty; they have quite as much as they, poor things, can do to take care of their dress. I also believe (and this is the serious point of the matter) that many a young man is deterred from soliciting a maiden in marriage by knowing that his means would not enable him to let her dress as he is accustomed to see her, and this is doubtless one of the many reasons why so many of both sexes remain unmarried. I hold, too, that whatever forms an obstacle to marriage has a tendency at the same time to obstruct the entrance to heaven.

I will now allude to some of the duties which will devolve upon you as a wife; and recollect that it is on the faithful discharge of these duties that your happiness, here and hereafter, mainly depends. All labor is honorable, and you know who it is that says, "My Father worketh hitherto, and I work." Being married, you must make your husband feel

"THERE IS NO PLACE LIKE HOME."

His business will probably take him from home most of the day, and it should be your care, as I doubt not it will be your delight, to see to his comfort, both before he starts and when he returns. It may sometimes happen in his fighting the battle of life that he has to encounter much that is unpleasant, and he may return home depressed. You will then have to cheer him, and be assured no one can do it so effectually, so pleasantly—aye, and so easily—as yourself.

It is not to sweep the house, and make the bed, and darn the socks, and cook the meals, chiefly, that a man wants a wife. If this is all that he needs, hired help can do it cheaper than a wife. If this is all, when a young man calls to see a young lady, send him to the pantry to taste the bread and cake she has made. Send him to inspect the needlework and bedmaking; or put a broom into her hands and send him to witness its use. *Such things are important*, and the wise young man will quietly look after them. But what a true man most wants of a true wife is her companionship, sympathy, courage, and love. The way of life has many dreary places in it, and a man needs a companion to go with him. A man is sometimes overtaken with misfortune; he meets with failure and defeat; trials and temptations beset him; and he needs one to stand by and sympathize. He has some stern battles to fight with poverty, with enemies, and with sin; and he needs a woman that, while he puts his arm around her and feels that he has something to fight for, will help him fight; that will put her lips to his ear and whisper words of counsel, and her hands to his heart and impart new inspirations. All through life—through storm and through sunshine, conflict and victory, and through adverse and favoring winds—man needs a woman's love. The heart yearns for it. A sister's or a mother's love will hardly supply the need. Yet many seek for nothing further than success in housework. Justly enough, half of these get nothing more; the other half, surprised beyond measure, have got more than they sought. Their wives surprise them by bringing a nobler idea of marriage, and disclosing a treasury of courage, sympathy, and love.

And I would here caution you against giving way to little misunderstandings in early married life. Sometimes trifling matters, for want of some forbearance or concession on one side on the other, perhaps on both sides, accumulate into serious results. These differences might be avoided by married partners studying each other's peculiarities of character, with the aim of mutually correcting, in a kindly spirit, any wrong tendency or temper which may sometimes show itself. Should you find you have inadvertently given pain to your husband, do not rest until you have ascertained the cause of his disquiet and succeeded in allaying the unhappy feeling. The earnest desire to please each other should by no means terminate on the wedding day, but be studiously continued through married life. Each should always endeavor to think the best of the other, and instantly reject every thought that might tend to weaken the bond of mutual preference and perfect trust.

If he be wise, he will leave the housekeeping entirely to you; his time and attention can be better employed elsewhere. To enable you to do this wisely, you should, long before you marry, become familiar with the quality and prices of articles of consumption, and where they can best be obtained. Every wife should be able to cook well, whether she has to do it herself or not. Health and good humor greatly depend upon the food being of good quality, well cooked, and nicely served up. She should also be able, if needful, to make and mend her own and children's clothes.

Too much importance cannot be attached to cleanliness. Men may be careless as to their own personal appearance, and may, from the nature of their business, be negligent in their dress, but they dislike to see any disregard in the dress and appearance of their wives. Nothing so depresses a man and makes him dislike and neglect his home as to have a wife who is slovenly in her dress and unclean in her habits. Beauty of face and form will not compensate for these defects. The charm of purity and cleanliness never ends but with life itself. These are matters that do not involve any great labor or expense. The use of the bath, and the simplest fabrics, shaped by your own supple fingers, will be all that is necessary. These attractions will act like a magnet upon your husband. Never fear that there will be any influence strong enough to take him from your side.

An experience of many years of observation has convinced me that where a pure, industrious, and cheerful wife meets her husband with a bright smile on the threshold of her dwelling, that man will never leave the home for any other place.

As all people are liable to illness, every young woman should aim at being an efficient nurse. In case of illness, it is now generally admitted that good nursing is of more value than medicine. To a sick husband, a little gruel or other trifle prepared and given by his wife's own hands will confer much more benefit than if prepared and given by another. Should it happen to you to fall ill, you may expect your husband to do his best; but you must not be surprised if he is not your equal in that department. Nursing is one of the many useful things which women can do better than men. A practical knowledge of nursing will enable you to be useful beyond your own family, and will enhance your value as a neighbor.

You have often, I trust, experienced the pleasure of serving others from disinterested motives, and found that the pleasure has been deeper and purer when you have engaged in doing good to those who could not make you any return. This you have found to be the case wherever you have had charge of a baby—one of those little ones of whom the Lord says: "Their angels do always behold the face of my Father which is in heaven." You have perhaps been surprised to find how easy it was to perform such a duty, and let me assure you that you may always expect to find it easy to perform your duty in that state of life to which it shall please God to call you. He never requires anything from any of His creatures beyond what He gives them power to do. He is no hard task-master. You have only to look to Him and do your best, and then you may safely leave the result in His hands.

Of all God's creatures, I know no happier one than a young mother with a good husband and a healthy baby. I say a *healthy* baby, for that implies healthy parents, especially a healthy mother. She may justly feel proud that God has intrusted a young immortal to her care, and she should at all times bear in mind that it is His gift. While it is on all hands considered honorable to hold a commission from the President, and to fill a high office, contributing to the welfare of many people, a mother may feel her office at least as honorable, seeing she has intrusted to her the rearing and training of an immortal being, and that she holds her commission direct from the King of Kings. For, recollect, it is only by God's blessing that she becomes a mother; for such is the present state of society that many very worthy married people have not the privilege of offspring, although they are intensely fond of children and seem to have no other earthly want. They may, nevertheless, be very useful, and therefore happy, in a different sphere, by the adoption of nephews and nieces or in some similar way.

AT THE BIRTH OF HER FIRST CHILD

there is opened in the mother's heart a new well of love, such as she had not known before; and although she may fancy that this is all spent upon her babe, it is not so, for she loves her God, her husband, and everybody else better than ever. The father, too, is similarly affected; he also has a warmer love for his wife and for all his connections.

A similar idea is well expressed by Möhler, a German writer, who says: "The power of selfishness, which is inwoven with our whole being, is altogether broken by marriage, and by degrees love, becoming more and more pure, takes its place." When a man marries he gives himself up entirely to *another* being; in this affair of life he first goes out of himself, and inflicts the first deadly wound on his egotism. By every child with which his marriage is blessed, nature renews the same attack on his selfhood, causes him to live less for himself, and more—even without being distinctly conscious of it—for others; his heart expands in proportion as the claimants upon it increase, and, bursting the bonds of its former narrow exclusiveness, it eventually extends its sympathies to all around.

Whenever a mother is supplying her baby with the food which God has so wisely provided for it, or is ministering to any other of its numerous and increasing wants, she may feel that everything she does for it is pleasing to her Heavenly Father and has its immediate reward in the delight she experiences in the act.

I can fancy that when a mother has washed her baby, and before she dresses it has a good romp with it, smothering it with kisses, calling it all the beauties and darlings and pets and jewels she can think of, and talking any amount of nonsense at the top of her voice—the baby all the while cooing, chirping, or even screaming with delight—at such a time, I say, I can easily fancy that the angels are looking on approvingly and enjoying the scene. And why not? "Of such is the kingdom of heaven."

From the time that an infant first becomes conscious of its wants, and long afterwards, it looks to its mother to supply them all, fully believing her able to do so. She is, in fact, in place of God to it, and it would be well for many of us if we trusted our Heavenly Father as simply and as fully as the infant does its earthly mother.

Those who know no better, when they see a mother patiently watching her sleeping babe, might wonder that she does not feel the want of company. She has, however, company that they know not of, and of which even she herself may not be conscious. If only our eyes were open, we might see that she is not the only one that is so engaged—that angels are also occupied in watching the babe and in supporting her. I entirely agree with Dr. Watts, where, in his "Cradle Hymn," he makes the mother say:

> "Hush! my babe, lie still and slumber,
> Holy angels guard thy bed."

You probably know the beautiful Irish superstition that when a baby smiles in its sleep the angels are whispering to it.

"Before I became a father, I took little or no interest in babies; I rather thought them troublesome things. But the arrival of one of my own wrought a great change in me. It enlarged at once my views and my heart, and I had higher and stronger motives to exertion. My interest in them has not yet begun to weaken, and I have no reason to think it ever will."

Girls are differently constituted from boys. God makes the intellect predominate in males, and affection in females. Accordingly, a little girl early shows a love for a doll, regarding it quite as her baby and never taking into account that it is not alive. She has many of a mother's cares and anxieties, as well as pleasures, about it; indeed, as many as she is then capable of. It is a constant source of amusement and employment to her. In all this we may plainly see the hand of Providence. It forms a suitable introduction to some of the interesting and important duties which will devolve on her if it should be His good pleasure for her to become a mother.

You will, I dare say, readily see the object I now have in view. It is that I wish to impress on you how desirable it is that you should take every opportunity of becoming acquainted with the habits and wants of babies, and the best way of managing them. The more you have to do with them the more you will like the labors, and the easier and more delightful it will become. It is fair that, before you have children of your own, you should get your knowledge as to the management of them by experience with other people's. I take it for granted you will at all times do your best for them. You will then have but little cause to fear accident; and if accident should happen, as with all your care it sometimes will, you will have more confidence in your powers, and will be more likely to do what is best at the moment, than if you were unused to children. Much of the disease and early death that happens among children arises from the ignorance of the mothers, who, however, are much more to be pitied than blamed in the matter. They had never been taught their duties toward their future offspring.

Few mothers are, perhaps, sufficiently aware of the great influence which their manners, habits, and conversation have upon the tender minds of their children, even from birth. The child should grow up with a feeling of reverence for its parents, which can only be the case when wisdom, as well as affection, is exercised in its bringing up. Hence the necessity of the mother fitting herself, both *intellectually* and *morally*, for her sacred office, that the child may become accustomed to yield perfect obedience to her wishes, from a principle of love, and may acquire, as it advances in life, the habit of yielding a like obedience to that which is right.

As you well know that you are not perfect yourself, you must be prepared to find that your husband has also his imperfections, and it is no unimportant part of your duty to help him to get rid of them. Indeed, it is one of the highest uses of marriage for each partner to assist the other on the journey to the heavenly Canaan. But before you attempt to point out a fault in him, consider how you had best proceed so as to attain your object; for unless you adopt a judicious mode, and an affectionate as well as earnest manner, you may do as much harm as good. You must also carefully watch your opportunity; for what would be favorably received at one time and under certain circumstances, might under other circumstances give offence and altogether fail of the good effect intended and hoped for. You do not know how powerful you may be for good to your husband. There is much truth in the saying, "A man is what a woman makes him."

Previous to your marriage it will be expedient for you not to give your lover that full and unlimited confidence which it will be your duty—and your inclination, too—to give him when he becomes your husband. I refer chiefly to family and other private matters, not to anything he ought to know to enable him to judge of your character and position. Many unhappy marriages have been brought about through the young woman letting it be known that she has "great expectations." A worthless fellow may, in consequence, have succeeded in winning her hand.

There is another point to which I must just allude before concluding this address. It is doubtless the order of Providence for marriage to take place, when possible, on our arriving at years of maturity. But I would guard you against the evil results of *too early* marriage, before either body or mind is perfectly matured. We scarcely need consult either medical or moral science to satisfy ourselves on this by no means trifling point. We may find in society too many sad instances of such immature and indiscreet unions. The minds of young persons should be expanded by a certain amount of experience in the world before entering upon engagements involving so many momentous duties.

In your daily walks abroad, if you examine the countenances of those you meet, you will doubtless be led to conclude that there is a great deal of disease and misery in the world; but judging from my own observation, I think you will find that the greater number of persons exhibit signs of health and happiness. Much of the disease, and misery with which the world is afflicted is the direct result of the misconduct of the individuals themselves; but no little of it is attributable to their parents, who have neglected or violated God's laws of health, their misconduct thus affecting their descendants to the "third and fourth generation." I cannot, therefore, too much impress upon you the importance of your honestly trying to find out any bad habits to which you are inclined, with a view to getting rid of them, one by one, and supplying their place by good habits. By pursuing this course you will not only do much for your own happiness, but also for that of your children, if God should bless you with a family. Children, you know, are often striking likenesses of their parents, and in their minds and habits they likewise often resemble them. You should strive, then, to be good—not from mere self-love and that you may get to heaven, but because your duty to others requires it.

Earl Granville, when laying the foundation-stone of the Alexandria Orphanage, in England, thus expressed himself in reference to the great value of children: "Few will deny that a child is 'an inestimable loan,' as it has been called, or refuse to acknowledge, with one of our greatest poets, that the world would be a somewhat melancholy one if there were no children to gladden it." Children, more than any other earthly thing, equalize the conditions of society—to rich and poor they bring an interest, a pleasure, and an elevation which nothing else that is earthly does.

Now, young people, before they think of engaging themselves, should clearly know each other's peculiar views of religion; because if they differ seriously on this point there is danger of it interfering with that full confidence which is so essential to happiness.

CHAPTER IV.

LOVE AND MARRIAGE.

Love and marriage; The attraction of the sexes for each other; What
love is; What causes love; Individual loves; Fondness for cousins; Different kinds of love; Flirtation; Monogamy; Polygamy; The
special object of marriage; Should marriage be for life.

The attraction of the sexes for each other, though based upon the dual principle of generation which pervades the living world and which has its analogies in
the attractive forces of matter, yet pervades the whole being.

LOVE IS NOT MERELY

the instinctive desire of physical union, which has for its object the continuation of the species—it belongs to the mind as well as to the body. It warms, invigorates, and elevates every sentiment, every feeling; and in its highest, purest, most
diffusive form unites us to God and all creatures in Him.

ALL LOVE IS

essentially the same, but modified according to its objects and by the character of the one who loves. The love of children for their parents, of parents for
offspring, brotherly and sisterly love, the love of friendship, of charity, and the
fervor of religious love, are modifications of the same sentiment—the attraction
that draws us to our kindred, our kind; that binds together all races and humanity
itself, resting on the fatherhood of God and the brotherhood of man. It is but natural that this love should vary in degrees. Attractions are proportional to proximity.
Family is nearer than country; we prefer our own nation to the rest of the race.

Each individual has, also, his own special attractions and repulsions. There is
love at first sight and friendship at first sight. We feel some persons pleasant to us;
to be near them is a delight. Generally such feelings are mutual—like flows to like,
or as often, perhaps, differences fit into each other. We seek sympathy with our
own tastes and habits, or we find in others what we lack. Thus the weak rest upon
the strong, the timid are fond of the courageous, the reckless seek guidance of the
prudent, and so on. The sentiment of

LOVE FOR THE OPPOSITE SEX

—tender, romantic, passionate—begins very early in life. Fathers and daughters, mothers and sons, have a special fondness for each other, as, also, have brothers and sisters; but the boy soon comes to admire someone, generally older than himself, who is not a relation. Very little girls find a hero in some friend of an elder brother.

FONDNESS FOR COUSINS

generally comes more from opportunity than natural attraction, though a cousin may have very little appearance of family relation. The law appears to be that free choice seeks the diverse and distant. A stranger has always a better chance with the young ladies of any district than the young men with whom they have always been acquainted. Savages seek their wives out of their own tribe.

It is my belief that naturally (I mean in a state of pure and unperverted nature, but developed cultivated, and refined by education) every man loves womanhood itself, and all women so far as they approximate to his ideal; and that in the same way every woman loves manhood, and is attracted and charmed by all its gentle, noble, and heroic manifestations. By such a man, every woman he meets is reverenced as a mother, sister, daughter, or, it may be, cherished in a more tender relation, which should be at first, and may always remain, free from any sensual desire. Such love may have many objects, each attracting the kind and degree of affection which it is able to inspire. Such love of men for women, and women for men, may be free and will be free just in the degree in which it is freed from the bondage of sensual passion.

SUCH LOVE HAS A DIRECT TENDENCY

to raise men above the control of their senses. The more of such love one has and the more it is diffused, the less the liability to sink into the lower and disorderly loves of the sensual life.

The idea that every attraction, every attachment, every love between the sexes must lead to marriage—that no love can be tolerated but with that end in view—is a very false and mischievous one. It deprives men and women of the strength and happiness they might have in pure friendships and pure loves, and it leads to a multitude of false and bad marriages. Two persons are drawn together by strong attractions and tender sentiments for each other who have no more right to be married than if they were brother and sister, but who have the same right to love each other. But their true sentiments for each other, and consequent relation to each other, are not understood by those around them and perhaps not by themselves. They are urged by the misapprehension of others, by their expectation, by ignorant gossip, by the prejudice of society, based upon low and sensual estimates of life, to marry; they find that they must either marry or lose the happiness they have in each other's society, and they make the irrevocable mistake.

When it is understood that there are

OTHER LOVES

than that of marriage; when the special attraction that justifies union for life, and the begetting of offspring, is discriminated from all the other attractions that may bring two souls into very near and tender relations to each other, there will be more happiness in the world and fewer incomplete, imperfect, and, therefore, more or less unhappy, marriages. Nothing can be more detestable than that playing with fire which goes by the name of

FLIRTATION;

but there are men and women who have the happiness of living and of being tenderly and devotedly loved by persons of the opposite sex—loved purely, nobly, happily—without injury and with great good. When such loves are accompanied by perfect trust in the goodness, purity, truth, and honor of the beloved, there can be no jealousy, no desire for selfish absorption, no fear of deprivation of any right. There is no reason why a husband or a wife should limit the range of pure and spiritual affection to near relatives.

THE MAN WHO CAN LOVE

a sister as sisters are often loved, may love in the same way, or as purely, any woman who might be his sister. As men and women learn to purify their lives, the world will grow more tolerant and love will become more universal. The tender and fervent exhortations to mutual love to be found in the Gospels and Epistles of the New Testament are now almost without a meaning. But they had a meaning to those to whom they were addressed, and when we are better Christians, and bring our lives to the purity of Christian morality, they will have a meaning to us and we shall learn that, in a sense we have not dreamed of, God is Love.

IN THE HUMAN RACE ALL CIRCUMSTANCES POINT TO MONOGAMY

as the lawful or natural condition. Males and females are born in almost equal numbers. If there are two or three per cent. more of males than females, the risks of life with males soon make the number even. Therefore, as a rule, no man can have more than one wife without robbing his neighbor.

Polygamy is therefore a manifest injustice, and may become the most grievous of all monopolies.

Children are the most helpless of all young creatures and require the care of parents for the longest period. The care of a husband for his wife, and of a father for his child, is an evident necessity. The proper care and education of a single child should extend over at least fifteen years, and that of a family may reach to thirty years, or throughout the greatest part of an ordinary life. During all periods of pregnancy, childbearing, nursing, and the education and care of a family, every woman has a right to the sympathy, sustaining love, and constant aid of her husband. No man has a right to desert or leave helpless, or even dependent upon others, except in extraordinary cases, the mother of his children.

Marriage, like celibacy, should be a matter of vocation.

THE SPECIAL OBJECT OF MARRIAGE

is to have children; the co-operating motive is that two persons drawn to each other by a mutual affection may live helpfully and happily together. A selfish marriage, for its merely animal gratifications—a marriage in which strength, health, usefulness, often life itself, are sacrificed to sensuality and lust—is a desecration of a holy institution, and somewhat worse in its consequences than promiscuous profligacy, for the consequences of that may not fall upon one's children and posterity.

There are many persons who have no right to marry. There should be a kind and amount of love that will justify and sanctify such a relation. There should be a pure motive and the fixed intention of making the relation what it ought to be to husband, wife, and children. There should be a reasonable assurance of the power to provide for a family. There should be that amount of health, that freedom from bodily and mental disease, that physical and moral constitution which will give a reasonable prospect of children whose lives will be a blessing to themselves and to society.

When there is deformity of body, or an unhappy peculiarity of temper or mind liable to be inherited, people should not marry, or if they live together, should resign the uses of marriage. People should conscientiously refrain from propagating hereditary diseases. Persons near of kin are wisely forbidden to marry, for there is in such cases the liability of imperfect generation—the production of blind, deaf, idiotic or insane offspring.

SHOULD MARRIAGE BE FOR LIFE?

As a rule, undoubtedly. Every real, proper, true marriage must be. It takes a lifetime for a husband and wife to make a home and rear and educate and provide for a family of children. But what if people make mistakes and find that they are not suitably married? These are mistakes very difficult to remedy. If a man, after deliberately making his choice of a woman, ceases to love her, how can he honorably withdraw from his relation to her, and enter upon another,

WHEN SHE STILL LOVES HIM,

and is ready to fulfill her part of the contract? Laws cannot very well provide for mistakes. If the distaste for each other be mutual, and both parties desire to separate, a separation may of course be permitted; but it is a serious question whether two such persons can go into the world and find new partners, with justice to the rest. The law which permits of no divorce certainly bears hard upon individual cases; but if it leads to greater seriousness and care in forming such relations, it may be, on the whole, the best thing for society that it should be strictly observed.

CHAPTER V.

WHEN TO MARRY—HOW TO SELECT A PARTNER ON RIGHT PRINCIPLES.

When to marry; How to select a partner on right principles; Very early
marriages; The best age to marry; When marriages are most happy; The attributes of a handsome couple.

The proper age to marry is a somewhat vexed question, but needlessly so, because that age varies much, according to temperament and other circumstances relating to the individual. Although after puberty the sexual organs are capable of reproduction, yet it by no means follows that they should be used for that purpose. Their early activity is intended for the perfection of the body and mind, and not for the continuation of the species.

VERY EARLY MARRIAGE,

therefore, should be avoided, because the nervous force expended in amative indulgence is imperatively required in both sexes for developing the physical and mental faculties. The zoösperms produced by the male in the first years of puberty are inferior in power and less capable of producing healthy offspring than those of mature years. The early germs, also, of the female are less fitted for fecundation than those that appear later in life; nature evidently intending these early efforts to be used on the individuals themselves in building up their bodies, strengthening their minds, and preparing them to reproduce their species in maturer years. There is a serious day of reckoning for early indulgence; for precocious persons (unless their constitutions are as powerful as their desires) who give way to their passions at their first exactions, barter their youth for their enjoyment, and are old and weary of the world at an age when people of more moderate habits are only in the meridian of pleasure and existence.

GENERALLY THE BEST AGE TO MARRY,

where the health is perfect, is from twenty-one to twenty-five in the male and from eighteen to twenty-one in the female. As a general rule, marriages earlier than this are injurious and detrimental to health. Men who marry too young, unless they are of cold and phlegmatic constitution, and thus moderate in their conduct, become partially bald, dim of sight, and lose all elasticity of limb in a few years; while women in a like position rarely have any bloom on their cheek or fire in their eye by the time they are twenty-five. And all profound physiologists agree that from the same cause the mental faculties suffer in the same ratio.

A medium, however, is to be observed. It is not well to defer till middle age the period of connubial intercourse; for too tedious spinsterhood is as much calculated to hasten the decay of beauty as too early a marriage. Hence, there is rarely any freshness to be seen in a maiden of thirty; while the matron of that age, if her life has been a happy one, and her hymeneal condition of not more than ten years' standing, is scarcely in the heyday of her charm's. And the same rule will apply with equal force to the other sex; for, after the first prime of life, bachelors decay and grow old much faster than married men.

The rich are qualified for marriage before the poor. This is owing to the superiority of their aliment; for very nutritious food, and the constant use of wines, coffee, etc., greatly assists in developing the organs of reproduction; whereas the food generally made use of among the peasantry of most countries—as vegetables, corn, milk, etc.—retards their growth. Owing to this difference of diet, the daughter of a man of wealth, who keeps a good table, will be as adequate to certain duties of married life at eighteen as the daughter of a humble peasant at twenty-one. Singular as it may seem, it is none the less true, that love novels, amorous conversations, playing parlor games for kisses, voluptuous pictures, waltzing, and, in fact, all things having a tendency to create desire, assist in promoting puberty and preparing young persons for early marriage. Those who reach this estate, however, by artificial means and much before the natural period will have to suffer for it in after life.

The female who marries before the completion of her womanhood—that is, before her puberty is established—will cease to grow and probably become pale and delicate, the more especially if she become pregnant soon after marriage. A person who is thus circumstanced will also be liable to abortions and painful deliveries.

MARRIAGE, UNLESS

under very peculiar circumstances, should not take place until two or three years after the age of puberty. Many instances could be cited of the injurious effects resulting from not observing this rule. The case of the son of Napoleon I. is a notable instance, who, at the age of fifteen or sixteen, began his career of sexual indulgence, which ended his life at the early age of twenty-one years. He was an amiable, inoffensive, and studious youth, beloved by his grandfather and the whole Austrian court; and though the son of the most energetic man that modern times has produced, yet, from his effeminate life, he scarcely attracted the least public attention.

Let me, therefore, advise the male reader to keep his desires in leading-strings until he is at least twenty-one, and the female not to enter the pale of wedlock until she is past her eighteenth year; but after these periods marriage is their proper sphere of action, and one in which they must play a part or suffer actual pain as well as the loss of one of the greatest of earthly pleasures.

MARRIAGES ARE MOST HAPPY

and most productive of handsome and healthy offspring when the husband and wife differ, not only in mental conformation, but in bodily construction. A melancholy man should mate himself with a sprightly woman, and *vice versa*; for otherwise they will soon grow weary of the monotony of each other's company. By the same rule should the choleric and the patient be united, and the ambitious and the humble; for the opposites of their natures not only produce pleasurable excitement, but each keeps the other in a wholesome check. In the size and form of the parties the same principles hold good. Tall women are not the ideals of beauty to tall men; and if they marry such, they will soon begin to imagine greater perfections in other forms than in those of their own wives. And this is well ordered by nature to prevent the disagreeable results which are almost certain to grow out of unions where the parties have a strong resemblance.

For instance, tall parents will probably have children taller than either, and mental imbecility is the usual attendant of extreme size. The union of persons prone to corpulency, of dwarfs, etc., would have parallel results; and so, likewise, of weakly and attenuated couples. The tall should marry the short, the corpulent the lean, the choleric the gentle, and so on, and the tendency to extremes in the parents will be corrected in the offspring.

Apart from these considerations, there are reasons why persons of the same disposition should not be united and wedlock. An amiable wife to a choleric man is like oil to troubled waters; an ill-tempered one will make his life a misery and his home a hell. The man of studious habits should marry a woman of sense and spirit rather than of erudition, or the union will increase the monotony of his existence, which it would be well for his health and spirits to correct by a little conjugal excitement; and the man of gloomy temperament will find the greatest relief from the dark forebodings of his mind in the society of a gentle, but lively and smiling partner.

However, in some particulars the dispositions and constructions of

MARRIED PEOPLE MUST ASSIMILATE

or they will have but few enjoyments in common. The man of full habits and warm nature had better remain single than unite his destinies with a woman whose heart repulses the soft advancements of love; and the sanguine female in whose soul love is the dominant principle should avoid marriage with a very phlegmatic person, or her caresses, instead of being returned in kind, will rather excite feelings of disgust. Thus the discriminations to be made in the choice of a partner are extremely nice.

Nature generally assists art in the choice of partners. We instinctively seek in the object of our desires the qualities which we do not possess ourselves. This is a most admirable arrangement of Providence, as it establishes an equilibrium and prevents people from tending to extremes; for it is known that unions of dwarfs are fruitful of dwarfs, that giants proceed from the embrace of giants, and that offspring of parents alike irritable, alike passive, alike bashful, etc., inherit the prominent qualities of both to such a degree as to seriously interfere with their prospects in the world.

It has another advantage. Through its means "Every eye forms its own beauty"; hence, what one person rejects is the *beau ideal* of another's conceptions, and thus we are all provided for.

In fine, with man as with animals, the best way to improve the breed is to cross it, for the intermarriage of like with like and relative with relative not only causes man to degenerate, but if the system became universal would in time bring the human race to a termination altogether.

A male or female with a very low forehead should carefully avoid marriage with a person of like conformation, or their offspring will, in all probability, be weak-minded or victims to partial idiocy.

The system of crossing is so perfect that marriages between persons of different countries are likely to be pleasant and fruitful. Speaking on this subject, an English writer says: "The Persians have been so improved by introducing foreigners that they have completely succeeded in washing out their Mongolian origin." And the same author adds to the effect that in those parts of Persia where there is no foreign intercourse the inhabitants are sickly and stunted, while in those that are frequented by strangers they are large and healthy.

To make what is called

"A HANDSOME COUPLE,"

the female should be about three inches less than the male, and the parties should be proportionately developed throughout their system.

"A WELL-FORMED WOMAN,"

says a modern physiologist, "should have her head, shoulders, and chest small and compact; arms and limbs relatively short; her haunches apart; her hips elevated; her abdomen large and her thighs voluminous. Hence, she should taper from the center, up and down. Whereas, in a well-formed man the shoulders are more prominent than the hips. Great hollowness of the back, the pressing of the thigh against each other in walking, and the elevation of one hip above the other, are indications of the malformation of the pelvis."

From the same writer I take the following, which is applicable here. It is very correct in its estimates of beauty in both sexes:—

"The length of the neck should be proportionately less in the male than in the female, because the dependence of the mental system on the vital one is naturally connected with the shorter courses of the vessels of the neck.

"The neck should form a gradual transition between the body and head—its fullness concealing all prominences of the throat.

"The shoulders should slope from the lower part of the neck, because the reverse shows that the upper part of the chest owes its width to the bones and muscles of the shoulders.

"The upper part of the chest should be relatively short and wide, independent of the size of the shoulders, for this shows the vital organs which it contains are sufficiently developed.

"The waist should taper a little farther than the middle of the trunk, and be marked, especially in the back and loins, by the approximation of the hips.

"The waist should be narrower than the upper part of the trunk and its muscles, because the reverse indicates the expansion of the stomach, liver, and great intestine, resulting from their excessive use.

"The back of woman should be more hollow than that of man; for otherwise the pelvis is not of sufficient depth for parturition.

"Women should have more extended loins than men, at the expense of the superior and inferior parts, for this conformation is essential to gestation.

"The abdomen should be larger in woman than in man, for the same reason.

"Over all these parts the cellular tissue, and the plumpness connected with it, should obliterate all distinct projection of muscles.

"The surface of the whole female form should be characterized by its softness, elasticity, smoothness, delicacy, and polish, and by the gradual and easy transition between the parts.

"The moderate plumpness already described should bestow on the organs of woman great suppleness. Plumpness is essential to beauty, especially in mothers, because in them the abdomen necessarily expands, and would afterwards collapse and become wrinkled.

"An excess of plumpness, however, is to be guarded against. Young women who are very fat are cold and prone to barrenness.

"In no case should plumpness be so predominant as to destroy the distinctness of parts."

A male and female formed on the above models would be well matched and have fine children.

CHAPTER VI.

SEXUAL INTERCOURSE—ITS LAWS AND CONDITIONS—ITS USE AND ABUSE.

Sexual Intercourse—Its laws and conditions—Its use and abuse: A prevalent error; The law of sexual morality; What men expect; How men and women should live; Age of puberty to marriage; The law of marriage; What a man who truly loves a woman will do; A true union; Seduction; How women are protected; The false and the true sense of duty. What is the most powerful restraint from evil.

There is an increasing and alarming prevalence of nervous ailments and complicated disorders that could be traced to have their sole origin from this source. Hypochondria, in its various phases, results from the premature and unnatural waste of the seminal fluid. Then speedily ensues a lack of natural heat, a deficiency of vital power, and consequently indigestion, melancholy, languor, and dejection ensue; the victim becomes enervated and spiritless, loses the very attributes of man, and premature old age soon follows.

IT IS A PREVALENT ERROR

that it is necessary for the semen to be ejected at certain times from the body; that its retention is incompatible with sound health and vigor of body and mind. This is a very fallacious idea. The seminal fluid is too precious—nature bestows too much care in its elaboration for it to be wasted in this unproductive manner. It is intended, when not used for the purpose of procreation, to be reabsorbed again into the system, giving vigor of body, elasticity and strength to the mind, making the individual strong, active, and self-reliant. When kept as nature intended, it is a perpetual fountain of life and energy—a vital force which acts in every direction, a motive power which infuses manhood into every organ of the brain and every fiber of the body.

THE LAW OF SEXUAL MORALITY

for childhood is one of utter negation of sex. Every child should be kept pure and free from amative excitement and the least amative indulgence, which is unnatural and doubly hurtful. No language is strong enough to express the evils of amative excitement and unnatural indulgence before the age of puberty; and the dangers are so great that I see no way so safe as

THOROUGH INSTRUCTION

regarding them at the earliest age. A child may be taught, simply as a matter of science, as one learns botany, all that is needful to know, and such knowledge may protect it from the most terrible evils.

The law for childhood is perfect purity, which cannot be too carefully guarded and protected by parents, teachers, and all caretakers. The law for youth is perfect continence—a pure vestalate alike in both sexes. No indulgence is required by one more than the other—for both nature has made the same provision. The natures of both are alike, and any—the least—exercise of the amative function is an injury to one as to the other.

MEN EXPECT

that women shall come to them in marriage chaste and pure from the least defilement. Women have a right to expect the same of their husbands. Here the sexes are upon a perfect equality.

On this subject, Dr. Carpenter (physiological works) has written like a man of true science, and, therefore, of true morality. He lays it down as an axiom that *the development of the individual and the reproduction of the species stand in an inverse ratio to each other*. He says: "The augmented development of the generative organs at puberty can only be rightly regarded as *preparatory* to the exercise of the organs. The development of the *individual* must be completed before the procreative power can properly be exercised for the continuance of the race." And in the following extract from his "Principles of Human Physiology," he confirms my statement respecting the unscientific and libertine advice of too many physicians: "The author would say to those of his younger readers who urge the wants of nature as an excuse for the illicit gratification of the sexual passions, 'try the effects of *close mental application* to some of those ennobling pursuits to which your profession introduces you, in combination with *vigorous bodily exercise*, before you assert that appetite is unrestrainable and act upon that assertion.' Nothing tends so much to increase the desire as the continual direction of the mind toward the objects of its gratification, whilst nothing so effectually represses it as a determined exercise of the mental faculties upon other objects and the expenditure of nervous energy in other channels. Some works which have issued from the medical press contain much that is calculated to excite, rather than to repress, the propensity; and the advice sometimes given by practitioners to their patients is immoral as well as unscientific."

EVERY MAN AND EVERY WOMAN,

living simply, purely, and temperately—respecting the laws of health in regard to air, food, dress, exercise, and habits of life—not only can live in the continence of a pure virgin life when single, and in the chastity which should be observed by all married partners, but be stronger, happier, and in every way better by so living.

Chastity is the conservation of life, and the consecration of its forces to the highest use. Sensuality is the waste of life, and the degradation of its forces to pleasure divorced from use. Chastity is life; sensuality is death.

FROM THE AGE OF PUBERTY TO MARRIAGE

the law, is the same for both sexes—full employment of mind and body, temperance, purity, and perfect chastity in thought, word, and deed. The law is one of perfect equality. There is no license for the male which is not equally the right of the female. There is no physiological ground for any indulgence in one case more than in the other. No man has any more right to require or expect purity in the woman who is to be his wife than the woman has to require and expect purity in her husband. It is a simple matter of justice and right. No man can enter upon an amative relation with a woman, except in marriage, without manifest injustice to his future wife, unless he allow her the same liberty; and also without a great wrong to the woman, and to her possible husband.

It is contended that the sins of men against chastity are more venial than those of women, because of the liability of women to have children. But men are also liable to be the fathers of children, who are deeply wronged by the absence of paternal care. The child has its rights, and every child has the right to be born in honest, respectable wedlock, of parents able to give it a sound constitution and the nurture and education it requires. The child who lacks these conditions is grievously wronged by both father and mother.

THE LAW OF MARRIAGE

is, that a mature man and woman, with sound health, pure lives, and a reasonable prospect of comfortably educating a family, when drawn to each other by the attraction of mutual love, should chastely and temperately unite for offspring. The sexual relation has this chief and controlling purpose. The law of nature is intercourse for reproduction. Under the Christian law, marriage is the symbol of the union of Christ with the Church; husband and wife are one in the Lord; they are to live in marriage chastity, not in lust and uncleanness; and there cannot be a more hideous violation of Christian morals than for a husband to vent his sensuality upon a feeble wife; against her wishes and when she has no desire for offspring and no power to give them the healthy constitutions and maternal care which is their right.

The law of Christian morality is very clear. It is the sexual union first and chiefly for its principal object. It is for the husband to refrain from it whenever it is not desired; whenever it would be hurtful to either; whenever it would be a waste of life; whenever it would injure mother or child, as during pregnancy and lactation.

A MAN WHO TRULY LOVES A WOMAN

must respect and reverence her, and cannot make her the victim of his inordinate and unbridled, selfish and sensual nature. He will be ever, from the first moment of joyful possession to the last of his life, tender, delicate, considerate, deferent, yielding to her slightest wishes in the domain of love, and never encroaching, never trespassing upon, never victimizing the wife of his bosom and the mother of his babes. We have romance before marriage, we want more chivalry in marriage.

This is not the world's morality, yet it seems to one the world must respect it. This, high and pure Christian morality is not always enforced by Christian ministers, some of whom yield too much to human sensuality and depravity, instead of maintaining the higher law of Christian purity, which is but nature restored or freed from its stains of sin. The world requires that unmarried women should be chaste, while it gives almost unbridled license to men. A girl detected in amours is disgraced and often made an outcast. In young men such irregularities are freely tolerated. They are "a little wild"; they "sow their wild oats"; but open profligacy, the seduction of innocence, the ruin of poor girls, adultery, harlotry and its diseases do not hinder men from marrying, nor from requiring that those they marry should have spotless reputations. It is not for a moment permitted that women in these matters should behave like men, and a pure girl is given to the arms of a wasted debauchee, and her babes are perhaps born dead, or suffer through life with syphilitic diseases, while she endures a long martyrdom from disordered, diseased, and unrestrained sensuality. For the unmarried, young men, soldiers, sailors, and all who do not choose to bear the burdens of a family, society has its armies of prostitutes—women like others, and more than others, or in less reputable fashion, the victims of the unbridled lust of men. They are everywhere tolerated as

"NECESSARY EVILS,"

and, in some places, protected or regulated; and, from economical or philanthropic considerations, or both, combined efforts are made to free them from the contagious diseases which for some centuries have been a curse attending this form of the violation of the laws of nature—one of the consequences of lust which is the divorce of the sexual instinct from its natural use and purpose.

The Christian

LAW OF MARRIAGE,

as set down in the Holy Scriptures, and defined by the best writers on moral theology, is in harmony with nature, in consonance with the higher nature of man. "God hath set the earth in families." Adultery is a sin, because it disorders that divine arrangement. Fornication is a sin, because it prevents pure marriages. Prostitution is a sin, because it is a sacrifice of women, who might be wives and mothers, to the selfish lusts of men. All useless indulgence is a waste of life, and a kind of suicide. In a pure marriage union, men and women unite themselves with God in acts of creative power. The progress of humanity depends upon individual development and the conditions at generation and gestation. With culture and a harmonized development, we acquire a higher and more integral life. When two parents are in their highest condition and in

A TRUE UNION

with each other, the child combines the best qualities of both parents. When parents are not in the unity of a mutual love, the child may be inferior to either parent. The intensity of mutual love tends to the reproduction of the best faculties of both parents in the child. When men or women are exhausted or diseased the race deteriorates. Health is therefore one of the conditions of progress.

"It is all very fine," I shall be told, "to talk of purity and chastity; but we must take men as they are. How are you going to make men pure and chaste, and respectful of the purity of women? How can you get men with strong amative propensities to live like anchorites?"

How can you get men to do anything right, or refrain from any wrong thing? There are three motives—fear of punishment, hope of reward, and sense of right or the principle of duty. The first of these is the lowest, but often the most effectual; the second is higher, and appeals to hope and the love of happiness; the third, the highest of all motives, pure and unselfish as the love of truth, as in mathematics, acts on noble minds with great power. Men of real conscientiousness love the right for its own sake. They are just from love of justice; pure from a sense and love of purity. They love good, and God as the source of all good; and do right, not from fear or hope, but from pure love.

We must appeal to all motives. Men refrain from theft and other dishonest conduct from the dread of disgrace and punishment, because they see that "honesty is the best policy," and from a sense of justice and regard to the rights of property, or a sense of honor which makes a mean action impossible. By similar motives great numbers are restrained from drunkenness and other vices. Children are to be restrained from impurity by the fear of the terrible consequences of unnatural indulgence in causing disease and pain, by the hope of a pure, healthy and happy life of love in manhood and womanhood, and by a sense of the beauty and holiness of chastity and the sacredness of the functions by which the race is recreated and preserved. The religious feelings that our bodies are to be kept pure, healthy, and holy in every way as the temples of the Holy Ghost cannot be too early instilled into the infant mind, which is open to the highest sentiments of veneration, devotion, and heroic religion. In youth there are the same motives. Indulgence in solitary vice is self-destructive of all that youth most values—a profanation of his own body.

SEDUCTION

is a desecration of what he should hold in the most tender reverence. To the young man, womanhood should be sacred, and every woman, mother, sister, beloved of the present or the future, should never be wronged by one thought of impurity. In this matter instinct goes with right. The inward voice supports the outer law of morality. Before men can become bad, their instinctive modesty must be broken down. Unless very badly born, with disordered amativeness, hereditary from a diseased and lustful parentage, they must be perverted and corrupted before they can act immodestly and impurely.

WOMEN ARE PROTECTED

by a strong public sentiment around them. They have the dread of disgrace. For them to yield to their own affectionate desires, or the solicitations of a lover, is a fall, is ruin. They have the hope of a loving husband, a happy home, and the respect of society. And in woman passion has commonly less force, and the sentiment of modesty and purity more power. Women are weak in yielding to solicitation, giving

EVERYTHING FOR LOVE;

but we see how protective of female virtue are these motives to vast numbers.

Men can perfectly restrain the sensual part of their natures whenever they have a strong motive to do so. A child would be simply mad who was not controlled by the presence of father, mother, and persons he respected or feared. Young men have no difficulty when they are in the company of pure women. They are in no trouble when their lives are full of mental and muscular activity, and particularly if their habits of eating simply and temperately, of refraining from heating and exciting stimulants, and sleeping in cold beds and fresh air, are such as health requires. There needs but the strong will to live purely in any one, and at any age, the will that comes from the high motives of conscience and religion, or all motives combined. A strong sense of what is just and right controls even the motions of our bodies and actions which seem to be involuntary. A man who has a vivid sense of the right and duty of refraining from sensuality, and preserving his own purity of mind and body and the chastity of all women, will do so even in his dreams. When the will is right, all things are soon brought into its subjection. The mind controls the organization, and the life forces are directed into other channels. A strong man, full of

LIFE AND LOVE,

can safely hold a virgin in his arms, and respect her virginity, if he have but the motives and the will to do so. If he be pure in his will, how can he commit impurity? If a woman be sacred in his eyes, how can he profane her? It is not that men have not the power of restraint, the power to do right; it is that they lack the motive. They have lost the sense of right; they are even impelled to do wrong by the pressure of opinion around them. Boys and young men are driven into libertinage by the ridicule of their companions. Vice is considered manly. They seek sensuality in an evil emulation, as they learn to smoke, or gamble, or drink; and, later on, vanity has often more to do with excess than the force of lust. Young men seduce girls that they may boast of it. They keep mistresses because it is the fashion. They exhaust themselves because they wish to give a high idea of their manly powers. Even in marriage, women are injured and have their health destroyed by yielding weakly, or from

A FALSE SENSE OF DUTY,

to a husband whose own motive is the desire to acquit himself manfully in what he considers his marital duties. Men and women are, in thousands of cases, wretched victims to what they imagine to be the wants or expectations of each other. A man, ignorant of the nature of women and the laws of the generative function, goes on in a process of miserable exhaustion, to please his wife. She submits, sometimes in pain, often in disgust, weariness, and weakness, to what she dare not, from

LOVE OR FEAR,

refuse. Men have to know what is right and to will to be right. This will is omnipotent. God helps those who have the will, who have even the desire, to do right.

If the presence of those we fear or reverence, respect or love, restrain us from sin and stimulate us to right action, faith in the existence and presence of God and angels, and the spirits of the departed, must have a more powerful and pervading influence. No one who really believes in the existence of a Supreme Being, no one who is strongly impressed with the reality of a spiritual life, can go on doing what he knows to be wrong. A religious faith is therefore the most powerful of all restraints from evil and incitement to good.

CHAPTER VII.

MARRIAGE.

Marriage: What marriage is; How far back the marriage tie has existed; Polygamy—What it is; Monogamy—What it is; Polyandry—What it is; Marriage customs; The basis of a happy marriage.

WHAT IS MARRIAGE?

Marriage is in law the conjugal union of man with woman, and is the only state in which cohabitation is considered proper and irreprehensible. The marriage relation exists in all Christian communities, and is considered the most solemn of contracts, and, excepting in Protestant countries, it is regarded as a sacrament. In some countries its celebration falls under the cognizance of ecclesiastical courts only, but in the United States it is regarded as merely a civil contract, magistrates having, equally with clergymen, the right to solemnize it, though it is usually the practice to have it performed by a clergyman and attended with religious ceremonies. Marriage, as a legalized custom, is of very ancient origin. It is doubtful whether even the primitive man was not governed in the intercourse of the sexes by some recognition of the union being confined to one chosen one. No greater promiscuity can certainly be supposed than occurs in the lower animals, where pairing is the law. The nobler animals, as the lion, elephant, etc., never have but one mate, and even in case of death do not remate. As men advanced, civil codes were inaugurated and certain protection given to the choice of the parties. The earliest civil code regulating marriage, of which we have any account, was that of Menes, who, Herodotus tells us, was the first of the Pharaohs, or native Egyptian kings, and who lived about 3,500 years before Christ. The nature of his code is not known.

The Biblical account extends further back, but it does not appear that any laws existed regulating marriage, but each one was allowed to choose his wife and concubines, and it is supposed that common consent respected the selection. Next, Moses gave laws for the government of marriage among the Israelites. The early Greeks followed the code of Cecrops, and the Romans were also governed in their marital relations by stringent laws. In fact, the necessity of some law regulating the intercourse between the sexes must have become very apparent to all nations or communities at a very early period. It certainly antedates any legal regulations with regard to the possession of property. It is very probable that every community did by common consent afford to each male one or more females, and the presumption is that such choice or assignment, as the case may have been, was respected by common agreement as inviolable. It is doubtful if ever promiscuity was the law or privilege with any community of men, even in their primitive state. The possession of reason is antagonistic to such a belief; and man was most probably elevated above the beast by the faculty of reason in this respect as in others. Promiscuous indulgence is always evidence of debauchery, and a departure from that natural course which is prompted by an innate sense of propriety characterizing mankind. The law is very indefinite with regard to what constitutes a legal marriage. It is an unsettled question, both in England and this country, whether a marriage solemnized by customary formalities alone is legal, or if one characterized by the mere consent of the parties is illegal. The latter has been held as legal in some instances in both countries. Kent, in his "Commentaries," lays down the law that a contract made so that either party recognizes it from the moment of contract, and even not followed by cohabitation, amounts to a valid marriage, and also that a contract to be recognized at some future period, and followed by consummation, is equally valid. It is unfortunate that the law is so undecided in this respect. The decisions arrived at, for or against, were not dependent upon any recognized law, but seem to be influenced by the character of the cases, either for favor or discountenance. As long as the law recognizes cohabitation legal only in marriage, it seems to me that if consummated under consent of the parties to bear marital relations with each other, or promise of marriage, the act should be unhesitatingly pronounced as the equivalent of a valid marriage in all instances. If cohabitation is only a marital prerogative, the law should not stultify itself by recognizing it as possible to occur in any other relation. If either of the parties is married, the law defines it as adultery, and very properly defines the punishment. It is necessary to the progress of the age that some such principle should be recognized in common law so as not to subject the decision of the question to the individual opinion of any judge. It would at once obviate the confusion of sentiment now held in regard to it and besides arrest the decision in test cases from mere caprice of the tribunal. It is certainly as correct a principle as any in common law, and would, in its operations as a statute law, be free from injustice, and capable of doing much good.

POLYGAMY—WHAT IT IS.

Polygamy is a state in which a man has at the same time more than one wife. It has existed from time immemorial, especially among the nations of the East. The custom was tolerated by the laws of Moses, and, in fact, no positive injunction against it is found in the whole of the Old Testament. It is questionable whether more than one was recognized as the *bona fide* wife, the others simply being wives by right of concubinage. But if polygamy was in its strictest sense the legal custom, it soon grew unpopular, for no trace of it is met in the records of the New Testament, where all the passages referring to marriage imply monogamy as alone lawful. The custom has been almost universal in the East, being sanctioned by all the religions existing there. The religion of Mohammed allows four wives, but the permission is rarely exercised except by the rich.

In Christian countries polygamy was never tolerated, the tenets of the Church forbidding it, though Charlemagne had two wives, and Sigbert and Chilperich also had a plurality. John of Leyden, an Anabaptist leader, was the husband of seventeen wives, and he held that it was his moral right to marry as many as he chose.

In England the punishment of polygamy was originally in the hands of the ecclesiastics. It was considered a capital crime by Edward I., but it did not come entirely under the control of the temporal power until a statute of James I. made it a felony, punishable by death. George III. made it punishable by imprisonment or transportation for seven years.

It is the offspring of licentiousness, and its advocates merely wish to give legal color to licentious habits. Every student of history will find that as soon as a nation became morally depraved, polygamy was practiced, and that monogamy was the rule in all countries truly civilized.

Polygamy has, of late years, been most shamefully revived and outrageously practiced in face of law by the Mormons. They claim it as a religious duty, and defend the system by claiming that unmarried women can in the future life reach only the position of angels who occupy in the Mormon theocratic system a very subordinate rank, being simply ministering servants to those more worthy, thus proclaiming that it is a virtual necessity of the male to practice the vilest immorality in order to advance the female to the highest place in heaven.

Mormonism is a religion founded by Joseph Smith, who was born in Sharon, E. V., Dec. 23rd, 1805, and killed at Carthage, Ill., June 27th, 1844.

It is a most singular fact that a sect like the Mormons could have been established in a country peopled with such law-abiding people as of the United States, and maintain a system of marriage, antagonistic to the law and religion of the land. Neither could they have done so if they had not possessed two great virtues, temperance and industry. It is to be hoped that the legal process now instituted for its abolition will effectually remove the blot from the national escutcheon.

The "Oneida Communists" are essentially polygamic, although they have no marriage system. They do not marry, and ignore all marriage codes. Cohabitation is under no restrictions between the sexes. Marriage is also not observed among the "Shakers."

MONOGAMY—WHAT IT IS.

This is the conjugal union of a male with one female only. We have seen that monogamy was coequal with civilization, and that most probably the majority of the males had but one wife, even among polygamic nations. Universal polygamy is practically impossible, the scarcity of females and the poverty of the males forbidding it. The excess of females is not so great in any country as to allow to each male more than one wife, except the male portion is depleted by long and disastrous wars. Monogamy has done more for the elevation of the female than any other custom of civilization. The rich could only afford to practice polygamy, and should the poor imitate the example it would necessarily subject the wives to a state of serfdom. In the economy of nature it is designed that the male should be the protector of the female, and that by his exertions the provision of food and raiment should be secured. In polygamous nations the female has not attained that social state that she has reached in countries where the male is entitled to but one female as his wife. Woman's highest sphere is not in the harem or zenana, but in that dignified state in which she is the sole connubial companion of but one man. It is debasing to her nature, and subversive of her dignity in the rank of humanity, to make her the equal only with others in the marital union with one male. She becomes only the true, noble and affectionate being when she is conscious of a superiority to others in the connubial companionship with her accepted one. The female bird chirps but for her single mate, and she is pugnaciously monogamic, as well as virtuous, allowing neither male or female at or near her home. The spirit of independence she gains by being the mate of but one male gains for her the victory over the intruders.

The physical and mental welfare of the female is also dependent upon monogamic marriage. We have demonstrated that temperate indulgence is conducive to the sanitary condition of the sexes, and that absolute abstinence is opposed to the designs of nature. It is also evident that the male is not endowed with greater power, vigor or capacity than the female; therefore, confinement or limitation of the congress to the companionship of one male with one female, as in monogamic marriage, gives the healthy balance to the marital union. The polygamic husband must either suffer from the consequences of excessive indulgence or his wives from poverty of sexual gratification; probably both would be the case.

POLYANDRY

is equally as proper as polygamy, yet it never in the history of man obtained a foothold. The system is more logical than polygamy, because the wife's dependence would be distributed between two or more husbands, in which case she would be better insured against poverty and her support would be guaranteed by greater probability.

We have now described the history and aspect of the two customs, and will conclude the subject by remarking that a man is morally and physically entitled to but one wife, and that a plurality is a great wrong to the female and in total opposition to the ordinance of nature. Wherever polygamy is the custom the female is held in slavish subjection. It only prospers in proportion to the ignorance of the sex. Intelligent and civilized woman will always rebel against such debasement and servitude.

MARRIAGE CUSTOMS.

It would probably be interesting to many to describe the marriage ceremonies observed by different nations, but to enter into a descriptive detail would occupy too much space. It is sufficient to say that while some wives are wooed and won, others are bought and sold; while in some countries the husband brings the wife to his home, in others, as in Formosa, the daughter brings her husband to her father's house, and he is considered one of the family, while the sons, upon marriage, leave the family forever. In civilized countries, the ceremonies are either ministerial or magisterial, and are more or less religious in character; while in others, less civilized, the gaining of a wife depends upon a foot-race, in which the female has the start of one-third the distance of the course, as is the custom in Lapland. In Caffraria, the lover must first fight himself into the affections of his ladylove, and if he defeats all his rivals she becomes his wife without further ceremony. Among the Congo tribes, a wife is taken upon trial for a year, and if not suited to the standard of taste of the husband, he returns her to her patents. In Persia, the wife's status depends upon her fruitfulness; if she be barren, she can be put aside. In the same country they have also permanent marriages and marriages for a certain period only—the latter never allowed to exceed ninety years.

In fact, the marriage ceremonies differ in nearly all countries. To us some may appear very absurd, and yet our customs may be just as amazing to them. It matters but little how a conjugal union is effected so long as sanctioned by law or custom and it obligates the parties, by common opinion, to observe the duties pertaining to married life.

THE BASIS OF A HAPPY MARRIAGE.

The state of conjugal union should be the happiest in the whole of the existence of either man or woman, and is such in a congenial marriage. Yet in the history of very many marriages contentment or happiness is palpably absent and an almost insufferable misery is the heritage of both parties. It is therefore important that previous to the marital union the parties should take everything into consideration that fore-shadows happiness after marriage, as well as everything calculated to despoil conjugal felicity.

The first requisite of congenial marriage is love. Without being cemented by this element the conjugal union is sure to be uncongenial. It is the strongest bond, the firmest cord, uniting two hearts inseparably together. Love for the opposite sex has always been a controlling influence with mankind. It is the most elevating of all the emotions and the purest and tenderest of all sentiments. It exerts a wonderful power, and by its influence the grandest human actions have been achieved. Of what infinite worth it is to either sex to be compensated with a worthy and satisfying love, and how ennobling to the impulses and actions it is to bestow the sentiment upon one worthy to receive and willing to return.

LOVE IS THE MAINSPRING

that regulates the harmony of conjugal life, and without it there is a void in the machinery, productive only of jars, convulsive movement, and a grating and inharmonious action. The soul yearns for love and to love, and unless the desire is compensated human life is a blank and becomes a purposeless existence. Love ever stimulates the good and suppresses the bad, if kept in a proper channel and guided by pure affections.

Another requisite of a happy marriage is health. No person has a moral right to engage in wedlock who cannot bring to his partner the offering of good health.

Another consideration is *evenness of temper*. In the wooing days everyone is a lamb, and only becomes the howling wolf after marriage. Circumstances that ruffle the temper in the presence of the intended are but like the harmless squib, but would become like the explosive torpedo in his or her absence or in after-marriage. Quarreling caused by matrimonial differences is the most frequent cause of infelicity, and most of it is caused by an innate irate temper of either husband or wife.

The *tastes* should not be dissimilar. Some of them may be unimportant, but others are a fruitful source of disagreement. The social wife will never be contented with the unsocial husband, and the gay husband, though his gayety may not be commendable, will always accuse his wife if she lacks a social disposition to a great extent. The religious wife will never excuse a tendency to irreligion in her husband, and though he may be far from being immoral, she is unhappy if he does not participate in her devotions. The one devoted to children will never be happy with one having a natural repugnance for them. In this way we might multiply facts illustrative of the importance of an investigation into the similarity of taste previous to marriage. Great love, however, overcomes almost every obstacle.

THE PARTIES SHOULD BE NEARLY OF ONE AGE.

The husband should be the elder. The union of the old husband to the young wife, or the reverse, is seldom a happy one. It is seldom that such a marriage occurs in which the incentive is not the wealth of either of the parties.

Marriages are usually contracted to gratify various desires, as love, fortune or position. The results are more truthfully stated by an eminent divine in the following:

"Who marries for love, takes a wife; who marries for fortune, takes a mistress; who marries for position, takes a lady."

To a man there is but one choice that he can rationally make, a marriage of love. My female readers, I hope, will decide rather to wed a husband than the master or the elegant gentleman.

A little foresight, a little prudence, and a little caution will prevent in most cases the entrance into a marriage which, by the very nature of the alliance, is certain to be an unhappy and improper one.

CHAPTER VIII.

PREGNANCY—LABOR—PARTURITION.

Pregnancy—Labor—Parturition: The signs of pregnancy; The changes that take place in the appearance; How soon after conception these changes take place; The period of gestation; Changes in the breasts; What causes labor; How labor may be rendered safe and easy; What the diet should consist of; The period of quickening; How to relieve the toothache, cramping of the legs, palpitation of the heart, morning sickness, etc., with which pregnant women are liable to be troubled; Sure test for the detection of pregnancy; Parturient Balm, a very important medicine; Abortion; Premature labor; The cause of abortion; Symptoms of threatened abortion; What to do for a threatened abortion; What to do for miscarriage; To prevent miscarriage.

Perhaps there is no more eventful period in the history of woman than that in which she first becomes conscious that the existence of another being is dependent upon her own and that she carries about with her the first tiny rudiments of an immortal soul.

THE SIGNS OF PREGNANCY

are various. Many females are troubled with colic pains, creeping of the skin, shuddering, and fainting fits immediately on conception taking place. Where such symptoms occur immediately after connection, they are a certain indication of impregnation.

A REMARKABLE CHANGE

takes place in the face in most cases, varying in time from three days to three months. The eyes are dull and heavy, and present a glassy appearance; the nose pinched up; the skin becomes pale and livid, and the whole countenance appears as if five or ten years' advance in life had been taken at a single step.

Another important and remarkable sign, and one the most to be relied on, is an increase in the size of the neck. This often occurs at a very early period, and many females, by keeping a careful daily measurement of the neck, can always tell when they are pregnant.

A suppression of the menstrual flow is another strong presumptive sign. It is true a partial flow of the menses often occurs after pregnancy, from the lower part of the womb, but when the flow is suddenly stopped without any apparent cause, pregnancy is generally the predisposing cause.

SOON AFTER CONCEPTION

the stomach often becomes affected with what is called morning sickness. On first awaking, the female feels as well as usual, but on rising from her bed qualmishness begins and perhaps while in the act of dressing retching and vomiting takes place.

This symptom may occur almost immediately after conception, but it most frequently commences for the first time between two and three weeks after. Now and then it is experienced only during the last six weeks or two months of pregnancy, and subsides about the time the movements of the child begin to be felt.

CHANGES IN THE BREAST

are generally considered as strong signs of pregnancy. When two months of pregnancy have been completed, an uneasy sensation of throbbing and stretching fullness is experienced, accompanied by tingling about the middle of the breasts, centering in the nipples. A sensible alteration in their appearance soon follows, they grow larger and more firm. The nipple becomes more prominent, and the circle around its base altered in color and structure, constituting what is called the areola, and as pregnancy advances milk is secreted.

THE PERIOD OF GESTATION,

at which these changes may occur, varies much in different females. Sometimes, with the exception of the secretion of the milk, they are recognized very soon after conception; in other instances, particularly in females of a weakly and delicate constitution, they are hardly perceptible until pregnancy is far advanced or even drawing toward its termination.

The changes in the form and size of the breasts may be the result of causes unconnected with pregnancy. They may enlarge in consequence of marriage, from the individual becoming stout and fat or from accidental suppression of the monthly flow.

The changes which take place in the nipple, and around its base, are of the utmost value as an evidence of pregnancy.

ABOUT THE SIXTH OR SEVENTH WEEK

after conception has taken place, if the nipple be examined it will be found becoming turgid and prominent, and a circle forming around its base, of a color deeper in its shade than rose or flesh color, slightly tinged with a yellowish or brownish hue, and here and there upon its surface will be seen little prominent points from about ten to twenty in number. In the progress of the next six or seven weeks these changes are fully developed, the nipple becoming more prominent and turgid than ever, the circle around it of larger dimensions, the skin being soft, bedewed with a slight degree of moisture, frequently staining the linen in contact with it; the little prominences of larger size, and the color of the whole very much deepened.

Calculations of the

DURATION OF PREGNANCY,

founded upon what has been observed to occur after casual intercourse, or perhaps a single act, in individuals who can have no motive to tell us what is false, are likely to be correct. The conclusion drawn from these is, that labor usually, but not invariably, comes on about 280 days after conception, a mature child being sometimes born before the expiration of the forty weeks, and at other times not until that time has been exceeded by several days. A case is on record where the pregnancy lasted 287 days. In this case the labor did not take place until that period had elapsed from the departure of the husband for the East Indies, consequently the period might have been longer than 287 days.

CHILDBIRTH IS A NATURAL PROCESS,

and however complicated and painful habits or disease have made it, yet the work must be left to nature. Any efforts to assist or hurry matters will only end in harm. The only cases where interference is justifiable is where her powers are exhausted or some malformation exists or malpresentation occurs. When labor is about to commence, the womb descends into the bottom of the belly and the motions and weight of the child will be felt much lower down than usual. If in a natural position the head will fall to the mouth of the womb and press upon it. This drives forward the membranes which retain the water at the orifice, and at the proper moment they break and labor then commences.

Labor is caused by involuntary contractions of the uterus and abdominal muscles. By their force the liquor amnii flows out, the head of the fœtus is engaged in the pelvis, it goes through it, and soon passes out by the valve, the folds of which disappear. These different phenomena take place in succession and continue a certain time. They are accompanied with pains more or less severe, with swelling and softening of the soft parts of the pelvis and external genital parts, and with an abundant mucous secretion in the cavity of the vagina. All these circumstances, each in its own way, favor the passage of the fœtus.

It is proper here to remark that parturition is not necessarily either painful or dangerous. It is well known that women in an uncivilized state suffer very little pain or disablement in bringing forth children. Generally neither pregnancy nor labor interrupt the ordinary avocation of the mother, except for an hour or two at the birth itself. The suffering and debilitating influences that often attend childbirth now are caused by our unnatural modes of living and nonattention to the laws of health. Numerous well-authenticated instances are known where women who had previously suffered with severe labor in childbirth have, by attention to health and diet as here shown, been delivered of fine healthy children with comparative ease.

From the

BEGINNING OF PREGNANCY

more than ordinary care should be used in taking regular exercise in the open air, being careful to avoid fatigue and overexertion. During the whole period of pregnancy every kind of agitating exercise, such as running, jumping, jolting in a carriage, and plunging in cold water, should be carefully avoided, as well as the passions being kept under perfect control.

THE DIET

must chiefly consist of fruits and farinaceous food, as sago, tapioca, rice, etc. In proportion as a woman subsists upon aliment which is free from earthy and bony matter will she avoid pain and danger in delivery; hence, the more ripe fruit, acid fruit in particular, and the less of other kinds of food, but particularly of bread or pastry of any kind, is consumed, the less will be the danger and sufferings of childbirth. Nearly all kinds of fruit possess two hundred times less ossifying principle than bread or anything else made of wheaten flour.

Honey, molasses, sugar, butter, oil, vinegar, etc., when unadulterated, are entirely free from earthy matter. Common salt, pepper, coffee, cocoa, spices, and many drugs are much worse than wheaten flour in their hardening and bone-forming tendency, and should therefore be avoided. The drink should be tea or lemonade made with water, soft and clear, and, when practicable, distilled.

No mother who has adopted this mode of living but has blessed the knowledge of it, and it has saved many a young mother from needless terror.

In the third month of pregnancy, but not before, the belly begins to enlarge or swell, and gradually increases in size till the full term of pregnancy is completed. Between the sixteenth and twentieth week the womb rises up into the belly, and the motion of the child is felt, which is called

QUICKENING.

The first time a woman is with child this sensation of quickening is like that of a bird fluttering within her; at other times she feels a tickling or pushing sensation, or the child gives a kick or a jump, and this, too, with so much energy as to move the petticoats, a book, or any light article she may have in her lap.

It is important to remember these symptoms, and the order in which they occur: first, cessation of the menses; second, morning sickness; third, swelling and darting pains in the breast, and dark color around the nipples; fourth, gradual enlargement of the abdomen or belly; fifth, the movement of the child.

In ninety-nine cases out of a hundred, if these symptoms are present the woman is pregnant. Pregnant women are generally affected with heartburn, sickness of a morning, headache, and that troublesome disease, toothache, which accompanies pregnancy; all of which may usually be avoided by keeping the bowels gently open with seidlitz powders, caster oil, or pills of rhubarb, which should be taken occasionally, either alone or in combination with colocynth and soap. A clyster made of warm soapsuds will often be sufficient if repeated every few days; or senna and manna; and if there is any aversion to taking medicine, give some simple articles, such as roasted apples, figs, prunes, or anything that will quiet the stomach and prevent costiveness of the bowels.

THE TOOTHACHE

often complained of by pregnant women, and which may occur at any period, is seldom relieved by extraction, having its seat in the adjacent nerves of the face or jaws, and is neuralgic. The teeth ought not to be drawn during pregnancy, unless urgently required, but should be relieved by applying hot fomentations to the face, as a camomile poultice. Rubbing the jaw externally with spirits of camphor or laudanum, or applying mustard plasters or blisters behind the ears, will afford relief.

THE CRAMPS OF THE LEGS. ETC.,

in pregnancy, caused by the pressure of the enlarged womb on the nerves, are often troublesome, but not attended with any danger, and may be speedily relieved by a change of posture, and friction, or rubbing with opodeldoc, spirits of camphor, or hot whisky and salt. Palpitation of the heart occurs frequently, and usually about the period of quickening. In general, it is the result of a disordered stomach and may be relieved by attention to diet and moderate doses of magnesia and Epsom salts, of equal quantities.

THE PALPITATION OF THE HEART

may be produced by a morbid state of the nerves, and is then termed hysterical. Attention in all such cases should be paid to the diet, air, exercise, etc., with the view of improving the strength, the bowels being kept open by mild means. All exciting or agitating subjects should be carefully avoided, and the mind of the pregnant woman kept calm and tranquil; for the mind, in the early stages of pregnancy, exercises the most powerful influence over the child through life; and how many peculiar traits of character have been indelibly fixed upon their offspring from these exciting causes is evident in many families.

When the palpitation occurs from the state of the nerves, as before described, producing uncomfortable feelings, a teaspoonful of the tincture of castor or asafœtida, with an equal quantity of compound spirits of lavender, mixed in a little water, will seldom fail to afford relief, which may, if necessary, be repeated on its recurrence.

MORNING SICKNESS

is one of the most painful feelings attendant on the pregnant state, and it is one of those which medicine commonly fails to relieve. A cup of camomile or peppermint tea, taken when first awaking, and suffering the patient to be still for an hour, will frequently alleviate the distressing sickness; but should it recur during the day, and if these means fail, two or three teaspoonfuls of the following mixture should then be taken either occasionally or, when the vomiting and heartburn are more continual, immediately after each meal:

Take of—

Calcined magnesia,	One dram;
Distilled water,	Six ounces;
Aromatic tincture of rhatany,	Six drams;
Water of pure ammonia,	One dram.

Mix. The anxiety and sometimes despondency of mind—in other words, lowness of spirits—to which pregnant women are more or less liable greatly depends on the state of their general health and the natural temper and character of the individual; but it can be greatly aggravated, and may often be excited by circumstances or officious persons. Let me, then, urge upon you the *important necessity* of keeping the mind as tranquil and cheerful as possible, particularly during the first four months of pregnancy. A judicious course of this kind will produce the most beneficial and well-balanced mind in the child; while, if the contrary, a desponding and nervous temperament, with many other peculiarities, will be the consequence.

SURE TEST FOR THE DETECTION OF PREGNANCY.

M. Nauche has found that the urine of pregnant women contains a particular substance, which, when the urine is allowed to stand separates and forms a pellicle on the surface. M. Enguiser, from an extensive series of observations, has confirmed the fact, and ascertained that kisteine, as this particular substance has been called, is constantly formed on the surface of the urine of women in a state of pregnancy. The urine must be allowed to stand for from two to six days, when minute opaque bodies are observed to rise from the bottom to the surface of the fluid, where they gradually unite and form a continuous layer over the surface. This layer is so consistent that it may be almost lifted off by raising it by one of its edges. This is the kisteine. It is whitish, opalescent, slightly granular, and can be compared to nothing better than the fatty substance which floats on the surface of soups after they have been allowed to cool. When examined by the microscope, it has the aspect of a gelatinous mass without determinate form; sometimes cubical shaped crystals are discovered on it, but this appearance is only observed when it has stood a long time, and is to be regarded as foreign to it. The kisteine remains on the surface for several days; the urine then becomes turbid, and small opaque masses become detached from the kisteine and fall to the bottom of the fluid and. the pellicle soon becomes destroyed.

The essential character of the urine of pregnancy, then, is the presence of the kisteine; and the characters of the pellicle are so peculiar that it is impossible to mistake it for anything else. A pellicle sometimes forms on the surface of the urine of patients laboring under phthisis, abscess, or disease of the bladder, but may be easily distinguished by this circumstance, that it does not form in such a short time as the kisteine, and that in place of disappearing, as this last, in a few days, it increases in thickness and at last is converted into a mass of moldiness. There exists, likewise, a very marked difference between its mucous aspect and that of kisteine; a difference which is difficult to describe, but which is easily recognized.

Kisteine appears to exist in the urine from the first month of pregnancy till delivery. It has even been recognized in the urine of a few gravid animals.

"PARTURIENT BALM,"

For Rendering Childbirth Easy and Less Dangerous — A very Important Medicine.

Take blue cohosh root, four ounces; lady's-slipper root and spikenard root, of each one ounce; sassafras bark (of root) and clover, of each half an ounce. Bruise all, and simmer slowly for two hours in two quarts of boiling water. Strain, and add one pound of white sugar.

Dose: A wineglassful twice a day for two weeks or a month previous to expected confinement, for the purpose of rendering parturition, or childbirth, more easy.

Should be taken by every pregnant woman.

ABORTION.

Abortion, or miscarriage, means, in plain language, a woman losing her child previous to the seventh month of her pregnancy; that is, before its due time. When this occurs after that period it is called

PREMATURE LABOR.

Miscarriage involves pain and weakness in addition to the loss of offspring, and is often a severe trial to the maternal constitution. It may occur at any period of pregnancy, but particular stages are more liable to the accident than others. These are generally considered to be about the time of the first menstruation after conception; again at the twelfth week, and toward the seventh month; and the liability is increased at those times which correspond to the menstrual period. When abortion has once taken place it is more likely to occur again, and some have so strong a tendency to it that they never go beyond a certain stage, but then invariably miscarry.

THE CAUSE OF ABORTION

may exist in the constitution of the female herself, being the result of weakness and irritability, or of an overfull habit or a diseased condition of the womb; or the fœtus, or child, may die or be deficient in development, when it is cast off like a blighted fruit. Suckling after conception has taken place is not infrequently a cause of miscarriage. Active diseases occurring during pregnancy, such as fevers, severe inflammation, eruptive fevers, etc., are almost certain to occasion the expulsion of the uterine contents. Continued diarrhœa and the action of strong purgative medicines, particularly the aloetic, are dangerous. This is a very good reason for those who are pregnant avoiding all quack aperient medicines; they almost all contain aloes, and may be very injurious. All undue exertion or agitation of body or mind, sudden jerks or jumps, riding on horseback in the early stage, or in a shaking carriage in the latter stages of pregnancy, may any of them bring on miscarriage. To these may be added: exertion of the arms in doing anything on a level above the head; costive bowels and straining consequent therein; sexual indulgence, or, in plain language, too much connection with your husband; and luxurious habits. Those who have once suffered from abortion ought to be extremely careful during succeeding pregnancies, and all ought to bear in mind the possibility of the occurrence.

THE SYMPTOMS OF THREATENED ABORTION

vary with the constitution. In the strong and plethoric it is often preceded by shivering and febrile symptoms and by a feeling of weight in the lower bowels. In the weak there is languor, faintness, flaccidity of the breasts, general depression, and pains in the back and loins. Intermittent pains, and discharge of blood from the passage, tell that the process has begun. If miscarriage occurs within the first month or two after conception, the process may be accomplished with so little inconvenience as to escape notice and be mistaken for a menstrual period. More generally, however, the severity of the pain and an unusual clotted discharge of blood render the case evident. The pain, the discharge, and, at the same time, the danger of an abortion, are in proportion to the advancement of the pregnancy. When a miscarriage goes on, the pains increase in force and frequency, and continue, with discharge of blood, fluid or in clots, until the ovum, or first formation of the child, is expelled; after which both become moderated till they cease altogether and the red flow gives place to a colorless one. It is very important that those in attendance upon the patient should examine every clot that comes away. If large, tear it in pieces, that they may ascertain whether the contents of the womb are expelled or not, for there is no safety or rest, where miscarriage is progressing, till it has taken place and everything is cast off.

AS SOON AS A FEMALE

experiences threatenings of abortion she ought at once to retire to bed, upon a mattress, and keep perfectly quiet till every symptom has disappeared. Sometimes this simple measure, *promptly adopted*, is sufficient to avert the threatened evil. If there is much feeling of fullness, and the patient is of full habit generally, eight or a dozen leeches may be applied to the lower part of the bowels; if there is fever, saline medicines may be given, such as the common effervescing draft of carbonate of soda and tartaric acid or lemon juice; or, if the bowels are much confined, seidlitz powders, assisting the action by cold clysters, if necessary. When the pains are severe, particularly in the weak and irritable, twenty or thirty drops of laudanum should be given, and may be repeated in a few hours if the symptoms are not improved. In the case of profuse discharge, the patient should be kept very lightly covered, movement avoided, and every article of food or drink given cold, or iced if possible, provided the vital powers are not excessively reduced. Cloths dipped in cold or iced water should also be applied to the lower part of the body and frequently changed. Acid drinks, with cream of tartar, may be freely given.

Ten or fifteen drops of elixir vitriol may be given in a wineglassful of water every two or three hours. Should slight faintness come on, it is better not to interfere with it, but use outward remedies—camphor, cold water, vinegar, etc.—as they maybe salutary. If it reaches to an extent to threaten life, stimulants, as brandy and water, and others, must be had recourse to. Profuse and continued discharge, though it may not threaten life, must occasion a weakness which will take a long time to overcome, and which may ultimately, if not properly attended to, promote the development of other diseases of the womb.

IF THE FLOODING IS PROFUSE

and uncontrolled by the means before mentioned, one grain and a half of sugar of lead may be given every two or three hours, and washed down with a drink of vinegar and water, to which, if there is much pain, add from five to ten drops of laudanum.

Pieces of linen or cotton cloth should be soaked in a strong solution of alum, or a decoction of oak bark; and then well oiled; with this cloth plug the passage or birthplace; or, some of this astringent wash may be thrown up with a syringe.

But, during the time and after miscarriage, the general strength must be supported by a strengthening diet, such as soups, meat, etc., avoiding stimulants as much as possible. Nevertheless, in some cases wine or malt liquors may be necessary in convalescence, or when recovering, and if so may be assisted by tonic or strengthening medicines, such as contain mineral acid. Bark or iron are generally given as the most appropriate remedies. The bowels will, in some cases, require strict attention, as indeed they do throughout, and for this purpose castor oil is a good medicine, or clysters of cold or tepid water are most useful. A teaspoonful of Epsom salts dissolved in half a pint of water, either cold or slightly warmed, to which add fifteen drops of elixir vitriol, forms a most excellent and mild purgative, which should be taken before breakfast. In all cases where the constitution of the woman has a tendency to miscarriage or abortion, a quiet state of mind should be observed, avoiding all violent exertions, particularly lifting heavy weights. These principles of treatment are to be kept in mind in the management of miscarriage:

The first, to prevent it, if possible, by rest, opiates, etc.

The second, to allay pain, moderate the discharge of blood, and to save and support the strength of the patient.

The third, when abortion must take place, to expedite the separation of the ovum and free the contents of the womb. This is generally done by simply occasionally drinking cold water, and in difficult cases, if necessary, by the administration of spurred rye. The dose is a strong infusion or tea given every twenty or thirty minutes until the desired effect is produced, as long as the stomach will bear it.

The health of pregnant females should at all times be an object of great care and interest; and they should be impressed with the conviction that while

BEARING THE FIRST CHILD

they may, by proper care and attention, lay the foundation for their future health and that of their offspring; while by neglect and imprudence in this matter, they may not only enfeeble their constitution, but entail upon their children an inheritance of infirmity and disease.

Miscarriage, or abortion, which includes all cases in which delivery takes place before the sixth month, seldom occurs without being preceded, or accompanied, or followed, by a morbid discharge of blood from the womb, which is commonly known by the name of *flooding*. Abortion, or miscarriage, takes place with the first pregnancy, and during the first two months; therefore, great care should be observed during this period, as any cause which either destroys the life of the child in the womb or brings on morbid or premature contractions in that organ may induce miscarriage. Coughing severely, or vomiting, a blow or fall, or a misstep leading to an effort to prevent falling, may, and does frequently, result in miscarriage; and this having once occurred, it is, without proper care, exceedingly liable to be the case again at the same period of a subsequent pregnancy. The same result may follow any vivid moral impression; for fright, or mental excitement by passion, or witnessing any accident, will be found often to end in miscarriage. In some healthy females, however, it occurs without any other cause than mere fullness of blood. A bleeding from the womb is often in such cases a first symptom of abortion, and should be attended to as early as possible before it goes to any considerable extent. The amount of flooding, in most cases, is in proportion to the early period of pregnancy at which it takes place, for in the latter months there is seldom much blood lost. But there are cases in which pregnant women will lose blood repeatedly from the womb and yet not miscarry, but these are very rare cases.

In most cases, the occurrence of a woman's flooding between the first and fourth months, unless very slight, or quickly relieved, is usually followed by a miscarriage; but as soon as the child and its membranes are both expelled by the contraction of the womb the flooding soon ceases. In many such cases it is often very difficult, and sometimes impossible, to deliver the afterbirth and membranes, which remain and finally pass off after putrefaction has taken place, resulting in long and offensive discharges from the womb, and which, unless treated by the most skillful management, frequently result in many internal mischiefs of a serious character, such as ulcers, cancers, etc.

In all cases, those who are constitutionally disposed to abortion, or have a tendency to miscarriage, should take great care to preserve a quiet state of mind and to avoid all violent exertion; and all active purgatives should be avoided, and exposure to great heat or cold, during the time of gestation or pregnancy.

When the miscarriage has really taken place, and the fœtus, or child, is expelled, together with the contents of the womb, the same precautions should in general be observed as in childbirth.

TO PREVENT MISCARRIAGE,

when it is threatened, or on the appearance of the first symptoms, the patient should lie down and be as quiet as possible; live on very light diet; bowels be kept freely open; and an injection of thirty drops of laudanum should be given in half a pint of slippery elm tea. Should flooding be present, cold lemonade should be drank freely, and cloths wet with cold or ice water applied to the thighs and lower part of the birthplace, which should be repeated until the flooding is relieved.

MEANS OF PREVENTING ABORTION.

To prevent abortion, women of weak or relaxed habit should use solid food, avoiding great quantities of tea, coffee, or other weak or watery liquors. They should go soon to bed and rise early, and take frequent exercise, but avoid fatigue. They should occasionally take half a pint of the decoction of lignum-vitæ, boiling an ounce of it in a quart of water for five minutes.

If of a full habit, they ought to use a spare diet and chiefly of the vegetable kind, avoiding strong liquors and everything that may tend to heat the body or increase the quantity of blood; and when the symptoms appear, should take a dram of powdered nitre in a cup of water gruel every five or six hours.

In both cases the patient should sleep on a hard mattress and be kept cool and quiet; the bowels should be kept regular by a pill of white walnut extract or bitterroot.

CHAPTER IX.

MENSTRUATION.

Menstruation: The time of life at which it should appear; Signs of approaching puberty; Duty of mothers; Delayed and obstructed menstruation—What to do for it; Chlorosis, or green sickness—What to do for it—What it is caused by; Too profuse menstruation—How to treat it; Painful menstruation, or menstrual colic—How to treat it; Amenorrhœa, or suppressed menstruation—What causes this, and how to treat it.

Cessation of the menses, or change of life: Very important advice is given as to the way in which the patient should treat herself, which, if followed, will be of great benefit.

Falling of the Womb: What causes it, and how the patient should be treated.

Leucorrhœa—Whites—Flour Albus: What this disease is; What causes it; How to relieve and cure it.

Though this is not a disease, but a healthy function, and as, from various causes, derangement of the function occurs, it is proper that it should be perfectly understood. Menstruation is the term applied to the phenomenon that attends the rupture of what is called the *Graafian follicles* of the ovaries and the discharge of an ova, or egg. It is a bloody discharge from the female genitals; not differing from ordinary blood, excepting that it does not coagulate, and in its peculiar odor. The blood comes from the capillaries of the womb and vagina.

MENOPHANIA, OR THE FIRST APPEARANCE

of the menses, is usually preceded by a discharge of a fluid whitish matter from the vagina, by nervous excitement, and by vague pains and heaviness in the loins and thighs, numbness of the limbs, and swelling and hardness of the breasts. The first appearance is an evidence of capacity for conception. It generally appears about the age of fourteen, but varies from nine to twenty-four years. In warm climates women begin to menstruate earlier and cease sooner than in temperate regions; in the cold climates the reverse of this holds as a general rule. The manifestations of approaching puberty are seen in the development of the breasts, the expansion of the hips, the rounded contour of the body and limbs, appearance of the purely feminine figure, development of the voice, and the child becomes reserved and exchanges her plays for the pursuits of womanhood.

More or less indisposition and irritability also precede each successive recurrence of the menstrual flux, such as headache, lassitude, uneasiness, pain in back, loins, etc. The periods succeed each other usually about every twenty-eight days, although it may occur every twenty-two, twenty, eighteen, fifteen, or thirty-two, thirty-five, or forty days. The most important element is the regularity of the return. In temperate climates each menstrual period ordinarily continues from three to six days, and the quantity lost from four to eight ounces. The menses continue to flow from the period of puberty till the age of forty-five or fifty. At the time of its natural cessation the flow becomes irregular, and this irregularity is accompanied occasionally by symptoms of dropsy, glandular swellings, etc., constituting the *critical period, turn* or *change of life*; yet it does not appear that mortality is increased by it, as vital statistics show that more men die between forty and fifty than women.

It should be the

DUTY OF EVERY MOTHER

or female in charge of a child in whom age or actual manifestations suggest the approach of puberty to acquaint her with the nature of her visitation and the importance of her conduct in regard to it. She should be taught that it is perfectly natural to all females at a certain period, and that its arrival necessitates caution on her part with regard to exposure to wet or cold. The author has made the acquaintance of the history of many cases of consumption and other diseases which were directly induced by folly and ignorance at the first menstrual flow. The child is often kept in extreme ignorance of the liability of womanhood occurring to her at a certain age, and, hence, when she observes a flow of blood escaping from a part, the delicacy attached to the locality makes her reticent with regard to inquiry or exposure; she naturally becomes alarmed, and most likely attempts to stanch the flow by bathing or applying cold water to the part, thus doing incalculable mischief.

This purely feminine physiological function should be well studied and understood by all females. At least, they should know that the phenomenon is a natural one, liable to disorder, and that the best interests of their general health demands care and prudence on their part to maintain regularity, etc., of the flow. Disregard of such a duty will surely entail much misery.

DELAYED AND OBSTRUCTED MENSTRUATION.

When the menses do not appear at the time when they may naturally be expected, we call it delayed or obstructed menstruation. It is, however, of great importance to know whether a girl is sufficiently developed to make it necessary for the menses to appear, although she may have reached the proper age. As long as the girl has not increased physically, if she has not become wider across the hips, if her breasts have not become enlarged, and if she experience none of the changes incident to this period, an effort to force nature is positively injurious. In this case a general treatment will be called for. She should be required to exercise freely in the open air, retire early to bed and rise at an early hour in the morning. She should not be allowed to be closely confined to school, if attending. Her diet should be generous but free from all rich food, which will disorder the stomach. If, however, she is fully developed, and she suffers from time to time from congestions of the head, breast or abdomen, it will be necessary to interfere. The following are symptoms which will generally be found in these cases: Headache, weight, fullness, and throbbing in the center of the cranium and in the back part of the head; pains in the back and loins; cold feet and hands, becoming sometimes very hot; skin harsh and dry; slow pulse, and not infrequently attended with epilepsy.

TREATMENT.

It is well for the patient, a few days before the period, to take a warm hip bath or foot bath twice a day, and at night, when retiring, to apply cloths wet in warm water to the lower part of the abdomen.

The bowels should be kept open by some mild catharsis, as castor oil or a pill of aloes. If there is pain and fullness of the head during the discharge, or before it, use the following:

Tincture of aconite leaves,	Two drams;
Tincture of belladonna,	One dram;
Tincture of cantharides,	One dram;
Morphia,	Three grains;
Simple syrup,	Quarter ounce.

Mix. Dose: One teaspoonful three times a day. If the pain is severe it may be taken every two hours.

Between the monthly periods, if the system is weak, the following may be taken:

Precip. carbonate of iron,	Five drams;
Extract of conium,	Two drams;
Balsam Peru,	One dram;
Alcohol,	Four ounces;
Oil wintergreen,	Twenty drops;
Simple syrup,	Eight ounces.

Dose: Two teaspoonfuls three times a day. Shake the mixture before using.

CHLOROSIS, OR GREEN SICKNESS.

This disease generally occurs in young unmarried females who are weak and delicate. It manifests itself about the age of puberty, and is accompanied by feeble appetite and digestion. There is no menstrual discharge, or else it is very slight.

It is caused by innutritious food and residence in damp and ill-ventilated apartments. It may be hereditary, all the females of the family being liable to the same disease. Those who drink largely of tea, coffee, diluted acids, bad wines, and indulge in tight lacing; are predisposed to this disease. Among the exciting causes may be mentioned disturbing emotions, unrequited love, homesickness, depression of spirits, etc. When we take into consideration the fact that the cause of the disease is impoverishment of the blood, the treatment will not be difficult.

TREATMENT.

Exercise freely in the open air; protect the body from chilliness with warm clothing and plenty of it. The patient should sleep on a mattress in a well-ventilated room. The diet should be nourishing without being stimulating. It is important that the habits should be regular, and the mind kept cheerful by society and innocent amusements. Before the medical treatment is commenced the exciting causes of the disease must be removed. A complete change must be made in the existence of the patient. If she is confined closely at school, she must be removed; if she is inclined to confine herself to the house, send her to the country. Picture to her the danger she is in by the continuance of such a life; give her plenty of outdoor exercise. The mental and moral causes are the most difficult to remove, but a change of scenery and new friends will do much towards it. For those who are shut up in factories, or who work all day in a stooping position, a change of employment must be made. A bath of tepid water in the morning, followed by a brisk rubbing, will be beneficial; also the frequent use of the sitting-bath, and the sponge bath in the evening. Active exercise should precede and follow all baths. During menstruation all applications of water should be omitted. The following remedies are recommended by a famous Philadelphian doctor. They are to be taken on alternate days; that is, take No. 1 one day, No. 2 the next day, etc.:

No. 1.—Precip. carbonate of iron, five drams; extract of conium, two drams; balsam Peru, one dram; oil cinnamon, twenty drops; simple syrup, eight ounces; pulverized gum arabic, two drams. Mix. Dose: Two teaspoonfuls three times a day, every other day, after meals. Shake before using.

No. 2.—Tincture of nux vomica, one dram; syrup iodide of iron, one ounce; simple syrup, four ounces. Mix. Dose: One teaspoonful three times a day, every other day, after meals.

Another treatment is as follows:

Clear the bowels with the following mixture: Sulphate of magnesia, one ounce; nitrate of potash, ten grains; extract of liquorice, one scruple; compound infusion of senna, five and one-half ounces; tincture of jalap, three drams; spirit of sal volatile, one dram. Mix. Dose: Two or three tablespoonfuls at a time, at intervals of two hours until an effect is produced. This is to be followed by sulphate of iron, five grains; extract of gentian, ten grains. Make into three pills and take a pill twice a day, with the compound aloes or rhubarb pill every night.

PROFUSE MENSTRUATION—MENORRHAGIA:

By menorrhagia we understand an immoderate flow of the menses. There is no fixed amount of blood which is lost at the menstrual period, but it varies in different women. It will average, however, from four to eight ounces. The quantity discharged may be estimated by the number of napkins used. Each napkin will contain about half an ounce, or one tablespoonful, so that eight napkins would contain four ounces; twenty, ten ounces; etc. In some females the discharge may be excessive without impairment of the general health.

Some females are predisposed to uterine hemorrhages, from a relaxed or flabby state of the texture of the uterus. Frequent childbearing, abortion, high living, too prolonged and frequent suckling, may induce flooding. Among the exciting causes we may mention overexertion, dancing, falls, lifting heavy weights, cold, and mental excitement.

TREATMENT.

The patient must lie down on a hard bed, and abstain from all stimulating food and drinks. The room should be cool and she should be lightly covered with bedclothes. Soak the feet in warm water, and if the flowing is excessive apply cloths wrung out in vinegar and water to the lower bowels. The hips must be elevated higher than the head. Only in extreme cases should plugging be resorted to. This may be done by pieces of linen, about four inches square, thrust into the vagina until it is full, and a bandage applied between the legs. Cold hip baths and vaginal injections of cold water will be beneficial when the hemorrhage is slight.

Use also the following:

Diluted sulphuric acid,	Two drams;
Syrup of orange peel,	Two ounces;
Cinnamon water,	One ounce.

Mix. Dose: A teaspoonful in a wineglassful of water two or three times a day.

If there is much pain administer the following every two or three hours:

Morphia,	Quarter grain;
Cayenne,	Four grains;
Rosin,	Four grains.

Mix. Give in blackberry syrup.

PAINFUL MENSTRUATION—MENSTRUAL COLIC—DYSMENORRHEA.

Dysmenorrhea means a difficult monthly flow, and is always preceded by severe pains in the back and lower part of the abdomen. It is caused by taking cold during the period; fright, violent mental emotions, obstinate constipation, sedentary occupations, smallness of the mouth and neck of the womb. Females subject to this trouble are generally relieved by marriage. The symptoms are severe bearing-down pains in the region of the uterus, like labor pains; restlessness, coldness, flashes of heat, with headache; aching in the small of the back, lower part of the abdomen, and thighs; the discharge is scanty, and contains shreds of fiber and clotted blood.

TREATMENT.

The patient should immediately go to bed and cover up warmly. Stimulating food and drinks should be avoided. Use a warm foot bath and sitting-bath, with hot poultices of hops or cloths wet in hot water applied to the abdomen.

In the interval of the menses, take active exercise, with a tepid hip bath three nights in the week, injecting some of the water high up in the vagina. Keep the bowels open by a pill of aloes and myrrh, and take a small teaspoonful of the volatile tincture of guiacum three times a day, in water. On the approach of the period, take the following at night:

Calomel,   Three grains;

Opium,   One grain.

In the morning a dose of caster oil, and on the appearance of the menses, the Dover's Powder and mixture as before. Repeat this treatment, in each interval, until permanently relieved.

The following is recommended by an eminent physician, to be taken a few days before the period:

Acetous tincture of colchicum,	Three drams;
Magnesia,	One dram;
Sulphate of magnesia,	Three drams;
Distilled mint or cinnamon water,	Four ounces.

Mix. Dose: A small wineglassful every two or three hours until it operates. This should be preceded the night before by a small dose of blue pill.

SUPPRESSION OF THE MENSES—AMENORRHŒA.

By suppression is meant a disappearance of the menses after they have become established, and may be either acute or chronic. It is caused by cold caught during the flow, by exposure to night air or by wetting the feet; fear, shocks, violent mental emotions, anxiety, fevers and other acute diseases. Chronic suppression may be either a consequence of the acute, or caused by delicate health; also, from diseases of the ovaries or womb. It may also be occasioned by an imperforate hymen, in which case it must be cut open by a physician.

TREATMENT.

When the suppression is caused by some disease in the system, that disease must be cured before the menses will return. For sudden suppression, use the warm sitting-bath or foot bath. Apply cloths wet in warm water to the lower part of the abdomen, and drink freely of warm water. If the suppression is chronic and the patient is delicate, in the interval between the menses use the shower or the full bath of cold or tepid water, rubbing the body briskly with a coarse towel, especially around the abdomen, loins, and genital organs.

As soon as the discharge has ceased, a warm hip bath will generally bring it on. If there is much inflammation of the uterus give the following:

Tincture aconite leaves,   Two drams;

| Sweet spirits of nitre, | One ounce; |
| Simple syrup, | Three ounces. |

Dose: One teaspoonful every two or three hours.

If the discharge cannot be brought on, wait until the next period. A few days before the term the bowels should be freely opened and kept open until the period for the discharge has arrived. A pill of aloes and iron is one of the best that can be given. Give from one to three pills daily. If there is no evident reason for the discharge not appearing, such as pregnancy, inflammation of the neck of the womb, and the woman is suffering from the suppression, use the following:

Caulophyllin,	One dram;
Extract aconite,	Eight grains;
Aloes,	Ten grains;
Sulphate of iron,	Ten grains.

Make into forty pills. Dose: Two or three pills, taken night and morning.

The remedies should always be taken a few days before the period arrives for the menses. If the chronic suppression is the result of any acute disease, the health must first be re-established, otherwise it would be wrong to force the menses. When this has been done, immediately before the return of the period a warm hip bath should be taken every night for six nights, and one of the following pills taken three times a day:

Fresh powdered ergot of rye,	Fifty grains;
Barbadoes aloes,	Twelve grains;
Essential oil of juniper,	Twelve drops.

Make into twelve pills with syrup or mucilage, washing down each pill with a cupful of pennyroyal tea.

CESSATION OF THE MENSES—CHANGE OF LIFE.

By the phrase, "change of life," or, the critical period, we understand the final cessation, or stoppage, of the menses. It usually takes place between the ages of forty and fifty, although in some cases it may occur as early as thirty, and in others not until sixty. However, we can expect the change about the forty-fifth year.

The symptoms will vary according to the constitution of the woman. In some the change occurs by the discharge gradually diminishing in quantity; in others, by the intervals between the periods being lengthened. A woman may pass this period without having any more unpleasant symptoms than an occasional rush of blood to the head, or a headache. Others, however, may have very severe symptoms arise, which will require the care of an intelligent physician. These disagreeable sensations should receive a careful consideration and not be hushed up with the reply that these complaints arise from the "change of life" and will vanish whenever that change takes place. The foundation of serious trouble may be laid which will make the remainder of her existence a burden and cut short a life which might have been conducted to a good old age. While this change is in progress, in probably the majority of cases there is more or less disturbance of the health. It is sometimes quite impossible to say exactly what is the trouble with the patient, except that she is out of health. The following are some of the symptoms which may arise: Headache, dizziness, biliousness, sour stomach, indigestion, diarrhœa, piles, costiveness, itching of the private parts, cramp and colic of the bowels, palpitation of the heart, swelling of the limbs and abdomen, pains in the back and loins, paleness and general weakness.

TREATMENT.

Eat and drink moderately; sleep in airy, well-ventilated rooms; exercise daily in the open air, either by walking or riding; avoid violent emotions; shun exposure to wet, stormy weather, wet feet, etc.

Keep the bowels regulated with the following:

Mercurial pill, one grain; ipecac powder, one-half grain; compound rhubarb pill, three grains. Mix for a pill to be taken every night.

Or, one ounce of hicra picra, or powdered aloes with castella, mixed in a pint of gin, which should stand for four or five days, after which a tablespoonful in a glass of water may be taken every morning or second morning, as the case may be.

If the patient is large and fleshy, of full habit, the following is recommended:

Sulphate of magnesia, one and one-half ounces; compound infusion of roses, five ounces; cinnamon water, one ounce. Mix, Dose: Two tablespoonfuls once a day.

If there are nervous symptoms prominent, give valerianate of zinc, eight grains; tincture of valerian, two drams; orange flower water, three and a half ounces; syrup of red poppies, two drams. Mix. Dose: A tablespoonful every six hours.

FALLING OF THE WOMB
(Prolapsus uteri).

Falling of the womb is simply a sinking down of the organ, and may be so slight as not to be noticed or so great that the organ will protrude between the legs through the external opening. It is not a disease of the womb itself, but of some of its supports.

So long as the vagina retains its natural size and the ligaments are but two and a half inches long the organ will not be displaced. Whatever tends to relax and weaken the system may cause the complaint. The muscles of the abdomen which support the intestines being weakened from any cause will allow the intestines to press down upon the womb and its ligaments, and, in consequence of this constant pressure, they give way. Another cause is too early exercise after childbearing. Flooding and leucorrhœa, or whites, if allowed to continue for a long time, will produce it; in delicate females, continued running up and down stairs, also tight lacing, dancing, leaping, and running, particularly during the period of menstruation, when the womb is increased in weight by the blood contained in it. The use of medicines to loosen the bowels, which is very common among many, is still another cause of the disorder.

Most females who are troubled with falling of the womb think that it is necessary to a cure that they should wear some kind of a support to the abdomen. These supporters, however, do a vast amount of harm, for by being worn tightly around the abdomen they increase the pressure on the bowels, thus forcing down, more and more, the womb and its appendages. All that is necessary is to raise up the womb to its natural position, and use an instrument that will keep it in place. This instrument is called a pessary. This pessary is a ring or hollow cup-shaped globe, made of gold, silver, ivory, wood or gutta-percha, and is placed in the vagina or birthplace, thus supporting the womb. The cold hip bath should be used once a day, at the same time injecting cold water into the vagina with a syringe. Lie down as much as possible, and avoid becoming fatigued. Apply cold bandages to the abdomen on going to bed.

If the womb has descended to the external orifice it is often necessary to restore it to its natural position by pressing it upward and backward by a finger or two pressed into the vagina. If the process be accompanied with pain, the vagina should be well washed by injections of thick flax seed or slippery elm bark tea for a day or two before the astringent washes are used.

Avoid tight corsets and heavy skirts, suspend the under-garments from the shoulders and not from the waist, as is usually done. Use plain vegetable diet, and avoid tea, coffee, spirituous drinks, and all sensual indulgences. Allow the clothes to be loose. These things must be attended to closely. The diet should be plain and nourishing, but not stimulating.

Use an injection of an infusion of white oak bark, geranium, or a solution of alum, in the proportion of one ounce to the pint of water. If there is inflammation of the womb, this must be subdued before using the pessary. Give tincture of aconite, compound powder of ipecac and opium, with injections of an infusion of hops and lobelia, or an infusion of belladonna.

If there is heat and difficulty in passing water, drink an infusion of marsh mallow and spearmint. If the patient is weak, give the following tonic:

Sulphate quinine, twenty-five grains; citrate of iron (soluble), thirty-five grains. Make into twenty-four powders. Take a powder three times a day, after each meal, in sweet wine.

LEUCORRHŒA—WHITES—FLOUR ALBUS.

The word leucorrhœa is derived from two Greek words, and means literally a "white discharge." It is also known as "flour albus," "whites," and "female weakness," and consists of a "light colorless discharge from the genital organs, varying in hue from a whitish or colorless to a yellowish, light green, or to a slightly red or brownish; varying in consistency from a thin, watery, to a thick, tenacious, ropy substance; and in quantity from a slight increase in the healthy secretion to several ounces in the twenty-four hours." This discharge generally occurs between the ages of fifteen and forty-five, seldom during infancy or old age. When it occurs in young female children, it will not infrequently be produced by the presence of pinworms in the vagina, which make their way there from the rectum. There will be intense itching of the parts, and the worms can be removed with a small piece of cloth, after separating the lips.

This disease may be either acute or chronic. The acute form generally results from taking cold, and is simply a catarrhal inflammation of the mucous membrane lining the vagina. The chronic form is but a continuation of the acute, and is generally caused by the acute stage having been neglected or improperly treated. Ulceration of the neck of the womb sometimes results. There are two forms of leucorrhœa: Vaginal leucorrhœa, when the discharge comes from the walls of the vagina; and cervical leucorrhœa, when the discharge proceeds from the neck of the womb.

Causes: Taking cold from sitting on the ground, or exposure of the neck and shoulders; over sexual excitement, and sexual intercourse; tight lacing; piles, miscarriages, and abortions; displacements of the womb; purgatives, improper articles of diet; warm injections, or injections of any kind; late hours, etc. It may also be hereditary.

TREATMENT.

The treatment, to be successful, requires that the patient should first be placed in a favorable condition. Anything which tends to excite the disease must be avoided, as dissipations, late suppers, etc. The diet must be plain and nourishing without being stimulating, and be taken regularly. Exercise, short of fatigue, will be beneficial. The clothing should be warm and worn loosely, especially about the waist. Water is of great importance in the treatment of this trouble. The sitting-bath may be used every day, and injections of cold or tepid water should be used three or four times a day, according to the severity of the discharge.

An injection of weak green tea will be found good in some mild cases, as also sweet cider or a weak solution of alum.

One of the best tonics is the muriated tincture of iron, of which take twenty or twenty-five drops in half a tumbler of water three or four times a day. An excellent injection is made by taking three drams of tannic acid and an ounce of alum, dissolving in a quart of water, and inject one-third three times a day. The bowels should be kept open by Rochelle or Epsom salts, or seidlitz powder. When there is great debility of the organs, or when the disease has been brought on by exposure to cold, pregnancy, abortions, etc., the following will be found very successful:

Tincture of aloes, two ounces; muriated tincture of iron, four drams. Mix. Dose: Thirty-five drops in water three times a day. At the same time use the following injection: Sulphate of zinc (white vitriol), two drams; sugar of lead, two drams. Mix in one quart of water, and use one-fourth for each injection.

CHAPTER X.

COLLECTION OF VALUABLE MEDICAL COMPOUNDS.

Collection of valuable Medical Compounds: Magic kidney and liver restorer; Hop bitters; Alterative or liver powders; Anti-dyspeptic pills; Dyspeptic ley (sure cure for dyspepsia); Ague pills; Certain remedy for ague or intermittent fever; Fever powders; Ague drops; Pills for neuralgia; Sick headache pills; Anodyne headache pills; Rheumatic pills; Pills for dysentery; Epileptic pills; Pills for asthma; Hysteric pills; Pills for neuralgia; Cure for bleeding of the lungs; Cure for consumption; Cough syrup; Soothing cough mixture; Expectorant tincture; Sure remedy for bowel complaints; Cordial for summer complaint; Scrofulous syrup; Eyewater; Tincture for rheumatism; Worm elixir; Dr. Jordan's cholera remedy; Pile ointment (sure cure); To cure warts and corns; Cure for deafness; Cure for inverted toe-nail.

Do you have—

* A frequent headache over the eyes?
* A susceptibility to chills and fever?
* A bitter or oily taste in the mouth?
* A sour stomach?
* A complexion inclined to be yellow?
* A great depression of spirits without known cause?
* Specks before the eyes, and flushed face?
* A done out, tired feeling?

Besides many other symptoms too numerous to mention? If you have you are affected in your liver and kidneys, and should do something for it. The following preparation, "Magic Kidney and Liver Restorer," acts on these organs and, when diseased or out of order, restores them to a healthy state. Everyone should keep a bottle of this preparation in the house, as it is an invaluable medicine. Splendid to take in the spring to tone up the system:

MAGIC KIDNEY AND LIVER RESTORER.

* Two ounces of alcohol;
* One and a half ounces of glycerine;

- One ounce of liverwort;
- Three hundred and twenty grains of saltpetre;
- Forty drops of wintergreen.

Steep the liverwort in a quart of water down to half the quantity, then throw in the other ingredients while hot. Dose: One tablespoonful about four times a day.

HOP BITTERS.

- One ounce mandrake root;
- One ounce gentian root;
- One ounce dandelion root;
- One ounce buchu leaf;
- One ounce sarsaparilla leaf;
- One ounce blackberry leaf;
- One ounce hops.

Infuse in cold water, three quarts, two or three days. Add a pint of whisky, and bottle. Dose: A teaspoonful three times a day.

ALTERATIVE, OR LIVER POWDER.

Take podophyllin and sanguinaria, of each ten grains; leptandrin, twenty grains; white sugar, forty grains. Triturate or rub the whole well together in a mortar and divide into twenty powders, and take one night and morning. If they operate much on the bowels take but one a day.

Uses: Valuable in liver complaint, torpidity of the liver, and as an alterative to act on the secretions of the system generally. A complete substitute for blue pill and free from any danger.

HEPATIC AND ALTERATIVE POWDER.

Take equal parts, say of each half an ounce, of finely powdered blue flag root, bloodroot, May apple root, golden seal root, and bitterroot. Mix all together and pass through a fine sieve. Dose: As an alterative and to act on the liver and secretions, from two to five grains two or three times a day.

CATHARTIC AND LIVER PILLS.

Take podophyllin, sixty grains; leptandrin and sanguinaria, ipecac and pure cayenne, each thirty grains. Make into sixty pills with a little soft extract of mandrake or dandelion. This is the best pill that can be used as a cathartic and liver pill and to act on the secretions generally. As a purgative the dose is from two to four pills for a grown person, and as an alterative and substitute for blue mass and to act on the liver, one pill once a day or every other day.

ANTI-DYSPEPTIC PILLS.

Take Socotrine aloes, two drams; colocynth, gamboge, rhubarb, and castile soap, each one dram; cayenne, thirty grains; oil cloves, thirty drops. Make into one hundred and twenty pills with extract of gentian or dandelion. Dose: For dyspepsia, inactive liver or costiveness, one or two pills once a day; as a cathartic, three to five pills at a dose. This is a splendid pill. It cleanses the stomach, gives tone and energy to the digestive organs, restores the appetite, excites the liver and other secretory organs, without causing any debility.

ANOTHER ANTI-DYSPEPTIC PILL.

Take Quevenne's powdered metallic iron, forty grains; rhubarb, twenty grains; extract of nux vomica, one grain. Triturate well in a small mortar, so as to mix them perfectly, and make into twenty pills with extract of boneset or gentian. Take one pill before each meal. This is one of the best anti-dyspeptic pills known.

DYSPEPTIC LEY.

Take hickory ashes, one pint; soot, three or four ounces; boiling water, two quarts. Pour on in a suitable vessel or crock, stir, and let stand, over night, then pour off clear and bottle. Dose: Half a teacupful three times a day, and if too strong weaken with water until palatable. A sure remedy for dyspepsia.

AGUE PILLS.

Take quinine, twenty grains; piperine, ten grains; Dover's Powder, ten grains; cayenne, ten grains. Mix, pulverize, and make into twenty pills with a little gum arabic or extract of gentian or boneset. To be taken at the rate of one pill an hour when there is no fever, or during intermission, until twelve pills are taken, the balance to be taken on the third day or next well day. Good as a remedy for the chills or fever and ague.

CERTAIN REMEDY FOR THE AGUE OR INTERMITTENT FEVER.

Take quinine, twelve grains; ipecac and cayenne, of each six grains; pulverized opium, three grains. Make into twelve pills with precipitated extract of Peruvian bark, or if you cannot get this, use either extract of dogwood or boneset, sufficient to form into pill mass. Two or three pills to be taken every two or three hours, during the well day or intermission, till all are taken. A very certain and effectual remedy for the ague or intermittent fever.

FEVER POWDER.

Take finely pulverized gum myrrh, bloodroot, and lobelia seed, or ipecac, of each half an ounce; gum camphor and nitre, of each two drams. Pulverize, mix, and rub well together in a mortar, and bottle for use. Dose: Three to five grains every hour of two during fever. Good to allay the excitement, act on the skin and promote perspiration; also a good expectorant powder in coughs, colds, pneumonia, and oppressed breathing.

AGUE DROPS.

Take quinine, twenty grains; water, one ounce; sulphuric acid, twenty drops.

Mix in a vial. Dose: A teaspoonful every hour or every two hours during the well day till all is taken. A certain cure for the ague, or chills and fever.

SICK HEADACHE PILLS.

Take Socotrine aloes, gamboge, and castile soap, of each one dram; ipecac and scammony, of each thirty grains; oil of anise, thirty drops. Make into sixty pills with a little mucilage, gum arabic or extract dandelion. Dose: One to three pills. Useful in sick headache, habitual costiveness, dizziness, sour stomach, and indigestion, and may be used whenever a good vegetable cathartic is needed. For an attack of headache, take three pills, and repeat in three hours if the first does not operate. Will invariably give relief.

ANODYNE HEADACHE PILLS.

Take extract of hyoscyamus, thirty grains; extract stramonium, ten grains; quinine, twenty grains; morphine, two grains. Mix well and make into twenty pills, adding a little powdered liquorice root, or any other innocent powder, if necessary, to thicken the mass. The pills are one of the best remedies known for nervous headache, neuralgia in the face or head, toothache and nervous and neuralgic pains in any part of the system, that I have ever used. Dose: One pill, for a grown person, and may be repeated every two or three hours till relief is obtained. The extract of belladonna may be used instead of the stramonium, in the same proportion, with equally good effect.

RHEUMATIC PILLS.

Take jalap, colchicum seeds, and gum guaiac, of each one dram. Pulverize and mix veil, and make into sixty pills with extract of poke root (or berries). The dose is one or two pills three or four times a day. Good in all cases of chronic rheumatism, neuralgia, sciatica, and the like.

ANOTHER FOR SAME.

Take macrotin and pulverized gum guaiac, of each one dram; podophyllin, ten grains. Make into sixty pills with extract of poke root. Dose: One pill two or three times a day. An excellent pill for rheumatism and neuralgia.

PILLS FOR DYSENTERY.

Take rhubarb, ipecac, and castile soap, each thirty grains; pulverized opium, fifteen grains. Make into thirty pills with mucilage, gum arabic, or any other suitable substance. Dose: One pill every three to six hours for diarrhœa and dysentery. After three or four are taken they should not be taken oftener than once in six hours.

ANOTHER FOR SAME.

Take leptandrin, forty grains; rhubarb, twenty grains; morphine, four grains. Mix, and triturate well in a mortar so as to mix perfectly, and make into twenty pills with mucilage of gum arabic. Dose: In dysentery and diarrhœa, one pill every six to twelve hours. Two or three pills are generally sufficient to cure any ordinary case, if given during the early stage. They may be relied on in all cases and stages of bowel diseases, and especially in dysentery. A second pill may be given three hours after the first, a third six hours after the second; after that not oftener than once in twelve hours, and never more than one pill at a time.

EPILEPTIC PILLS.

Take sulphate of zinc, sixty grains; rhubarb and ipecac, each thirty grains; cayenne, sixty grains. Make into sixty pills with extract of hyoscyamus. Dose: One pill night and morning for one week, then leave off for a week, and then resume again, and so on every other week. An important remedy, and has cured many cases of epileptic fits when taken in the early stages.

PILLS FOR ASTHMA.

Take powdered elecampane root, powdered liquorice root, powdered anise seed, and sulphur, of each one dram. Make into ordinary sized pills with a sufficient quantity of tar, and take three or four pills at night on going to bed. This is an admirable remedy for asthma and shortness of breath.

HYSTERIC PILLS.

Take asafœtida and carbonate of ammonia, of each one dram; pulverized opium and macrotin, of each thirty grains. Melt the first two articles over the fire, and then stir in the others. Mix well and make into sixty pills. Dose: One or two pills, in cases of hysteric fits, every two or three hours; also good in female nervous attacks and spasmodic affections.

PILLS FOR CHRONIC BRONCHITIS.

Take pulverized skunk cabbage root, two drams; pulverized extract of liquorice, one dram; sanguinaria and macrotin, of each thirty grains. Make into large sized pills (say from eighty to one hundred) with a sufficient quantity of tar, and take one pill from three to six times a day, and continue for several weeks if necessary. One of the best remedies known for chronic bronchitis, and what is sometimes called "clergyman's sore throat."

PILLS FOR NEURALGIA.

Hyoscyamus, extract of, one dram; extract of aconite, thirty grains; macrotin, twenty grains; morphine, five grains. Make into forty pills, thickening the mass, if necessary, with a little powdered liquorice or ginger. Dose: One pill every three hours till relief is obtained. Good in neuralgia and all severe nervous pains.

BLEEDING AT THE LUNGS.

Eat freely of raw table salt, or take a teaspoonful three or four times a day of equal parts of powdered loaf sugar and rosin, or boil an ounce of dried yellow dock root in a pint of milk. Take a cupful two or three times a day.

FOR CONSUMPTION.

Take a teaspoonful of the expressed juice of horehound (the herb) and mix it with a gill of new milk. Drink it warm every morning. If persevered in it will perform wonders.

COUGH SYRUP.

Take horehound herb, elecampane root, spikenard root, ginseng root, black cohosh, and skunk cabbage root, of each a good-sized handful. Bruise and cover with spirits or whisky, and let stand ten days; then put all in a suitable vessel, add about four quarts of water and simmer slowly over a fire (but don't boil) for twelve hours, or till reduced to about three pints, then strain and add one pint of strained honey, half a pint each of number six, tincture lobelia, and tincture bloodroot (the vinegar or acetic tincture of bloodroot is the best) and four ounces of strong essence of anise, and you will have one of the best cough syrups known. Dose: A tablespoonful three to six times a day, according to circumstances. Good in all kinds of coughs and incipient consumption.

SOOTHING COUGH MIXTURE.

Take mucilage of gum arabic, oil of sweet almonds, syrup of balsam tolu, and wine of ipecac, of each one ounce; tincture of opium, half an ounce. Dose: For a grown person, one to two teaspoonfuls as often as required.

COUGH MIXTURE.

Take extract of liquorice, one ounce, powdered; nitrate of potash (saltpetre) and muriate of ammonia, of each two drams. Dissolve in half a pint of boiling water, and when cool add wine of ipecac, syrup of balsam tolu, and essence of anise, of each one ounce. Dose: From a teaspoonful to a tablespoonful several times a day. An excellent remedy for bronchitis, colds, and catarrhal coughs.

EXPECTORANT TINCTURE.

Take pulverized lobelia (seed or herb), powdered bloodroot, and powdered rattleroot (black cohosh), of each three ounces; alcohol and good vinegar, of each one pint. Digest for ten days or two weeks, then strain or filter and add four ounces each of wine of ipecac and tincture balsam of tolu and one ounce strong essence of anise. A portion of honey may be added if preferred. Dose: One to two teaspoonfuls repeated as often as circumstances require. Highly useful as an expectorant in coughs, colds, and all affections of the lungs.

COMPOUND TINCTURE OF MYRRH.

Take best gum myrrh, eight ounces; cayenne, balsam of fir, and nutmegs, of each one ounce; good brandy, two quarts. Bruise the solid articles, and let stand two weeks to digest (shake it once or twice every day), then strain or filter. Or, it may be made for immediate use by putting the whole in a stone jug and placing this in a warm sand bath or in a vessel of boiling water for twenty-four hours, shaking frequently. Dose: A teaspoonful is an ordinary dose for a grown person. Good in colic, pains in the stomach and bowels, diarrhœa, headache, sick stomach, and wherever a powerful stimulant is indicated. It is also valuable as a wash or external application for sprains, bruises, and foul ulcers and old sores. It is a preparation that no family should be without.

SURE REMEDY FOR BOWEL COMPLAINTS.

Take half an ounce bruised turkey rhubarb and half an ounce saleratus, steep or simmer slowly for fifteen minutes in a pint of water, strain and add a teacupful of white sugar, and heat again to dissolve; then add sixty drops oil of peppermint dissolved in one ounce of alcohol. Dose: From a teaspoonful to a tablespoonful every hour till relieved. An excellent remedy for diarrhœa, dysentery, and especially adapted to the bowel complaints of young children.

CORDIAL FOR SUMMER COMPLAINTS.

Take cloves, allspice, and cinnamon bark, of each half an ounce; white oak bark, one ounce. Bruise all, and boil in one quart of water down to half a pint; strain, add four ounces white sugar, dissolve by melting, then add half as much good brandy as there is of the liquid. Dose: One, two or three teaspoonfuls three to six times a day or oftener, according to age and urgency of symptoms. An infallible cure for cholera infantum, or summer complaints of children, and for all bowel complaints.

SCROFULOUS SYRUP.

Take yellow dock root, two pounds; stillingia root and bark of bittersweet root, of each one pound. Boil slowly in three or four gallons of water down to three quarts; strain, and add six pounds of white sugar. Dose: Half a wineglass three times a day. A valuable remedy for scrofula, and all scrofulous skin diseases, as tetter, herpes, leprosy, and the like; also a valuable alterative in all constitutional diseases.

EYEWATER.

Take half an ounce each of green tea and lobelia herb, and tincture a few days in four ounces of alcohol and water, equal parts. An invaluable eyewater for weak eyes and all kinds of sore and inflamed eyes. Use it two or three times a day.

TINCTURE FOR RHEUMATISM.

Take pulverized gum guaiac and allspice, of each four ounces; bloodroot, pulverized, two ounces; pearlash, one ounce; fourth proof brandy, one quart. Let stand and digest three or four days, shaking it two or three times a day. Dose: A teaspoonful three or four times a day, in a little milk, syrup or wine. An almost infallible remedy for rheumatism.

WORM ELIXIR.

Take gum myrrh and aloes, of each one ounce; saffron, sage leaves, and tansy leaves, of each half an ounce. Tincture in a pint of brandy for two weeks, and give to children a teaspoonful once a week to once a month as a preventive. They will never be troubled with worms as long as you do this.

DR. JORDAN'S CHOLERA REMEDY.

Take gum guaiac, prickly ash berries (or double as much bark of the root), cloves, and cinnamon bark, of each two ounces; gum camphor and gum myrrh, of each one ounce; gum kino, half an ounce. Reduce all to a coarse powder and add to one quart of best French brandy. Let it stand ten days or two weeks to digest, shaking the bottle two or three times a day to keep the ingredients from becoming impacted at the bottom; then strain and press out, and then take oil anise and oil peppermint, of each two drams; alcohol, four ounces. Mix the oils and alcohol together in a bottle and shake well till they are cut, then add to the former, and it is ready for use. Dose: From one to two teaspoonfuls every five, ten, fifteen or thirty minutes, according to the urgency of the symptoms. In cholera it should be given frequently, and if there are nausea and vomiting small doses are preferable; a single teaspoonful every five minutes till urgent symptoms are checked, then give it less frequently. It should always be given alone, unmixed with anything else. In ordinary diarrhœa, one or two teaspoonfuls taken once an hour will be sufficient. It is also an excellent remedy for colic and pains in the stomach and bowels, and will generally settle the stomach very soon in case of vomiting or nausea. It should always be kept in the house. Where it is needed for immediate use, it may be made in an hour or less by using alcohol instead of brandy and by boiling all in a stone jug, uncorked, by placing the jug in a vessel of boiling water, shaking or stirring frequently.

PILE OINTMENT.

Take say a teacupful of hog's lard, put in a flat or pewter dish, and take two bars of lead, flattened a little, and rub the lard with the flat ends and between them till it becomes black or of a dark lead color. Then burn equal parts of cavendish tobacco and old shoeleather in an iron vessel till charred. Powder these and mix into the lard till it becomes a thick ointment. Use once or twice a day as an ointment for the piles. An infallible cure.

WARTS AND CORNS.

The bark of the common willow burnt to ashes, mixed with strong vinegar and applied to the parts, will remove all warts, corns, and other excrescences.

DEAFNESS.

It is seldom that the power of hearing once entirely lost can ever be restored, and not always that even partial deafness can be cured, though it may often be relieved. Partial deafness is frequently owing to the accumulation and hardening in the ear of the ear wax, which may generally be remedied by dropping into the ear such articles as are calculated to soften, relax, and stimulate. For this purpose the following preparations are recommended as the best:

Take sulphuric ether, one ounce, and add to it one dram pulverized carbonate of ammonia. Let it stand a few days to form a solution. If it does not all dissolve, pour off carefully the liquid from the dregs, and of this liquid drop into the ear once a day from three to six drops. The patient should lay his head upon the opposite side at the time, and remain in that position a few minutes to allow the liquid to penetrate. This preparation is highly recommended, and if persevered in will, it is said, overcome almost any partial deafness or greatly relieve it.

ANOTHER.

Take pure olive oil, say one ounce, and half an ounce each of the tincture of lobelia and tincture of cayenne. Mix; and from a warm teaspoon drop into the ear four to six drops of this twice a day, shaking the vial well always before using it. This is relaxing, softening, and stimulating, and in all ordinary cases will answer the purpose. Turkey oil (or grease) is said to be still better than olive oil and may be used instead of it in this preparation. The following remedy, long kept a secret, is said to be infallible where it is possible for anything to effect a cure:

Take a common eel, remove the skin and intestines, and hang it up before the fire and let the oil drip into a pan or vessel. When done dripping, bottle the oil, and of this drop into the ear once a day or twice a day five or six drops from a warm teaspoon. I have heard remarkable accounts of the efficacy of this remedy, and doubt not but it is good. I believe it has never been published but once before. The secret was obtained with some difficulty from an old negro.

INVERTED TOE-NAIL.

This is a very troublesome and often painful affection. The edges or sides of the nail are disposed to turn down and grow into the flesh, giving rise to inflammation, ulceration, and often great pain and suffering. The best remedy I have ever known in this difficulty is to scrape with some sharp-pointed instrument, as the point of a penknife, a sort of groove or gutter in the center of the nail lengthways from the root to the end. It must be scraped down to near the quick, or as thin as it can be borne. This renders the nail "weak in the back," so that it will gradually and ultimately turn up at the sides until the edges come above and over the flesh. Continue this as fast as the nail grows out and grows thicker, and you will eventually succeed in getting the nail in its proper shape and position. It will be proper to poultice if there is much inflammation, and also apply healing salve. If ulceration, bathe the part also occasionally with tinctures aloes, myrrh, and opium, equal parts mixed. — *Gunn's Domestic Physician.*

CHAPTER XI.
THINGS FOR THE SICK ROOM.

Things for the Sick Room. Tells how to prepare the following articles
for the sick and convalescent: Barley water; Sage tea; Refreshing
drink for fevers; Arrowroot jelly; Irish moss jelly; Isinglass jelly;
Tapioca jelly; Toast; Rice; Bread jelly; Rice gruel; Water gruel;
Arrowroot gruel; Beef liquid; Beef tea; Panado; French milk por-
ridge; Coffee milk; Drink for dysentery; Crust coffee; Cranberry
water; Wine whey; Mustard whey; Chicken broth; Calves'-foot
jelly; Slippery elm jelly; Nutritive fluids; Gum acacia restorative;
Soups for the convalescent; Eggs; Milk for infants; Water gruel.

Many people are ignorant of what constitutes good, nourishing, refreshing
food and drink for sick people. The following dishes are all palatable and nourishing, and are very refreshing to an invalid. Every one should have these recipes for
"Things for the sick room":

BARLEY WATER.

Pearl barley, two ounces; boiling water, two quarts. Boil to one quart, and
strain. If desirable, a little lemon juice and sugar may be added. This may be taken
freely in all inflammatory and eruptive diseases: measles, scarlet fever, small-pox,
etc.

RICE WATER.

Rice, two ounces; water, two quarts. Boil one hour and a half, and add sugar
and nutmeg to suit the taste. When milk is added to this it makes a very excellent
diet for children. Should the bowels be too loose, boil the milk before adding.

SAGE TEA.

Dried leaves of sage, half an ounce; boiling water, one quart. Infuse for half
an hour, and strain. May add sugar if desired. Balm, peppermint, spearmint, and
other teas are made in the same way.

A REFRESHING DRINK IN FEVERS.

Boil one ounce and a half of tamarind, two ounces of stoned raisins, and three
ounces of cranberries in three pints of water until two pints remain. Strain, and
add a small piece of fresh lemon peel, which must be removed in half an hour.

ARROWROOT JELLY.

Stir a tablespoonful of arrowroot powders into half a cupful of cold water, pour in a pint of boiling water, let it stand five or ten minutes and then sweeten and flavor it to suit the taste.

IRISH MOSS JELLY.

Irish moss, half an ounce; fresh milk, one and a half pints. Boil down to one pint. Strain, and add sugar and lemon juice sufficient to give it an agreeable flavor.

ISINGLASS JELLY.

Isinglass, two ounces; water, two pints. Boil to one pint; strain, and add one pint milk and one ounce of white sugar. This is excellent for persons recovering from sickness, and for children who have bowel complaints.

TAPIOCA JELLY.

Tapioca, two large spoonfuls; water, one pint. Boil gently for an hour, or until it appears like a jelly. Add sugar, wine, and nutmeg, with lemon juice to flavor.

RICE JELLY.

Mix a quarter of a pound of rice, picked and washed, with half a pound of loaf sugar and just sufficient water to cover it. Boil until it assumes a jellylike appearance; strain, and season to suit the taste and condition of the patient.

GRAPES.

In all cases of fever, very ripe grapes of any kind are a beneficial article of diet, acting as both food and drink and possessing soothing and cooling qualities. They are also extremely grateful to every palate.

TOAST.

To make a most excellent toast for a reduced or convalescent patient, take bread twenty-four or thirty-six hours old, which has been made of a mixture of fine wheat flour and Indian meal and a pure yeast batter mixed with eggs. Toast it until of a delicate brown, and then (if the patient be not inclined to fever) immerse it in boiled milk and butter. If the patient be feverish, spread it lightly with cranberry jam or calves' foot jelly.

RICE.

In all cases where a light and nice diet for patients who have been or are afflicted with diarrhœa or dysentery is required, rice, in almost any cooked form, is most agreeable and advantageous. It may be given with benefit to dyspeptics, unless costiveness accompanies the dyspepsia. To make rice pudding, take a teacupful of rice, and as much sugar, two quarts of milk, and a teaspoonful of salt. Bake, with a moderate heat, for two hours. Rice flour made in a batter and baked upon a griddle makes a superb cake; and rice-flour gruel, seasoned to the taste, is most excellent for the sick room.

BREAD JELLY.

Boil a quart of water and let it cool. Take one-third of a common loaf of wheat bread, slice it, pare off the crust, and toast it to a light brown. Put it in water in a covered vessel and boil gently till you find, on putting some in a spoon to cool, the liquid has become a jelly. Strain and cool. When used, warm a cupful, sweeten with sugar, and add a little grated lemon peel.

RICE GRUEL.

Ground rice, one heaping tablespoonful; water, one quart. Boil gently for twenty minutes, adding, a few minutes before it is done, one tablespoonful of ground cinnamon. Strain and sweeten. Wine may be added when the case demands it.

WATER GRUEL.

Oat or corn meal, two tablespoonfuls; water, one quart. Boil for ten minutes and strain, adding salt and sugar if desired by the patient.

SAGO GRUEL.

Sago, two tablespoonfuls; water, one pint. Boil gently until it thickens; stir frequently. May add wine, sugar, and nutmeg, according to taste.

ARROWROOT GRUEL.

Arrowroot, one tablespoonful; sweet milk and boiling water, each one half pint. Sweeten with loaf sugar. This is very good for children whose bowels are irritable.

TAPIOCA.

Tapioca is a very delightful food for invalids. Make an ordinary pudding of it, and improve the flavor agreeably to the desire of the patient or convalescent by adding raisins, sugar, prunes, lemon juice, wine, spices, etc.

BEEF LIQUID.

When the stomach is very weak, take fresh lean beef, cut it into strips and place the strips into a bottle with a little salt; place in a kettle of boiling water and let it remain one hour; pour off the liquid and add some water. Begin with a small quantity, and use in the same manner and under similar circumstances as beef tea. This is even more nourishing than beef tea.

BEEF TEA.

Cut one pound of lean beef into shreds, and boil for twenty minutes in one quart of water, being particular to remove the scum as often as any rises. When it is cool, strain. This is very nourishing and palatable, and is of great value in all cases of extreme debility where no inflammatory action exists, or after the inflammation is subdued. In very low cases a small teaspoonful may be administered every fifteen or twenty minutes, gradually increasing the amount given as the powers of life return. In cases of complete prostration, after the cessation of long exhausting fever it may be used as directed above, either alone or in conjunction with a little wine.

PANADO.

Put a little water on the fire, with a glass of wine, some sugar, and a little grated nutmeg; boil all together a few seconds, and add pounded cracker or crumbs of bread, and boil again for a few minutes.

FRENCH MILK PORRIDGE.

Stir some oatmeal and water together; let the mixture stand to clear, and pour off the water. Then put more water to the meal; stir it well, and let it stand till the next day. Strain through a fine sieve, and boil the water, adding milk while so doing. The proportion of water must be small. With toast this is admirable.

COFFEE MILK.

Put a dessertspoonful of ground coffee into a pint of milk; boil a quarter of an hour, with a shaving or two of isinglass; let it stand ten minutes, and then pour off.

RESTORATIVE JELLY.

Take a leg of well-fed pork just as cut up, beat it and break the bone; set it over a gentle fire, with three gallons of water and simmer to one. Let half an ounce of mace and the same of nutmeg stew in it. Strain through a fine sieve. When cold, take off the fat. Give a coffee cup of this three times a day, adding salt to the taste. This is very valuable in all cases of debility where animal food is admissible.

DRINK IN DYSENTERY.

Sheep's suet, two ounces; milk, one pint; starch, half an ounce. Boil gently for thirty minutes. Use as a common drink. This is excellent for sustaining the strength in bad cases of dysentery.

CRUST COFFEE.

Toast slowly a thick piece of bread cut from the outside of a loaf until it is well browned, but not blackened; then turn upon it boiling water of a sufficient quantity, and keep it from half an hour to an hour before using. Be sure that the liquid is of a rich brown color before you use it. It is a most excellent drink in all cases of sickness.

CRANBERRY WATER.

Put a teaspoonful of cranberries into a cup of water and mash them. In the meantime boil two quarts of water with one large spoonful of corn or oat meal and a bit of lemon peel; then add the cranberries and as much fine sugar as will leave a smart flavor of the fruit; also a wineglassful of sherry. Boil the whole gently for a quarter of an hour, then strain.

WINE WHEY.

Heat a pint of new milk until it boils, at which moment pour in as much good wine as will curdle and clarify it. Boil and set it aside until the curd subsides. Do not stir it, but pour the whey off carefully, and add two pints of boiling water with loaf sugar.

ORANGE WHEY.

Milk, one pint; the juice of an orange with a portion of the peel. Boil the milk, then put the orange into it and let it stand till it coagulates. Strain.

MUSTARD WHEY.

Bruised mustard seed, two tablespoonfuls; milk, one quart. Boil together for a few minutes until it coagulates, and strain to separate the curd. This is a very useful drink in dropsy. A teacupful may be taken at a dose, three times a day.

CHICKEN BROTH.

Take half a chicken, divested of all fat, and break the bones; add to this half a gallon of water, and boil for half an hour. Season with salt.

VEGETABLE SOUP.

Take one potato, one turnip and one onion, with a little celery or celery seed. Slice, and boil for an hour in one quart of water. Salt to the taste, and pour the whole upon a piece of dry toast. This forms a good substitute for animal food and may be used when the latter would be improper.

CALVES'-FOOT JELLY.

Boil two calf's feet in one gallon of water until reduced to one quart. Strain, and when cool skim carefully. Add the white of six or eight eggs, well beaten; a pint of wine, half a pound of loaf sugar, and the juice of four lemons. Mix them well, boil for a few minutes, stirring constantly, and pass through a flannel strainer. In some cases the wine should be omitted.

SLIPPERY ELM JELLY.

Take of the flour of slippery elm, one or two tablespoonfuls; cold water, one pint. Stir until a jelly is formed. Sweeten with loaf sugar or honey. This is excellent for all diseases of the throat, chest, and lungs; coughs, colds, bronchitis, inflammation of the lungs, etc. It is very nutritious and soothing.

NUTRITIVE FLUIDS.

Following will be found directions for preparing three nutritious fluids, which are of great value in all diseases, either acute or chronic, that are attended or followed by prostration; debility, whether general or of certain organs only; derangement of the digestive organs, weak stomach, indigestion, heartburn or sour stomach, constipated bowels, torpidity or want of activity of the liver, thin or poor blood. These fluids are highly nutritious, supplying to the blood, in such a form that they are most easily assimilated, the various elements which are needed to enrich it and thus enable it to reproduce the various tissues of the body that have been wasted by disease. In cases where the stomach has become so weakened and sensitive that the lightest food or drinks cannot be taken without causing much uneasiness and distress these fluids are invaluable. They strengthen the stomach and neutralize all undue acidity, while at the same time they soothe the irritation by their bland and demulcent qualities. When carefully and properly prepared, according to the directions following, they very nearly resemble rich new milk in color and consistency, while their taste is remarkably pleasant. Care should be taken that all the ingredients are of the best quality. Soft water must be used in all cases. Fresh rain water is to be preferred, but spring water may be used if perfectly soft. Hard water will cause the fluids to be of a yellow color, and if the milk is old they are apt to separate:

FLUID NO. 1.

Put a pint of new milk (the fresher the better) and two pints of soft water, in a vessel perfectly free from all greasy matter, over a slow fire. Rub two even teaspoonfuls of superfine wheat flour and two teaspoonfuls of carbonate of magnesia, together with a little milk, into a soft batter, free from lumps; add this to the milk and water as soon as they begin to boil. Boil gently for five minutes—*no longer*—stirring constantly. Pour into an earthen or glass dish to cool, adding at the same time two teaspoonfuls of loaf sugar and one teaspoonful each of saleratus and table salt, rubbed fine. Stir until cold. The fluid must not be allowed to remain in a metallic vessel of any kind, and it must be kept in a cool place.

FLUID NO. 2.

Put one pint of fresh milk and two pints of soft water in a vessel over a slow fire. Rub together with a little fresh cream into a soft batter, free from lumps, one tablespoonful each of good sweet rye flour, ground rice, and pure starch; which add to the milk and water as soon as they begin to boil. Boil for five minutes, stirring constantly. Remove from the fire and add three teaspoonfuls of loaf sugar and one teaspoonful each of saleratus and table salt. Observe the same precautions as in No. 1.

FLUID NO. 3.

Put in a vessel, over a slow fire, one pint of fresh milk and two pints of soft water. When they begin to boil, add one tablespoonful of wheat flour, two tablespoonfuls of pure starch, and two teaspoonfuls of carbonate of magnesia, rubbed, together with a little milk into a soft batter, free from lumps. Boil gently for five minutes, stirring constantly. Pour into an earthen vessel to cool, and add one teaspoonful of the best gum arabic dissolved in a little warm water, one teaspoonful each of saleratus and table salt, and one tablespoonful of pure strained honey. Stir until cold. The same precaution must be observed as in preparing No. 1.

DIRECTIONS.

One half pint or less of these fluids may be taken at a dose, and at least three pints should be taken during the day and the amount gradually increased to two or three quarts. Commence with No. 1 and use two weeks, then use No. 2 for the same length of time, after which No. 3 is to be used for two weeks. Continue their use as long as necessary, taking each for two weeks before changing. In all the diseases mentioned above, the use of these fluids, in connection with proper remedies, will insure a speedy restoration to health.

GUM ACACIA RESTORATIVE.

Take two ounces of pure white gum arabic (procure the lump, the powdered is very apt to be adulterated), pulverize it well, and dissolve by the aid of a gentle heat in a gill of water, stirring constantly. When it is entirely dissolved, add three tablespoonfuls of pure strained honey. Let it remain over the fire until it becomes of the consistency of a jelly. The heat must be very gentle, it must not boil. If desirable, flavor with lemon or vanilla. This will be found a very pleasant article of diet for a weak stomach. When the articles used are pure it will be transparent and of a light golden color. This will be borne by the weakest stomach when everything else is rejected. *It is highly nutritious.*

MALT INFUSION.

Infuse one pint of ground malt for two hours in three pints of scalding water. The water should not be brought quite to the boiling point. Strain; add sugar, if desired; flavor with lemon juice. This is an excellent drink in inflammatory fevers, acute rheumatism, etc.

PEAS.

Take young and fresh shelled green peas, wash them clean, put them into fresh water, just enough to cover them, and boil them till they take up nearly all the water. This dish, if prepared according to directions, and eaten warm, will not harm any invalid, not even one suffering from diarrhœa.

MILK.

In some cases where a milk diet is advisable, owing to the peculiar condition of the patient's stomach it will cause distress. This is frequently the case where there is undue acidity. In such cases, let it be prepared in the following manner and it will be found to set well: Take a teacupful of fresh milk, heat nearly to boiling; dissolve in it a teaspoonful of loaf sugar; pour into a large sized tumbler, and add sufficient plain soda water to fill it. Prepared in the above directed manner it will be free from all unpleasant effects.

SOUPS FOR THE CONVALESCENT.

To extract the strength from meat, long and slow boiling is necessary; but care must be taken that the pot is never off the boil. All soups should be made the day before they are used, and they should then be strained into earthen pans. When soup has jellied in the pan, it should not be removed into another. When in danger of not keeping, it should be boiled up.

EGGS.

In cases of extreme debility, eggs are most excellent. They should never be boiled hard. The best way to prepare them is to beat them well with milk and sugar. When it will be appropriate to the case, add some fine pale sherry wine.

MILK FOR INFANTS.

Fresh cow's milk, one part; water, two parts; sweeten with a very little loaf sugar. When children are raised by hand it is always necessary to dilute the milk. As the child advances in age the proportion of water stated above may be gradually lessened.

WATER GRUEL.

Corn or oat meal, two tablespoonfuls; water, one quart. Boil ten or fifteen minutes, and strain. Add salt and sugar to suit the taste of the patient. This should be used freely during and after the operation of cathartic medicines.

CHAPTER XII.

THINGS CURIOUS AND USEFUL.

Things Curious and Useful: To get clear of mosquitoes; To get rid of bedbugs; To obtain fresh-blown flowers in winter; To increase the laying of eggs in hens; The art of transferring on to glass; To prevent horses being teased by flies; To prevent flies lighting on windows, pictures, mirrors, etc.; To make leather wear forever; To prepare waterproof boots; To render paper fireproof; To cure drunkenness; To cure laziness; To take leaf photographs; To make lamp wicks indestructible; To make different kinds of perfumes; To write secret letters; To preserve flowers.

TO GET CLEAR OF MOSQUITOES.

Take of gum camphor a piece about one-third the size of an egg and evaporate it over a lamp or candle, taking care that it does not ignite. The smoke will soon fill the room and expel the mosquitoes.

HOW TO GET RID OF BEDBUGS.

Bedbugs cannot stand hot alum water; indeed, alum seems to be death to them in any form. Take two pounds of alum, reduce it to a powder—the finer the better—and dissolve it in about four quarts of boiling water. Keep the water hot till the alum is all dissolved; then apply it hot to every joint, crevice and place about the bedstead, floor, skirting or washboard around the room, and every place where the bugs are likely to congregate, by means of a brush. A common syringe is an excellent thing to use in applying it to the bedstead. Apply the water as hot as you can. Apply it freely, and you will hardly be troubled any more that season with bugs. Whitewash the ceiling with plenty of dissolved alum in the wash, and there will be an end to their dropping down from thence on to your bed.

TO OBTAIN FRESH-BLOWN FLOWERS IN WINTER.

Choose some of the most perfect buds of the flowers you would preserve, such as are latest in blowing and ready to open. Cut them off with a pair off scissors, leaving to each, if possible, apiece of stem about three inches long. Cover the end of the stem immediately with sealing wax, and when the buds are a little shrunk and wrinkled wrap up each of them separately in a piece of paper perfectly clean and dry and lock them up in a dry box or drawer, and they will keep without corrupting.

In winter or at any time when you would have the flowers blow, take the buds at night and cut off the end of the stem sealed with wax and put the buds in water wherein a little nitre or salt has been diffused, and the next day you will have the pleasure of seeing the buds opening and expanding themselves and the flowers display their most lively colors and breathe their agreeable odors.

TO INCREASE THE LAYING OF EGGS IN HENS.

Pulverized Cayenne pepper, half an ounce, to be given to one dozen hens, mixed with their food every second day.

THE NEW AND BEAUTIFUL ART OF TRANSFERRING ON TO GLASS.

Colored or plain engravings, photographs, lithographs, water colors, oil colors, crayons, steel plates, newspaper cuts, mezzotints, pencil, writing, show cards, labels, or, in fact, anything.

DIRECTIONS.

Take glass that is perfectly clear (window glass will answer), clean it thoroughly; then varnish it, taking care to have it perfectly smooth; place it where it will be perfectly free from dust; let it stand over night, then take your engraving, lay it in clear water until it is wet through (say ten or fifteen minutes), then lay it upon a newspaper, that the moisture may dry from the surface and still keep the other side damp. Immediately varnish your glass the second time, then place your engraving upon it, pressing it down firmly, so as to exclude every particle of air; next, rub the paper from the back until it is of uniform thickness, so thin that you can see through it, then varnish it the third time and let it dry.

These transferred pictures make lovely ornaments for table, bracket, mantel, etc.

MATERIALS FOR MAKING THE VARNISH.

Take two ounces balsam of fir to one ounce spirits of turpentine. Apply with a camel's-hair brush.

TO PREVENT HORSES BEING TEASED BY FLIES.

Boil three handfuls of walnut leaves in three quarts of water; sponge the horse (before going out of the stable) between and upon the ears, neck, and flank.

TO PREVENT FLIES LIGHTING ON WINDOWS, PICTURES, MIRRORS, ETC.

No fly will light on a window or other article which has been washed in water in which garlic has been boiled.

TO MAKE LEATHER WEAR FOREVER.

Let it receive as much neat's-foot oil as it will take. If regularly repeated every three months, leather so treated seems to be impervious to outward action and will last for years.

TO RENDER PAPER FIREPROOF.

Whether the paper be plain, written, printed, or even marbled, stained, or painted for paper hangings, dip it in a strong solution of alum water and thoroughly dry it. In this state it will be fireproof.

TO PREPARE WATERPROOF BOOTS.

Take three ounces of spermaceti and melt it in an earthen pot over a slow fire; add thereto six drains of India rubber cut into slices, and after it dissolves add of tallow, eight ounces; amber varnish, four ounces. Mix it, and it will be ready for use immediately.

TO CURE DRUNKENNESS.

Keep the patient for one week freely dosed with figwort. This is a sure cure.

TO CURE LAZINESS.

Give the patient an occasional dose of ferri. The sulphate of ferri is the best. It acts on the liver and vital organs, and is a sure cure for laziness.

TO EXTRACT THE ESSENTIAL OIL FROM ANY FLOWER.

Take any flower you like, which stratify with common salt in a clean glazed pot; when filled to the top, cover it well and carry it to the cellar; forty days afterwards put a crape over a pan and empty the whole to strain the essence from the flowers by pressure. Bottle this essence, and expose it for four or five weeks in the sun and dew of the evening to purify. One single drop of this essence is enough to scent a whole quart of water.

TO TAKE LEAF PHOTOGRAPHS.

A very pretty amusement, especially for those who have just completed the study of botany, is the taking of leaf photographs. One very simple process is this: At any druggist's get an ounce of bichromate of potassium. Put this into a pint bottle of water. When the solution becomes saturated — that is, the water has dissolved as much as it will — pour off some of the clear liquid into a shallow dish; on this float a piece of ordinary writing paper till it is thoroughly moistened, and let it dry in the dark. It should be of a bright yellow color. On this put the leaf, under it a piece of black soft cloth and several sheets of newspaper. Put these between two pieces of glass (all the pieces should be of the same size) and with spring clothespins fasten them together. Expose to a bright sun, placing the leaf so that the rays will fall upon it as nearly perpendicular as possible. In a few moments it will begin to turn brown; but it requires from half an hour to several hours to produce a perfect print. When it has become dark enough, take it from the frame and put it into clear water, which must be changed every few minutes until the yellow part becomes white. Sometimes the veinings will be quite distinct. By following these directions it is scarcely possible to fail, and a little practice will make perfect.

TO MAKE LAMP WICKS INDESTRUCTIBLE.

Steep common wicks in a concentrated aqueous solution of tungstate of soda, and then dry thoroughly in an oven.

TO MAKE DIFFERENT KINDS OF PERFUMES.

BALM OF A THOUSAND FLOWERS.

Deodorized alcohol, one pint; nice white bar soap, four ounces. Shave the soap when put in; stand in a warm place till dissolved; then add oil of citronella, one dram, and oils of neroli and rosemary, of each one-half dram.

FRANGAPANNI.

Spirits, one gallon; oil of bergamot, one ounce; oil of lemon, one ounce: Macerate for four days, frequently shaking; then add water, one gallon; orange flower water, one pint; essence of vanilla, two ounces. Mix.

JOCKEY CLUB.

Spirits of wine, five gallons; orange flower water, one gallon; balsam of Peru, four ounces; essence of bergamot, eight ounces; essence of musk, eight ounces; essence of cloves, four ounces; essence of neroli, two ounces. Mix.

LADY'S OWN.

Spirits of wine, one gallon; otto of roses, twenty drops; essence of thyme, one-half ounce; essence of neroli, one-quarter ounce; essence of vanilla, one-half ounce; essence of bergamot, one-quarter ounce; orange flower water, six ounces. Mix.

UPPER TEN.

Spirits of wine, four quarts; essence of cedrate, two drams; essence violets, one-quarter ounce; essence of neroli, one-half ounce; otto of roses, twenty drops; orange flower essence, one ounce; oil of rosemary, thirty drops; oils of bergamot and neroli, each one-half ounce. Mix.

If you wish to make a small quantity of any of the above perfumes, use small quantities of the ingredients, preserving the same proportions.

TO WRITE SECRET LETTERS.

Put five cents' worth of citrate of potassa in an ounce vial of clear cold water. This forms an invisible fluid. Let it dissolve, and you can use on paper of any color. Use goose quill in writing. When you wish the writing to become visible, hold it to a red-hot stove.

TO PRESERVE FLOWERS SO THAT THEIR BEAUTY WILL LAST FOR YEARS.

Make a strong solution of gum arabic, two ounces of the gum to one pint of boiling water; shake until dissolved; then take your flowers and immerse in the solution, taking care that every part is well wet with the solution. When dry, repeat the operation. Do this three times. Flowers treated thus will last for years.

CHAPTER XIII.

HOME DECORATION.

Home Decoration: On furnishing a house; How to furnish the Parlor, Library, Dining-room, Hall, Chambers, and Kitchen; Telling the proper way of arranging each room tastefully and economically.

The chief features to be observed in house furnishing are color, form, and proportion. All stiffness of design in furniture should be avoided. Do not attempt to match articles, but rather carry out the same idea as to color and form in the whole. It is not *en règle* to have decorations in sets or pairs; the arrangements should all be done with odd pieces. Every room in the house should be arranged for occupancy, having nothing too good for use, and the judicious housewife will follow a medium course and adopt no extreme of fashion.

The style and arrangement of the furniture should correspond with the size of the room, with a due regard to the place a piece of furniture or ornament will occupy. The order of arrangement in furnishing is subject to individual taste, but the following suggestions may not be inappropriate:—

In decorating a dining-room, deep, rich tones should be used; a drawingroom or parlor should have bright, cheerful shades; in a library use deep, rich colors, which give a sense of worth; a sleeping-room should have light, pleasing tints, which give a feeling of repose.

THE HALL.

The hall being the index to the whole house, due care should therefore be given to its furnishing. Light colors and gilding should be avoided. The wall and ceiling decorations now mostly used are in dark, rich colors, shaded in maroons or deep reds. Plain tinted walls and ceilings in fresco or wainscot are also frequently used. The latest shades of wall paper come in wood colors, dark olive-greens, stone color, and grays, in tile, arabesque and landscape designs, and with these are used a corresponding dado and frieze.

A tile or inlaid floor is the most appropriate, but if circumstances do not admit of one of these, a floor stained a deep wood-brown, base board and moldings to correspond, may be substituted; when India mattings and rugs may be used.

The colors now in vogue for hall carpets are crimson or Pompeiian reds, with small figures of moss-green or peacock-blue. The prevailing shades of the walls and floor should be incorporated in the stair carpet.

If the hall is narrow, none but the most essential pieces of furniture should be used; but if wide enough, there may be a lounge placed against one of the walls, an old-fashioned clock of the cuckoo style set in a quiet corner, two high-backed chairs upholstered in leather, a table, an umbrella-stand placed near the door, a jardinière filled with tropical plants set near the foot of the stairway, and a hall mirror with a deer's head and antlers placed above it and a wooden or marble slab underneath. The slab should be covered with a Roman scarf, allowing a fall of twelve inches at each end. The hatrack must also find a place. Family portraits or a few well-selected pictures are appropriate for these walls.

If the door-lights are not stained glass, lace shades in designs of birds, cupids, and garlands of flowers are used; also, etchings in various colors and designs are worked on different fabrics. Crimson silk shades lined with black netting are very desirable, as the light penetrating through them fills the hall with a rich, subdued glow.

THE PARLOR.

The furnishing of the parlor should be subject to its architectural finish. The first things to be considered are the walls and floor. The former may be decorated in fresco or papered, according to individual taste and means. The prettiest styles of parlor paper are light tints of gray, olive, pearl, and lavender grounds, and in small scroll patterns, panels, birds, and vines, finished in heavy gold traceries, with dado and frieze to correspond.

The styles of carpet mostly used are Brussels, Wilton, tapestry, and Axminster. A tapestry carpet in light canary ground, with clusters of lotus, or begonia leaves, makes a charming background to almost all the colors generally used in upholstery.

In selecting the furniture, the first thought should be given to its true worth. Chairs and couches should be chosen for comfort rather than for style. They should be of solid make, easy, graceful, and of good, serviceable colors and materials. The most serviceable woods to select in frames are ebony, oak, walnut, cherry, and mahogany. These frames are finished in different styles—plain, carved, inlaid, and gilt—and are upholstered in all shades of satin, plush, rep, silk, and damask. These come at prices within the means of a slender purse. That slippery abomination in the shape of haircloth furniture should be avoided. The latest design in parlor furniture is in the Turkish style, the upholstery being made to cover the frame. Rich Oriental colors in woolen and silk brocades are mostly used, and the trimmings are cord and tassels or heavy fringe.

Formerly the parlor appointments were all in sets or pairs, but this fashion is no longer observed, as the most tastefully arranged parlor has now no two pieces of furniture alike; but two easy-chairs placed opposite each other are never out of place. Here may stand an embroidered ottoman, there a quaint little chair, a divan can take some central position; a cottage piano, covered with some embroidered drapery, may stand at one end of the room, while an ebony or mahogany cabinet, with its panel mirrors and quaint brasses, may be placed at the other end, its racks and shelves affording an elegant display for pretty pieces of bric-a-brac.

Marble-topped center-tables are no longer in use. Tables in inlaid woods, or hand-painted, are used for placing books or albums on. A small, airy-looking table, elaborately mounted in gilt, may stand near a window or wall. The mantel mirror, with its beveled edges and small racks arranged on each side, looks very effective when decorated with pretty oddities—ferns, grasses, and pieces of old china. A jardinière filled with living plants and placed near a bay window makes an elegant ornament. Care should be taken in arranging that the room be not over-crowded. There should be a few good pictures or painted plaques mounted in plush hung on the walls; a portrait may be placed on a common easel and draped with a scarf in old gold or peacock-blue, and tiny lambrequins, painted or embroidered, may hang beneath a bracket supporting a bust or flower-vase.

An embroidered scarf with fringed ends may be placed on the back of a chair or sofa in place of the old lace tidy. A sack made of small pieces of bright-colored plush or silk in crazy work may be flung across the table, the ends drooping very low. The mantelpiece may be covered with a corresponding sash, over which place a small clock as centerpiece and arrange ornaments on each side—statuettes, bannerets, flower-holders, small Japanese fans, pieces of odd china, painted candles in small scenes, may all find a place on the mantel.

Window curtains of heavy fabric, hung from brass or plush mounted poles, may be gracefully draped to the sides, while the inner lace ones should be hung straight and be fastened in the center with some ornament or bow of ribbon corresponding in shade to the general tone of the room. The straight shades next to the glass may correspond in tone to the outside walls or window-facings; but this is a mere matter of taste. White or light-tinted shades, finished in etching or narrow lace, are always in vogue.

The dado shades are the latest innovation in window decoration. These come in all colors, from the lightest to the darkest shades, with dado in tile, arabesque and fresco patterns, finished in lace, fringe, and brasses.

Portières (curtain doors) have superseded folding doors. These should be in shades to contrast with the general blending of the colors in the room. The fabrics mostly used are India goods, but they may be of any material, from expensive tapestries, satins, and plushes, to ten-cent factory cottons. The curtains, if made from striped tapestry and Turcoman, will give the finishing artistic touches to almost any room, but the last softening polish comes only from the genial presence of trailing and climbing vines.

THE SITTING-ROOM.

The sitting or everyday room should be the brightest and most attractive room in the house. Its beauty of decoration should not be so much in the richness and variety of material as in its comfort, simplicity, and the harmony of its tints—the main features being the fitness of each article to the needs of the room. In these days of so many advantages much can be done in adornment by simple means.

The wall papers mostly used come in grounds of cream, amber, rose, pale olive, fawn, ceil blue and light gray, with designs and traceries of contrasting hues.

The carpet, if in tapestry, looks more effective if in grounds of pale canary or light gray, with designs in bright-colored woodland flowers and borders to match. The new ingrain carpets, with their pretty designs and bright colors, are very fashionable for rooms that are much used.

Whatever may be the prevailing tint of the carpet, the window curtains should follow it up in lighter tones or contrast with it. The curtains may correspond with the coverings of the chairs, sofa, mantel and table draperies in color and fabric. If the furniture is of wicker, bamboo or rattan, the curtains should be of Japanese or any kind of Oriental goods. Curtains of muslin (either white or tinted), gay-colored chintzes, lace or dotted Swiss muslin, looped back with bright-toned ribbons, look very pretty and are appropriate for the sitting-room at almost any season. That clumsy structure called the cornice, for putting up curtains on, has happily given place to the more light and graceful curtain pole.

One large table, covered with a pretty embroidered cloth, should be placed in some central location for a catch-all. A low divan, with a pair of square, soft pillows, may stand in some quiet nook; a rocker, handsomely upholstered, with a pretty tidy pinned to its back; a large, soft easy-chair; a small sewing-chair placed near a table; and a bamboo chair, trimmed with ribbons, will be tastefully arranged in the room. Window stands and gypsy tables may be draped with some rich fabric, the surrounding valance being caught up in small festoons and fastened with bows or tassels, finished around the edge of the table with cord or quilted ribbon.

If the furniture is old or in sets it can be covered with different patterns in cretonne or chintz, which not only protects the furniture but breaks up the monotony and lends a pleasing variety to the room. A Turkish chair is a grand accessory to the family room. This may be made by buying the frame and having it upholstered in white cotton cloth and covering it with a rich shade of cretonne, finishing it with cord and fringe.

A foot-rest frame can be made in the same way and covered with a piece of homemade embroidery, finishing it off with a cord or narrow gimp around the edge. Homemade easels, screens, and pedestals may be made out of black walnut, and when stained and draped look exceedingly pretty. An old second-hand cabinet may be bought at a trifle, and when polished up may be set in a corner on which to display some pieces of bric-a-brac.

If the house has no library, the sitting-room is just the place for the bookcase.

With house plants in the windows, a room of this character, with floods of sunshine, makes a most attractive and comfortable living-room.

THE LIBRARY.

The walls of the library should be hung with rich, dark colors, the latest style in wall paper being a black ground with old gold and olive-green designs.

The carpet comes in Pompeiian red, with moss-green and peacock-blue patterns. Statuary and the best pictures should find a place in the library. The library table should be massive and the top laid with crimson baize. There should be a few high-backed chairs, upholstered in leather, a reading-chair, soft rugs, foot-rests, a mantel mirror, a few mantel ornaments, and the *piece de resistance*—the bookcase. In large libraries the bookcases are built in the wall. It is quite in vogue to hang curtains on rods in front of bookcases instead of doors, but we think the old style is the best, inasmuch as the books may be seen and the glass doors exclude the dust.

Heavy curtains of raw silk, Turcoman, and canton flannel, with a full valance at the top, are used for the window drapery.

CHAMBERS.

The walls of bedrooms should be decorated in light tints and shadings, with a narrow rail and deep frieze. Most housekeepers prefer rugs and oiled floors to carpets, but this is a matter of individual taste. Rugs are as fashionable as they are wholesome and tidy. These floor-coverings should be darker than the furniture, yet blending in shade. If carpets are chosen they should be the lightest shades and in bright field-flower patterns. Avoid anything dark and somber for the sleeping-room. Pink and ceil blue combined are very pretty, scarlet and gray, deep red and very light blue. Dark blue with sprays of lily of the valley running through it is exceedingly pretty for bedrooms. Dark furniture will harmonize with all these colors, but the lighter shades are preferable. Cretonnes in pale tints and chintzes in harmonizing colors are used for light woods. Square pillows of cretonne on a bamboo or wicker lounge are very pretty. Canton matting is often used, either plain or in colored patterns.

Formerly the bed-coverings were spotlessly white, but the profluent tide of color has included these also. The coverings now in vogue are: Nottingham lace, darned net, applique, antique lace, and Swiss muslin. These are used over silk and silesia for backgrounds, and are exceedingly pretty, with pillow shams to match. Cretonnes, chintzes, dimities, and silk in crazy work and South Kensington patterns are also used.

Cheese cloth, bunting, Swiss muslin, cretonne, and Swiss curtains are used for window drapery. These may be trimmed with the same fabric or antique lace. They are hung on poles above the windows and draped back with ribbons.

The appointments of a bedroom are a low couch, a large rocker, a small sewing-chair, a workbasket, footstools, a toilet table prettily draped with muslin, or a dressing-case, brackets for vases, flowerpots, a few pictures, small table, hanging shelves for books, etc., and the bed.

The washstand should have a full set of toilet mats, or a large towel with a colored border may be laid on it; also, a splasher placed on the wall at the back of the stand is very essential. A screen is a very desirable part of the bedroom appointments. A rug should be placed in front of the bed and dressing-case.

THE DINING-ROOM.

The dining-room should be furnished with a view to convenience, richness, and comfort. Choose deep, rich grounds for the walls—bronze-maroon, black,

Pompeiian red, and deep olive—and the designs and traceries in old gold, olive or moss-green, with dado and frieze to correspond. Or, the walls may be wainscoted with oak, walnut, maple, etc. Some are finished in plain panels, with different kinds of wood; others, again, are elaborately carved, with fruit, flowers, and emblems of the chase.

The floor is the next point for consideration. It may be of tile or laid in alternate strips of different colored woods, with a border of parquetry. Rugs or carpets may be used on these floors or dispensed with, according to taste. If a carpet is used, the dark, rich shades found in the Persian and Turkish designs should be chosen.

The window drapery should be those deep, rich colors that hold their own despite time and use—the pomegranates, rich crimsons, dark blues, dull Pompeiian reds, and soft olives. These curtains may be hung on poles, and should fall in heavy folds to the floor, then looped back with a wide embroidered dado.

Screens of stained glass are now used in the windows. They are both useful and ornamental, for they exclude the strong rays of the sun, and the light filtering through them beautifies the room with its many mellow hues.

Dark wood should be used for the furniture. The chairs should be chosen in square, solid styles, and upholstered in embossed or plain leather, with an abundance of brass or silver headed nails which are used for upholstering leather and add much to the substantial appearance of the articles.

The dining-table should be low, square or bevel cornered, heavily carved, and when not in use should be covered with a cloth corresponding in shade to the window drapery.

A buffet may stand in one corner for the display of ceramics or decorated china. The sideboard should be of high, massive style, with shelves and racks for glassware and pieces of china.

A few pictures—two or three fruit pieces and one or two plaques of still life—are appropriate.

A case of stuffed birds, a few large pots of tropical plants, and a fernery are in keeping with the dining-room appointments. A three-leaf folding Japanese screen should not be forgotten; also, a lamp shade of antique lace, lined with crimson silk, is very desirable.

THE KITCHEN.

It is a remark too often made that this or that "is good enough for a servant." If all knew that unpleasant surroundings made unpleasant servants and ill-prepared meals, we think more pains would be taken to have pleasant and comfortable kitchens. There should be a pleasant window or two through which fresh air and floods of sunlight may come, a few plants on the window sill, a small stand for a workbasket, an easy-chair that the servant may "drop into" when an opportunity offers, the walls painted or calcimined with some cheerful tint, and a general air of comfort pervading the whole kitchen.—*The Popular Art Instructor.*

CHAPTER XIV.

FLORAL.

How to Care for House Plants: How to succeed with plants; A good collection of plants; To kill the spider; To start slips; To keep plants without a fire at night; To kill rose-slugs; On watering plants.

To prepare autumn leaves and ferns; To prepare skeleton leaves; Pretty hanging baskets.

HOW TO CARE FOR HOUSE PLANTS.

Plants that require a high or low temperature or a very moist atmosphere and plants that bloom only in summer are undesirable. Procure fresh sandy loam, with an equal mixture of well-rotted turf, leaf mold, and cow-yard manure, with a small quantity of soot. In repotting plants use one size larger than they were grown in. Hard-burned or glazed pots prevent the circulation of air. Secure drainage by broken crockery and pebbles laid in the bottom of the pot. An abundance of light is important, and when this cannot be given it is useless to attempt the culture of flowering plants. If possible they should have the morning sun, as one hour of sunshine then is worth two in the afternoon. Fresh air is also essential, but cold, chilling drafts should be avoided. Water from one to three times a week with soft, lukewarm water, draining off all not absorbed by the earth.

DO NOT PERMIT

water to stand in the saucers, as the only plant thriving under such treatment is the calla lily; and even for these it is not necessary, unless while blooming. Dust is a great obstacle to the growth of plants. A good showering will generally remove it, but all the smooth-faced plants (such as camellias, ivies, etc.) should be carefully sponged so as to keep the foliage clean and healthy.

PLANTS SUCCEED BEST

in an even temperature, ranging from sixty to seventy degrees during the day and from ten to twelve degrees lower at night. If troubled with insects, put them under a box or barrel and smoke from thirty to sixty minutes with tobacco leaves.

FOR THE RED SPIDER

the best remedy is to lay the plants on the side and sprinkle well or shower. Repeat if necessary. If manures are used, give in a liquid form.

Some of the plants most suitable for parlor culture are: Pelargoniums, geraniums, fuchsias, palms, begonias, monthly roses, camellias, azaleas, oranges, lemons, Chinese and English primroses, abutilons, narcissus, heliotrope, petunias, and the gorgeous flowering plant, *Poinsettia pulcherrima*. Camellias and azaleas require a cooler temperature than most plants, and the Poinsettia a higher temperature. Do not sprinkle the foliage of the camellia while the flower buds are swelling or it will cause them to droop, nor sprinkle them in the sunshine. They should have a temperature of about forty degrees and more shade. By following these rules, healthy flowering plants will be the result.

A good way

TO START SLIPS

is to partly break off the slip (but do not entirely sever it from the parent stock), leaving it hanging for ten or twelve days; then remove and plant in a box of half sand and half leaf mold and it will be well rooted in a week. Do not water too freely or the slip will rot.

If house plants are watered once a week with water in which is mixed a few drops of ammonia they will thrive much better. Sometimes small white worms are found in the earth—lime water will kill them. Stir up the soil before pouring it on, to expose as many as possible. For running vines, burn beef bones and mix with the earth.

TO KEEP PLANTS WITHOUT A FIRE AT NIGHT.

Have made, of wood or zinc, a tray about four inches deep with a handle on either end, water-tight. Paint it outside and in, put in each corner a post as high as the tallest of your plants, and it is ready for use. Arrange your flowerpots in it and fill between them with sawdust. This absorbs the moisture falling from the plants when you water them and retains the warmth acquired during the day, keeping the temperature of the roots even. When you retire at night spread over the posts a blanket or shawl, and there is no danger of freezing.

SURE SHOT FOR ROSE-SLUGS.

Make a tea of tobacco stems and a soapsuds of whale oil or carbolic soap; mix and apply to the bush with a sprinkler, turning the bush so as to wet the under as well as the upper part of the leaves. Apply, before the sun is up, three or four times.

TO PREPARE AUTUMN LEAVES AND FERNS.

Immediately after gathering take a moderately warm iron, smear it well with white wax, rub over each surface of the leaf once, applying more wax for each leaf. This process causes leaves to roll about as when hanging on the trees. If pressed more they become brittle and remain perfectly flat. Maple and oak are among the most desirable, and may be gathered any time after the severe frosts; but the sumac and ivy must be secured as soon after the first slight frost as they become tinted or the leaflets will fall from the stem. Ferns may be selected any time during the season. A large book must be used in gathering them, as they will be spoiled for pressing if carried in the hand. A weight should be placed on them until they are perfectly dry; then, excepting the most delicate ones, it will be well to press them like the leaves, as they are liable to curl when placed in a warm atmosphere. These will form beautiful combinations with the sumac and ivy.

TO PREPARE SKELETON LEAVES.

When properly prepared, skeleton leaves form a companion to the scrapbook or collection of pressed ferns, fronds, etc. This is a tedious operation and requires skill and great patience to obtain satisfactory results. Some leaves are easier to dissect and make better specimens than others, and, as a rule, a hard, thin leaf should be chosen; that is, when a special variety is not required.

Among those which are skeletonized most successfully are the English ivy, box elder, willow, grape, pear, rose, etc. They should be gathered during the month of June, or as soon as the leaf is fully developed. The leaves should be immersed in a vessel of rain water and allowed to remain till decomposed. When this takes place, press the leaf between pieces of soft flannel, and the film will adhere to the flannel, leaving a perfect network. Dry off gradually and clean the specimen with a soft hair pencil. Place between folds of soft blotting paper, and when perfectly dry place in your collection.

TO BLEACH THE LEAVES,

dissolve one half pound of chloride of lime in three pints of rain water, strain, and use one part of the solution to one of water. For ferns, use the solution full strength. When perfectly white remove to clear water, let stand for several hours, changing water two or three times, float out on paper, and press between blotting paper in books.

In mounting use mucilage made of five parts gum arabic, three parts white sugar, two parts starch, and very little water; boil and stir till thick and white.

HANGING BASKETS.

A correspondent of the *Gardener's Monthly* tells of a new style of hanging basket made of round maple sticks about one inch in diameter, eight inches in length at the bottom, increasing to fourteen at the top. In constructing, begin at the bottom and build up, log-cabin fashion; chink the openings with green moss and line the whole basket with the same. These are easily kept moist, and the plants droop and twine over them very gracefully. A good way to keep the earth moist in a hanging basket without the trouble of taking it down is to fill a bottle with water and put in two pieces of yarn, leaving one end outside. Suspend the bottle just above the basket and allow the water to drip. This will keep the earth moist enough for winter and save a great deal of time and labor. Plant morning glory seeds in hanging baskets in winter; they grow rapidly and are very pretty.—*Buckeye.*

CHAPTER XV.

THE LAUNDRY.

The Laundry: To make washing fluid; Gall soap; For washing woolens and fine prints; To take out scorch; To make bluing; To make coffee starch; To make flour starch; To make fine starch; Enamel for shirt bosoms; To clean articles made of white zephyr; To clean velvet; To clean ribbons; To take out paint; To remove ink stain; To take out fruit stains; To remove iron rust; To take out mildew; To wash flannels in tepid water.

TELLING OF A GREAT MANY USEFUL AND LABOR-SAVING PRACTICES FOR THE LAUNDRY.

TO MAKE WASHING FLUID.

Bring to a boil one pound of sal soda, half a pound of unslaked lime, a small lump of borax, and five quarts of water. Let cool, pour off, and bottle. Use one teacupful to a boiler of clothes. This is superior.

GALL SOAP.

For washing woolens, silks, or fine prints liable to fade. One pint beefs gall, two pounds common bar soap cut fine, one quart boiling soft water; boil slowly, stirring occasionally until well mixed. Pour into a flat vessel, and when cold cut into pieces to dry.

TO TAKE OUT SCORCH.

If a shirt bosom or any other article has been scorched in ironing, lay it where bright sunshine will fall directly on it. It will entirely remove it.

BLUING.

Take one ounce of Prussian blue, one-half ounce of oxalic acid; dissolve in one quart of perfectly soft rain water. Insert a quill through the cork of the bluing bottle to prevent waste or putting too much in clothes and you will be pleased with the result. One or two tablespoons of it is sufficient for a tub of water, according to the size of the tub. Chinese blue is the best and costs twelve and a half cents an ounce, and the acid will cost three cents.

COFFEE STARCH.

Make a paste of two tablespoons best starch and cold water; when smooth stir in a pint of perfectly clear coffee, boiling hot; boil five or ten minutes. Stir with a spermaceti or wax candle. Strain and use for all dark calicoes, percales, and muslins.

FLOUR STARCH.

Have a clean pan or kettle on stove with one quart boiling water, into which stir three heaping tablespoons flour, previously mixed smooth in a little cold water; stir steadily until it boils and thereafter enough to keep from burning. Boil about five minutes, and strain, while hot, through a crash towel. The above quantity is enough for one dress, and will make it nice and stiff.

TO MAKE FINE STARCH.

Wet the starch smooth in a little cold water in a large tin pan, pour on a quart of boiling water to two or three tablespoons of starch, stirring rapidly all the while; place on stove, stir until it boils and then occasionally. Boil from five to fifteen minutes, or until the starch is perfectly clear. Some add a little salt or butter or pure lard or stir with a sperm candle; others add a teaspoon of kerosene to one quart of starch. This prevents the stickiness sometimes so annoying in ironing.

Cold starch is made from starch dissolved in cold water, being careful not to have it too thick. Since it rots the clothes, it is not advisable to use it.

ENAMEL FOR SHIRT BOSOMS.

Melt together, with a gentle heat, one ounce white wax and two ounces spermaceti. Prepare in the usual way a sufficient quantity of starch for a dozen shirt bosoms, put into it a piece of this enamel the size of a hazelnut. This will give your clothes a beautiful polish.

TO CLEAN ARTICLES MADE OF WHITE ZEPHYR.

Rub in flour or magnesia, changing often. Shake off and hang in the open air a short time.

HOW TO CLEAN VELVET.

Invert a hot flatiron, place over it a single thickness of wet cotton cloth, lay on this the velvet (wrong side next the wet cloth), rub gently with a dry cloth until the pile is well raised, take off the iron, lay on a table, and brush it with a soft brush or cloth.

TO CLEAN RIBBONS.

Dissolve white soap in boiling water; when cool enough to bear the hand, pass the ribbons through it, rubbing gently, so as not to injure the texture; rinse through lukewarm water and pin on a board to dry. If the colors are bright yellow, maroon, crimson or scarlet, add a few drops of oil of vitriol to the rinse water; if the color is bright scarlet, add to the rinse water a few drops of muriate of tin.

TO TAKE OUT PAINT.

Equal parts of ammonia and spirits of turpentine will take paint out of clothing. Saturate the spot two or three times, and then wash out in soapsuds.

TO REMOVE INK STAIN.

Immediately saturate with milk, soak it up with a rag, apply more, rub well, and in a few minutes the ink will disappear.

TO TAKE GREASE OUT

of silk, woolens, paper, floors, etc., grate chalk thick over the spot, cover with brown paper, set on it a hot flatiron and let it remain until cool; repeat if necessary. The iron must not be so hot as to burn paper or cloth.

FRUIT STAINS.

Colored cottons or woolens stained with wine or fruit should be wet in alcohol and ammonia, then sponged off gently (not rubbed) with alcohol; after that, if the material will warrant it, washed in tepid soapsuds. Silk may be wet with this preparation when injured by these stains.

TO REMOVE IRON RUST.

While rinsing clothes, take such as have spots of iron, wring out, dip a wet finger in oxalic acid and rub on the spot, then dip in salt and rub on and hold on a warm flatiron, and the spot will immediately disappear; rinse again, rubbing the place a little with the hands.

TO TAKE OUT MILDEW.

Wet the cloth and rub on soap and chalk, mixed together, and lay in the sun; or, lay the cloth in buttermilk for a short time, take out and place in the hot sun; or, put lemon juice on and treat in the same way.

TO WASH WOOLEN GOODS.

Many woolen goods, such as light-colored, heavy sacques, nubias, etc., may be washed in cold suds and rinsed in cold water. The garments should be well shaken out and pulled into shape.

TO WASH FLANNELS IN TEPID WATER.

The usefulness of liquid ammonia is not as universally known among housewives as it deserves to be. If you add some of it to a soapsuds made of a mild soap it will prevent the flannel from becoming yellow or shrinking. It is the potash and soda combined in sharp soap which tend to color animal fibers yellow; the shrinking may be partially due to this agency, but above all to the exposure of the flannel while wet to the extremes of low and high temperature. Dipping it in boiling water or leaving it out in the rain will also cause it to shrink and become hard. To preserve their softness, flannels should be washed in tepid suds, rinsed in tepid water, and dried rapidly at a moderate heat. — *Buckeye*.

CHAPTER XVI.

HOW TO DO YOUR OWN STAMPING AND MAKE YOUR OWN PATTERNS.

How to do your own Stamping and make your own Patterns: The articles needed for stamping; To make perforated patterns; To enlarge designs; To stamp; To make blue powder; To do French indelible stamping; To make paint for stamping; The proper brush to use; To make a distributor; To care for patterns.

In the following chapter are given full instructions for dry and wet stamping, explaining how to make stamping powder, how to mix white paint for stamping dark goods and black paint for stamping light goods.

The articles necessary are a sheet of writing paper and a piece of transfer paper. The transfer paper can be made by rubbing white paper with a composition consisting of two ounces of tallow, one-half ounce powdered blacklead, one-quarter pint linseed oil, and sufficient lampblack to make it of the consistency of cream. These should be melted together and rubbed on the paper while hot. When dry it will be fit for use.

In order to make a perforated pattern of any engraving, procure a piece of writing paper larger than the design to be traced and put a piece of transfer paper on the writing paper, then place both sheets directly under the engraving and pin the three sheets together at one end, having the transfer paper between and dark side facing the writing paper. You then take a quill with a fine point (a knitting needle will do nicely) and without leaning too hard go over all the outline of the engraving. You must be careful not to press your fingers on the engraving, as this would cause a deposit of powder the same color as the transferring paper on the writing paper. Now remove the transfer paper and you have the design accurately traced and the pattern is ready to be perforated. Lay a couple of folds of velvet or felt on the table, place the pattern on this, and with a needle of medium size or tracing-wheel prick out the pattern, being careful to follow the outline closely and make the perforations quite close.

MECHANICAL ENLARGEMENT OF DESIGNS.

The simplest way is to enlarge by the eye, as the artists do. One method is to divide the whole design into squares and rule off the paper to be enlarged in corresponding squares of larger size. Each portion within the square is then exactly reproduced, copying the portion in the smaller square. For embroidery designs especially we should think this would be very good.

DRY STAMPING.

This is done by a process known as pouncing. The process is as follows: Place the pattern (rough side up) on the material to be stamped, placing heavy weights on the corner to keep it from slipping; then rub the powder over the perforations with the pouncet or distributor described below till the pattern is clearly marked on the material. This can be ascertained by lifting one corner of the pattern slightly. Then remove the pattern carefully, lay a piece of thin paper over the stamping and pass a hot iron over it. This melts the gum in the powder and fastens the pattern to the material. The iron should be as hot as possible without scorching the cloth. Should the heat change the color of the material, iron it all over. Do not do any stamping by this process on a hot or damp day if it can be avoided. Keep the powder in a cool, dry place. In stamping with light-colored powder, the best way to fasten it is to hold the back of the cloth against the stovepipe or the face of the iron. French stamping is better, however, for all dark materials. To take the powder up on the distributor, have a tin plate with a piece of woolen cloth glued on the bottom, sprinkle a little powder on the cloth, and rub the distributor over it, taking care to shake off all the powder you can—enough will remain to stamp the pattern clearly.

TO MAKE A DISTRIBUTOR.

Take a strip of fine felt almost an inch wide (a strip from an old felt hat is as good as anything), roll it up tightly into a roll, leaving the end flat, and rub the end over a piece of sand paper to make it smooth and even.

TO MAKE BLUE POWDER.

Take equal parts of gum damar and white rosin and just enough Persian blue to color it. Mix well together.

Other colors are made the same, using for coloring chrome yellow (for light-colored powder), burnt sienna, lampblack, etc. Black powder is improved by adding a little blue to it.

TO MAKE WHITE POWDER.

Take one ounce white lead; half ounce gum arabic, in the impalpable powder; half ounce white rosin, in the fine powder. All well mixed.

SUPERIOR DARK BLUE POWDER.

One ounce white rosin; one half ounce gum sandarac; one half ounce Prussian blue, in fine powder. Mix all thoroughly.

FRENCH INDELIBLE STAMPING.

This is the best process for all dark materials; in fact, this and the blue powder are all that will ever be needed. By this process a kind of paint is used instead of powder, and a brush instead of a pouncet. Place the pattern on the cloth, smooth side up if you can (though either side will work well), weight the pattern down as in stamping. Rub the paint evenly over the perforations, and it will leave the lines clean, sharp and distinct. After the stamping is done, the pattern must be cleaned immediately. This is done by placing the pattern on the table and turning benzine or naphtha over it to cut the paint and then wiping the pattern dry on both sides with an old cloth, or, better still, with common waste—such as machinists use to clean machinery; this is cheap and absorbs the paint and naphtha quickly. Hold the pattern up to the light to see if the holes are all clear; if they are not, wash it the second time. Do not use the pattern for powder immediately after it has been washed; let it dry a short time, otherwise the moistened gum will clog the perforations.

TO MAKE THE PAINT.

Take zinc white, mix it with boiled oil to about the thickness of cream, add a little drying, such as painters use. Keep in a tin pail (one holding about a pint is a good size); have a piece of board cut round, with a screw in the center for a handle, to fit *loosely* into the pail; drop this on the paint and it will keep it from drying up. Add a little oil occasionally to keep the paint from growing too thick, and it will always be ready for use.

THE BRUSH.

Take a fine stencil brush (or any brush with a square end), wind it tightly with a string from the handle down to within one half inch of the end; this will make it just stiff enough to distribute the paint well. Keep the brush in water, to keep it from drying up, taking care to wipe off the water before using.

THE CARE OF PATTERNS.

New patterns, before being used, should be rubbed over on the rough side with a smooth piece of pumice stone; this wears off the burr and makes the stamping come out cleaner and finer. When patterns are so large that they have to be folded, iron out the creases before using them. After using the patterns for powder stamping, snap the pattern to shake the powder from the perforations. After using the patterns for paint stamping they should be washed thoroughly with naphtha until the perforations are all perfectly clear. Keep the naphtha away from the fire. After the pattern has been washed, do not use it for powder until it has had time to thoroughly dry, otherwise it will gum up the holes and spoil the pattern.

If these directions are carefully followed the stamping will always be satisfactory.—*Popular Art Instructor.*

CHAPTER XVII.

BRONZE WORK.

Bronze Work: What bronze work is; The articles required for doing
bronze work; The art of making a vase in bronze; A motto; A floral
basket; Copper bronze statuary; The art of making exotic leaves;
To make leaves and flowers, etc.; Decalcomania—The uses to
which it may be put.

Bronzing is the latest improvement in waxwork, and if properly made cannot
be detected from the most expensive artistic bronze. It answers for table, mantel,
and bracket ornaments, and may be exposed to dust and air without sustaining
the slightest injury. It can be dusted with a feather duster like any piece of furniture, and is a very desirable and inexpensive ornament.

The colors required in bronze are: Silver bronze, gold bronze, copper bronze,
fire bronze, and green bronze.

THE ART OF MAKING A VASE IN BRONZE.

For instruction, let us take a vase to be finished in copper bronze. First the vase
must be molded. The casting material is one part wax, one part spermaceti, two
parts mutton tallow. Melt the three articles together and color with burnt umber.
Have a coil of fine hair wire, cut into one-half inch lengths, and when the mixture
is melted to the consistency of thick cream stir in the cut wire by degrees until
there is a sprinkling of it throughout the mixture; then pour into the elastic mold
and let stand till perfectly cold and solid; then loosen the sections of the mold and
take it out. Should any of the ends of the wire project, they can be cut with a pair
of sharp scissors. Trim the seams caused by the sections of the mold; then take a
piece of soft flannel cloth, dip it in the refined spirits of turpentine and polish the
vase with it, after which it is ready for bronzing.

Take copper bronze No. 4000, and with the tinting brush bronze the vase evenly, and polish it with a soft piece of white silk. Now take another brush and with
copper bronze No. 6000 give it the last coat The vase is now ready for draping. The
most simple drapery is an ivy vine. Take an embossed ivy leaf (or embossed muslin leaves, as they are named), lay a fine wire along its midrib, leaving two or three
inches of wire for stem; cover the leaf with brown sheet wax, press them together
well with the finger and thumb to make the wax adhere to the leaf, get the impression, and hold the wire firmly; then lay another piece of wax on the under side,
press the edges together and cut away the superfluous wax, leaving the edge plain

(the ivy leaf is not serrated), cover the wire stem with wax and the leaf is ready for bronzing. Rub both sides with turpentine, give one coat of bronze No. 4000, then the last coat of bronze No. 6000. When all the leaves are finished, weave them into a spray, grading them from large to small till the end of the vine is reached, then bronze and drape around the vase in an easy, natural way.

The natural fall leaves, pressed, make pretty draperies for these kinds of vases. Sprays of mixed leaves, oak leaves and acorns, small maple leaves, the holly leaf and berry, mixed ivy and fern leaves, and many other kinds of leaves and vines are equally pretty.

THE ART OF MAKING A MOTTO IN BRONZE.

Take a box frame of the ordinary motto-frame size (gilt face) and line it with either crimson or royal purple velvet, and it is ready for any design. The word "Welcome" is the simplest to begin with. Take a thick blotting pad, lay it on a table, rub some arrowroot or rice power over its upper surface, and lay a sheet of either calla or pond lily wax, *extra thick*, on this powdered surface. Select the style of letter preferred; German text is very appropriate for the motto "Welcome." Cut the pattern letters out in pasteboard, or any kind of thick paper, if tin letter-cutters are not convenient.

Begin with the letter W. Lay it on the sheet of wax and cut out the waxen letter after the pattern with a penknife previously dipped in water. Next cut the E, and so on till the seven letters are cut out, care being taken to powder the blotter every time a new sheet of wax is laid on. Lay the back of the box on the table, having melted glue ready, and with a camel's-hair brush apply a small portion of it to the back of each letter as it is set in its relative position, pressing it gently against the velvet with the palm of the hand. The letters should be set an inch apart, and when all on the frame should be set away until the glue is thoroughly dry and the waxen letters adhere firmly to the velvet, then they are ready for ornamenting. This is done in various ways, and all depends on the artist's taste, but a few suggestions may not be amiss.

Take a two-inch fern-cutter and cut the ferns out of double sheet wax; then bronze them as directed on both sides, either with gold or silver bronze. Begin with draping the letter W. Take the stem end of the fern leaf and with the bead end of the curling-pin fasten it to the lower side of the letter; then turn it over and fasten it down in the middle, letting the point turn outward. Set the ferns on the letters in such a way as not to obscure their form, *i. e.*, the form of the letters. If the motto is made in white wax it should be frosted with diamond dust.

A pretty style of motto is clasped hands in the center, of pure white wax, surrounded with sprays of fine flowers and buds, finished in fire bronze.

Another style of motto is a vase in the center, from which vines in different colors of bronze run. Green, fire, and copper bronzing should have a light background; silver and gold bronzing should have a dark background.

THE ART OF MAKING A FLORAL BASKET IN BRONZE.

Take a medium-sized basket (chip or any solid substance), brush it with glue on the inside, fill it with moss, and set it away to dry till the moss is stuck to the basket. The moss should be raised in the center in the form of a mound. Have the wax sheeted in carmine. Make the center of the basket in roses, rosebuds, and carnations, as they are the most durable. Mold the petals over the embossed muslin petals and bronze them with fire bronze—Nos. 4000 and 6000—as previously directed. Drape the basket and the handle in smilax, having the wax for the smilax sheeted in chrome green; then mold over the embossed muslin leaves, bronze in green bronze, and drape loosely. Such a basket makes a pretty table ornament.

DIRECTIONS FOR BRONZING.

All kinds of ornaments may be made in bronze—small animals, fish, shells, birds, statuary, etc. The mixture for casts should be the same shade as the bronze used.

Fish may be bronzed in silver, gold, and copper bronze; shells in silver, copper, gold, and some may be tinted with fire bronze on the exterior of the shell, but the interior of almost all shells must be tinted with paint; dogs in zinc, silver, and copper; birds in almost any shade.

GREEN BRONZE STATUARY.

Prepare the mixture in chrome green No. 1. A little rosin may be added and a thick sprinkling of cut wire. Trim the object and rub with spirits of turpentine, then apply the green bronze—the two numbers, as directed.

COPPER BRONZE STATUARY.

Prepare the mixture in burnt umber and proceed as directed.

BRONZING STATUETTES.

Statuettes, or any object in plaster of Paris, may be made to resemble bronze by first rendering the plaster nonabsorbent with drying linseed oil and then painting it with a varnish made by grinding waste gold leaf with honey or gum water.

Another method is by first painting the article, after it has been rendered nonabsorbent, of a dark color made of Prussian blue, yellow ochre, and verditer, ground in oil. Before this becomes quite dry, bronze powder of several colors should be dusted on those most prominent parts which may be supposed to have worn bright. Plaster casts may also be made to resemble bronze to a certain extent by merely brushing them over with graphite, which is a brilliant blacklead.

METHOD OF MAKING EMBOSSED MUSLIN LEAVES.

Take a piece of green muslin or calico and size it well with isinglass, then take the natural leaf, lay the sized piece of muslin over it on the under or veined side of the leaf, let the muslin remain on it till almost dry and the impression is set; then with a pair of sharp scissors cut the muslin around the leaf, either plain or serrated.

The impression may be taken of any leaf or flower in this way. The use of muslin leaves tends to make the work more durable and is found very convenient for the artist.

THE ART OF MAKING EXOTIC LEAVES.

The begonia rex makes a beautiful parlor plant. Five or seven leaves make a nice-sized plant: Select five or seven healthy begonia leaves of different sizes, as no two leaves of the rex are of one size on the same plant. Cut the leaves closely off the stem and immerse them in a solution of cold water and castile soap. Leave them in this twelve hours before using. Melt the wax to the consistency of cream, in chrome green, permanent green, dark olive-green, and verdigris-green. Now take a leaf out of the soapsuds and lay it on a marble slab, keeping the under surface or veined side uppermost; then with a camel's-hair brush lay on the melted wax in different shades, following the shades of the natural leaf. The soapsuds having made the leaf transparent, all the shades and spots can be plainly seen on the veined side, which is the side the waxen leaf has to be formed on. The belt of light green over the silvery markings of the leaf should be put on with verdigris-green. Begin the leaf in the center and continue on each side of the midrib till the edge is reached and the leaf has a thick coating of wax. Then lay a wire along the midrib or center of the leaf, fasten it in the wax by pressing, care being taken to leave it long enough for eight or nine inches of stem. Wire must also be laid on all the side ribs or veins leading to the midrib. These small wires are all brought to the center wire and laid evenly by its side till they all come to the stem, where they are all twisted around it to form one long, thick stem. Give the leaf another coating of dark olive-green wax (this covers the wires), then finish with a thin coating of burnt umber tinted with Vandyke brown, and the under surface of the leaf is finished. Remove the natural leaf from the waxen and tint the veins lightly with carmine. Brush a little carmine loosely on the darkest shade in the center of the leaf, and before it sticks blow off as much as possible, when enough will be left to give it that reddish-green tint peculiar to the begonia rex leaf. The next is to finish the silver belt or silvery leaf-markings midway between the center and the edge of the leaf. This strip must be rubbed with spirits of turpentine; then with the tinting brush apply a coating of silver bronze (Nos. 4000 and 6000), care being taken that the bronze does not scatter over the leaf. Now the leaf is finished.

If the work is done according to directions, the waxen leaf will be a true copy of the original. Continue in the same way till all the leaves are made, then wax the stems and run them through the begonia stemming, when they may be arranged in their natural growing manner in a flowerpot filled with moss; or, if preferred, the flowerpot may be filled with wax, in *terre-verte* green, and the stems must be placed in it before the wax gets hard.

HOW TO MAKE BEGONIA STEMMING.

Procure the bristles of a very young pig, five or six weeks old. After washing, put them in a very strong solution of chloride of lime and let them remain in it till whitened; then rinse well in warm water till free from chlorine. Color them while damp, some in different shades of green and some in different shades of brown. After the bristles are ready, the next thing is to make the stemming. Take a square piece of cambric and fasten it in a stretcher, then give it a thick coating of mastic varnish, and when the varnish is dry cut the cambric on a true bias into straight strips of different widths, from an inch to two inches, and half a yard in length. Lay one of these strips on a table or some smooth surface, add another coat of varnish, then cover it with glaucous green flock, care being taken to leave a narrow margin bare on one side to lap under the other when the piping is being made. Dip the bristles in mastic varnish, sprinkle them thickly over the flock, and leave for twenty-four hours to dry; when thoroughly dry, revarnish the bare edge, and turn it in underneath the other edge, thus forming the strip into a pipe, ready to receive the wire stems of the leaves. Brown and crimson flock may be used.

For begonia rex, use crimson flock; for the rubra, use glaucous flock; and for the palmata, use brown flock. Very good stemming may be made by tinting canton flannel, which has a very long nap or pile.

GERANIUM LEAVES—ROSE GERANIUM.

This leaf is of a dark chrome green. Prepare the wax in two shades, dark chrome green and light; immerse the leaves in soapsuds for six hours; take out of the soapsuds and lay it on the marble slab. As there is neither shading nor marking on the leaf, all that is required is to give it a coat of dark chrome green, thick enough to prevent the wires from showing; then lay the wires over the veins and coat them over with a light shade of green. Remove the natural leaf, and as the texture of the rose geranium leaf is rather rough, rub it over with green flock mixed with hair powder. The stems may be left in different lengths.

The best directions that we can give for the tinting and marking of leaves is to copy from nature. The cyclamen leaf is well adapted for the practice of marking and tinting.

The leaf of the pond lily, lotus, canna, maranta, rubber tree, magnolia, camellia, orange, and all leaves which have a waxy surface, should either be varnished or bronzed.

All kinds of leaves may be made by the foregoing directions.—*Popular Art Instructor.*

DECALCOMANIA.

This is another name for a style that has been in vogue for an indefinite, period of time, and comes under the head of transferring. It is almost superfluous to mention the variety of purposes to which decalcomania may be applied, as it can be transferred upon everything for which ornamentation is required, and the variety of designs which are printed especially for it is so great that something may easily be procured to suit the taste of the most fastidious.

A few of the articles that may be decorated can be mentioned by way of showing what a variety this style of ornamentation will embrace: All kinds of crockery, china, porcelain, vases, glass, bookcases, folios, boxes, lap desks, ribbons, dresses, etc. The method of transferring beautiful designs is so simple, and all the materials requisite for the art so easily procured, that it brings it within the means of everyone. Flat surfaces are more suitable than concave or convex ones for this style of decorating, for when the surface is curved the design has to be cut to accommodate the shape, and in this way is often spoiled unless done by the most careful and skillful hand. The materials required are cement, copal varnish, designs, a duck-quill sable, and a flat camel's-hair brush.

Cut your designs neatly with a small pair of scissors, apply the cement by means of the sable to the article to be decorated, place on your design and press equally over its entire surface to exclude the air; dampen it a little and keep pressing equally so that the design may adhere firmly in every part. When the cement is sufficiently dry dampen again with water (a little more freely) and remove the paper. Be careful in manipulating this process, or you will remove some of the colored part with it. If such should occur, instantly replace it as well as you are able, or, if you have a knowledge of Oriental painting, your panacea will be in that. You can retouch with these colors and bring it back nearly to its original beauty. In case you have no knowledge of Oriental painting, match the colors as nearly as possible with water-color paints, allow time to dry, and varnish with copal.

Sometimes the cement becomes too thick for use. It may be restored to its proper flowing consistency by placing the bottle in a bed of warm sand, and can then be applied while warm. If you apply your design to a dark groundwork, it would be desirable to give your picture a coating of Winsor and Newton's Chinese white. The reason for this is that some parts of the picture are semi-transparent, and these would lose their brilliancy if transferred directly upon a dark background without first painting.

TO TRANSFER ON WOOD.

Dissolve some salt in soft water, float your engraving on the surface—picture side uppermost—and let it remain about an hour. The screen, box or table on which you wish to transfer the design should be of bird's-eye maple or other light-colored hardwood, varnished with the best copal or transfer varnish.

Take the picture from the water, dry a little between blotters, place the engraving—picture side downwards—on the varnished wood and smooth it nicely. If the picture entirely covers the wood after the margin has been cut off so that no varnish is exposed, lay over it a thin board, on which place a heavy weight, and leave it for twenty-four hours. If you wish but a small picture in the center of the surface of the wood, apply the varnish only to a space the size of the picture. Dip your finger in the solution of salt and water and commence rubbing off the paper; the nearer you come to the engraving the more careful you must be, as a hole in it will spoil your work. Rub slowly and patiently until you have taken off every bit of the paper and left only the black lines and touches of your picture on the wood, in an inverted direction. Finish up with two or three coats of copal varnish.

TO TRANSFER ON SILK.

Apply a coating of mastic varnish to the design and allow it to dry; then with a brush wash the paper surrounding the design carefully; this removes from the paper the preparation, which would otherwise soil the silk. Apply a second coating of the same varnish, and when this is slightly dried place the design upon the silk or other fabric to be decorated, and with the roller press it well down. With the brush wet the back of the paper covering the design, when the paper may be at once lifted off. Another method is to cut out the design carefully and cover it with a thin coating of mastic varnish, and lay it upon the silk or other fabric (which should be dampened) and roll thoroughly with a rubber roller; dampen the back of the paper with the brush and lift it off as previously directed.

TO MAKE WAX FLOWERS.

The following articles will be required to commence waxwork: Two pounds white wax, one quarter pound hair wire, one bottle carmine, one bottle ultramarine blue, one bottle chrome yellow, two bottles chrome green No. 1, one bottle each of rose pink, royal purple, scarlet powder, and balsam fir; two dozen sheets white wax. This will do to begin with. Now have a clean tin dish, and pour therein a quart or two of water; then put in about one pound of the white wax and let it boil. When cool enough so the bubbles will not form on top it is ready to sheet, which is done as follows: Take half of a window pane, 7 × 9, and, after having washed it clean, dip into a dish containing weak soapsuds; then dip into the wax, and draw it out steadily and plunge it into the suds, when the sheet will readily come off. Lay it on a cloth or clean paper to dry. Proceed in like manner until you have enough of the white; then add enough of the green powder to make a bright color, and heat and stir thoroughly until the color is evenly distributed, then proceed as for sheeting white wax. The other colors are rubbed into the leaves after they are cut out, rubbing light or heavy according to shade.

For patterns you can use any natural leaf, forming the creases in wax with the thumb nail or a needle. To put the flowers together, or the leaves on to the stem, hold in the hand until warm enough to stick. If the sheeted wax is to be used in summer, put in a little balsam of fir to make it hard. If for winter, none will be required.

You can make many flowers without a teacher, but one to assist in the commencement would be a great help, though the most particular thing about it is to get the wax sheeted. The materials I have suggested can be procured at any drug store, and will cost from $3.00 to $4.50.

CHAPTER XVIII.

A chapter of useful things to know. How to prepare: Healing salve;
Magnetic croup cure; Worm elixir; Brilliant self-shining stove
polish; Wonderful starch enamel; Royal washing powder; Magic
annihilator; I X L baking powder; Electric powder; French polish,
or dressing for leather; Artificial honey. Table of poisons and their
antidotes.

Dear lady subscriber, if you are a housekeeper, or ever intend to be one, this chapter will more than repay you for what you have given for this book. It will tell you how to save a large percentage of your household expenses, and also how to have a great many of the articles you use in your daily household work of a superior quality — vastly better than the ones you are using at the present time.

It is a fact not generally known that a great many of the articles used in daily household work cost little more than one-tenth of the price the consumer pays for them. We propose to show the ladies of our great Continent how to have, in most instances, better articles than those they are in the habit of purchasing, and at a small percentage of the cost. To do this, we have, by our own personal investigation, gathered a number of valuable recipes together, and have paid for the privilege of using them. Remember, these are not common recipes, but a full explanation of the manufacture of different articles needed in every household; and they combine the embodied wisdom of practical and successful men and women of the past and present.

We give in this chapter a number of recipes which have never before been published, and which, once possessing, you will never wish to be without, as they are truly marvelous discoveries. The first three every mother should have; the remainder no housekeeper should be without.

No. 1 is

HEALING SALVE.

This salve heals all sores, chaps, cuts, bruises, sore lips, chafed limbs, roughness, etc. It is invaluable as a healing ointment and may be applied to the tenderest skin without injury, and yet it will heal the most painful sores. A three-ounce box will only cost you ten cents, and the directions are so plain that a child can follow them.

Recipe: Take one ounce of sweet oil, one-half ounce of camphor gum, and one-half ounce of mutton tallow. Melt all together over a slow fire, and stir continually until cold.

To use: Rub on part affected at night; wash off in the morning with warm water and castile soap.

No. 2 is

MAGNETIC CROUP CURE.

This is the best remedy for croup ever discovered. It will save parents much trouble and anxiety. With this remedy all that is necessary is (if you have any fear of croup on putting your child to bed) to take a piece of brown paper large enough to cover the throat and chest and spread it with the ointment and put across the throat and lungs; place over that several thicknesses of flannel so as to keep the stomach warm, and keep in place with a string or bandage. Put the child to bed, and you need have no fear of croup that night. This ointment is also excellent for cuts, bruises or sores. Twelve cents will make enough to last a year, even if you use it frequently.

Recipe: One-half pound of lard, quarter of a pound of raisins, quarter pound of fine cut chewing tobacco. In the morning place the tobacco in a tin can and cover it with water; set it on the stove and let it cook and boil all day, replacing the water when it is necessary; then squeeze all the juice from the tobacco. The next morning chop your raisins, put them in the tobacco water and cook well till noon; then again squeeze the raisins out of this water. Now to this water add the lard and let them simmer together until the water is evaporated. Now the croup remedy is ready for use. On putting the child to bed, if you fear an attack, take a piece of brown paper large enough to cover the throat and chest and spread it over with the ointment and put it across the throat and lungs. Place over that and tie several thicknesses of flannel; put the child to bed, cover up warmly, and you need have no fear of croup that night.

If taken with croup unexpectedly, on hearing the cough, spread a piece of brown paper with the ointment and lay it across the throat and chest; then heat flannel as hot as can be borne and lay over the paper; change in about ten minutes for another hot cloth. If no fire is on while waiting for it, heat cloths on a lamp chimney. As soon as you get the stomach covered and warm, give a teaspoonful of melted butter; repeat the dose in five minutes.

No. 3 is

WORM ELIXIR.

The best remedy for worms known. No mother should be without it. Also, if given occasionally it is a splendid preventive. Children will never be troubled with worms who are given a dose of this once a month, or fortnight.

Recipe: Take gum myrrh and aloes, of each one ounce; saffron, sage leaves, and tansy leaves, of each half an ounce; tincture in a pint of brandy two weeks, and give to children a teaspoonful once a week to once a month as a preventive. They will never be troubled with worms as long as you do this.

WORM VERMIFUGE.

Make a strong decoction of sage, two parts; wormseed, one part; strain, and add sugar enough to make into candy, and let the child eat of it. Infallible.

No. 4 is

BRILLIANT SELF-SHINING STOVE POLISH.

This is one of the greatest inventions of the age. It has been the result of a large amount of study on the part of the inventor to perfect a polish that would work easily and satisfactorily in a perfectly dry state, thereby obviating the disagreeable task of mixing and preparing. A good stove polish is an absolute necessity in every family. To be assured that this is the best you need give it only one trial. Now, remember, first, that this polish requires no water or mixing like the various cake and powder polishes; second, that it is self-shining and no labor is required; and third, that it has no equal in the world.

Below are the recipe and directions for preparing this polish. You can prepare enough in ten minutes to last a year. A box holding two ounces will cost but three cents.

Recipe: Get from the hardware store plumbago (blacklead), pulverize it finely and it is ready for use.

Directions for use: Use a damp woolen rag, dip in the polish and apply to the stove; then rub with a dry cloth, and a most beautiful polish will appear.

No. 5 is

WONDERFUL STARCH ENAMEL.

For polishing shirt bosoms, collars, cuffs, lace curtains, etc., putting on the same gloss and hard pearl finish as when bought at the store new. Every lady should use the wonderful enamel for the following reasons: It enables an ordinary ironer to compete with any laundry; it makes the clothes clear and white; it makes clothes iron smoothly, and prevents the iron sticking; it makes old linen look like new; and it saves a woman many hours' hard work each week. It is easily made, and five cents' worth will last an ordinary family six months.

Recipe: Melt half a pound of refined paraffine wax in a tin pan over a slow fire. When melted remove from the fire and add twenty drops of oil of citronella. Take a tin pan and oil with sweet oil, put the pan on a level table, and pour in enough of the hot wax to make a depth of an eighth of an inch. When cool, but not cold, cut in pieces about the size of an ordinary candy lozenge. Lay them aside to cool, but do not let them touch each other.

Directions for use: To a pint of boiling starch stir in one cake. Use starch while warm.

No. 6 is

ROYAL WASHING POWDER

—the laundress' assistant; warranted not to injure the finest fabric. No acid; no potash. In the wash room it saves time, labor, expense, muscle, temper, and hands. The clothes will come out cleaned and white, without wear or tear or rubbing on washboards, therefore will last twice as long. For housecleaning it is unequaled. One girl can wash more clothes, paint, walls, windows or floors in a day with perfect ease with this powder than she could in four days with hard labor, soap, and scrubbing brush, and the paint will look new and bright. It only requires to be tested to be appreciated. Packages of one pound will only cost seven cents.

Recipe: Mix any quantity of soda ash with an equal quantity of carbonate of soda crushed into coarse grains. Have a thin solution of glue or decoction of linseed oil ready, into which pour the soda until quite thick. Spread out in a warm apartment to dry. When dry shake up well and pack away for use. Use as other washing powders.

No. 7 is

MAGIC ANNIHILATOR.

Removes all kinds of grease and oil spots from every kind of wearing-apparel—such as coats, pants, vests, dress goods, carpets, etc.—without injury to the finest silks or laces. It will shampoo like a charm, raising the lather in proportion to the amount of dandruff and grease in the hair. A cloth wet with it will remove all grease from door knobs, window sills, etc., handled by kitchen domestics in their daily round of kitchen work. For cleaning silver, brass, and copper ware it cannot be beaten. It is certain death to bedbugs, for they will never stop after they have encountered the Magic Annihilator. It is useful for many other things. A quart bottle costs about ten cents.

Recipe: To make half a gallon, take aqua ammonia, one pint; soft water, one-half gallon; best white soap, one-half pound; saltpetre, one ounce. Shave the soap fine, add the water, boil until the soap is dissolved, then add the saltpetre, stirring until dissolved. Now strain, let the suds settle, skim off the dry suds, add the ammonia, and bottle and cork at once.

Directions for use: For grease spots, pour upon the article to be cleaned a sufficient quantity of the Magic Annihilator, rubbing well with a clean sponge and applying to both sides of the article. Upon carpets and coarse goods where the grease is hard and dry use a stiff brush and wash out with clear cold water. For shampooing, take a small quantity, with an equal quantity of water; apply to the hair with a stiff brush, brushing into the scalp, and wash out with clear water. For killing bedbugs, apply to the places they frequent.

No. 8 is

I X L BAKING POWDER.

An unsurpassed article. Can be relied on for strength and purity. So many of the baking powders sold contain injurious substances and are altogether unreliable. This powder can be relied on for strength and purity. It produces the most delightfully white, light and flaky biscuits. For cakes it is unsurpassed. Try it and be convinced. This powder is composed of the very best and purest substances, and therefore is perfectly wholesome. Any lady can prepare enough in a few minutes to last her six months. It will only cost a trifle—not one-quarter of what you would have to pay your grocer for the same amount.

Recipe: Take one pound of *tartaric* acid (in *crystals*), one and one-half pounds bicarbonate of soda, and one and one-half pounds of potato or corn starch. Each must be powdered separately, well dried by a slow fire, and well mixed through a sieve. Pack hard in a tin, or paper glazed on the outside. Buy the articles from a druggist.

Directions for use: For biscuits, pie crust, johnnycake, etc., use three teaspoonfuls to one quart of flour or meal; for cakes, two teaspoonfuls to a teacup of flour. Mix well with the flour.

No. 9 is

ELECTRIC POWDER.

This is one of the best articles on our list—something that every housekeeper needs. It is used for gold, silver, plated ware, German silver, copper, brass, tin, steel, window glass, or any material where a brilliant luster is required. To make two ounces costs but three cents, and it is the best article of its kind known.

Recipe: To one pound best quality whiting add one-half pound cream tartar and three ounces calcined magnesia. Mix thoroughly together and store away for use.

Directions for use: Use the polish dry, with a piece of canton flannel moistened with water or alcohol, and finish with the polish dry.

No. 10 is

FRENCH POLISH OR DRESSING FOR LEATHER.

This is a grand article. All that is necessary is to have your boots clean and apply this dressing with a sponge. The boots appear like the very best French leather. Much hard work is saved, as no brushing is required. To make a quart vessel full will only cost about twenty cents.

Recipe: Mix half a pint of the best vinegar with a quarter pint of soft water; stir into it one ounce of glue (broken up), two ounces log-wood chips, one-sixteenth ounce of finely-powdered indigo, one-sixteenth ounce of the best soft soap, one-sixteenth ounce of isinglass. Put the mixture over the fire, let it boil ten minutes or more; then strain, bottle and cork. When cold it is fit for use. Apply with a sponge.

No. 11 is

ARTIFICIAL HONEY.

Equal to bee honey, and often mistaken by the best judges to be genuine. It is palatable and luxurious. All persons are more or less aware that honey should be used in every household, and it would be so if every family could have it at a very moderate price. As a health-establishing nutriment in the chamber of the invalid, and as a delicious luxury for the well, honey cannot be too highly recommended. Any one using this honey regularly will find that he is strengthened and refreshed by it. He will have greater energy and if at all inclined to dyspepsia will find himself greatly helped. This honey costs but eight cents per pound to prepare, and our directions are so simple a child ten years old can follow them.

Recipe: Take two ounces of slippery elm bark and put into three quarts of warm water and let it stand four hours; strain and add eight pounds of white sugar; boil four minutes; then add one pound of bee honey while hot. Flavor with a drop of the oil of peppermint and a drop of the oil of rose.

Any lady will readily see what a saving the possession of the above recipes may cause in her household expense. Thus, you can get a ten cent box of stove polish for three cents, a twenty-five cent package of washing powder for seven cents, a twenty-five cent box of starch enamel for five cents, etc. Any of the articles contained in the list will take but a short time to prepare a large supply.

POISONS AND THEIR ANTIDOTES.

The first thing to do in a case of poisoning is to cause the ejection of the poison by vomiting. To do this, place mustard mixed with salt on the tongue and give large quantities of lukewarm water; or, tickle the throat with a feather. These failing, instantly resort to active emetics, like tartar emetic, sulphate of copper or sulphate of zinc. After vomiting has taken place with these, aid it, if possible, by copious draughts of warm water until the poison is entirely removed. Of course, if vomiting cannot be induced the stomach pump must be employed, especially if arsenic or narcotics have been taken. The following table may be useful for emergencies:—

POISONS.	ANTIDOTES.
Acids,	Alkalies: Soap and milk, chalk or soda.
Alkalies,	Vegetable acids, vinegar, oil in abundance.
Alcohol,	Common salt, moderately.
Arsenic,	Send for the doctor and his stomach pump.
Antimony,	Oak bark, strong green tea.
Baryta or lime,	Epsom salts, oils, magnesia.
Bismuth,	White of eggs, sweet milk.
Copper,	White of eggs, strong coffee.
Gases,	Cold douche, followed by friction.
Iodine,	Starch, wheat flour in water.
Creosote,	White of eggs, sweet milk.
Lead,	Strong lemonade, Epsom salts.
Opium and other narcotics,	Emetics, cold douche, and heat.

Phosphorus,	Magnesia in copious draughts.
Zinc,	White of eggs, sweet milk.
Mad-dog bite,	Apply fire in some form to the wound, thoroughly and immediately.
Bite of insect,	Ammonia, applied freely.
Bite of serpent,	Same as for mad dog, followed by whisky to intoxication.

The foregoing are the more common and more important poisons and their antidotes.—*Buckeye.*

TURKISH LOTION.

The New and Wonderful Discovery for Beautifying the Skin.

Gives to a woman of forty the fresh, bright complexion of a girl. No more wrinkles, crow's-feet or sallowness.

Turkish Lotion completely cures freckles, pimples, blackheads, moles and superfluous hair, tan, greasy skin, blotches, redness, sore or chapped lips, chapped and red, rough hands; and, best of all, completely eradicates and prevents wrinkles, crow's-feet, and sallowness.

Turkish Lotion creates a perfect complexion.

After using Turkish Lotion for a short time a lady's skin will be as exquisitely soft and velvety, as clear and pure, as that of a little child. It is not an artificial cosmetic, but a cleansing, refining, whitening tonic. It feeds and nourishes the skin, preventing and banishing wrinkles, crow's-feet, and sallowness. It is perfectly harmless and composed of the purest ingredients.

Turkish Lotion is invaluable to every lady. It conceals the evidences of age. By its use a lady of middle-age will have the charming, fresh look of a girl. Every womanly woman desires to appear fresh and youthful as long as possible, thereby making herself the wonder of her own sex and the admiration of the opposite. By using this lotion according to directions every lady may have a fresh, rosy tinted complexion of exquisite pearly fairness, free from wrinkles, crow's-feet, and sallowness.

One application will make the most stubbornly red and rough hands beautifully soft and white.

Turkish Lotion is not a paint or powder, but a new and great discovery—a cleansing, healing, whitening tonic that causes the cheek to glow with healthy action of the skin, and the neck, arms and hands to assume an exquisite pearly whiteness. By its use all redness and roughness is prevented and the skin is beautified and rendered soft, smooth, and white, thereby imparting a delicate, refined loveliness impossible to describe. Any lady using Turkish Lotion will present a fresh, youthful, natural appearance, with a pearly, rose-tinted complexion that is positively bewitching. It is without doubt the best face lotion ever discovered, being as it is a medicated lotion possessing healing qualities. Many ladies are troubled during cold weather with sore lips, rough, parched skin, and chapped hands upon the slightest exposure. By moistening at night with this wash the parts affected, all soreness and roughness will be completely cured and the face and hands will be as delicately soft and smooth as those of a little child.

No one need suffer any longer from any defect of the skin.

Recipe for Turkish Lotion: To one fluid ounce of tincture of gum benzoin add seven fluid ounces of distilled rose-water and one-half ounce of glycerine.

Directions for use: Bathe face, neck, and hands with Turkish Lotion at night, letting it dry on. Wash off in the morning with a very little pure white castile soap and soft water. If the water is hard, add a very little dissolved borax. This will prevent and cure greasy skin, freckles, tan, wrinkles, pimples, blackheads, crow's-feet, blotches, sunburn, chapped hands, sore lips, rough skin, etc.

To Cure Sallowness: Use as above directed, and ask your druggist for some good iron tablets. Take as directed. In a short time your complexion will be beautifully white and rose-tinted.

To Remove Hairy Moles and Superfluous Hair: Procure prepared pumice stone from your druggist; cut the hair as close as possible to the skin, dip the pumice in cold water and rub on the part on which the hairs grow, commencing gently at first (as it may cause slight irritation of the skin), then gradually increase the friction. After using the pumice stone, anoint freely each time with Turkish Lotion. Do this twice daily, and it will surely remove superfluous hair.

Always, after using Turkish Lotion, rub gently with the hands until the skin becomes dry. This will remove and prevent wrinkles and lines.

INDEX

S

T

W

Lector House believes that a society develops through a two-fold approach of continuous learning and adaptation, which is derived from the study of classic literary works spread across the historic timeline of literature records. Therefore, we aim at reviving, repairing and redeveloping all those inaccessible or damaged but historically as well as culturally important literature across subjects so that the future generations may have an opportunity to study and learn from past works to embark upon a journey of creating a better future.

This book is a result of an effort made by Lector House towards making a contribution to the preservation and repair of original ancient works which might hold historical significance to the approach of continuous learning across subjects.

HAPPY READING & LEARNING!

LECTOR HOUSE LLP
E-MAIL: lectorpublishing@gmail.com